EPHESIANS

Books in the PREACHING THE WORD Series:

(Unless otherwise indicated, all volumes are by R. Kent Hughes.)

GENESIS:
Beginning and Blessing

EXODUS:
Saved for God's Glory
by Philip Graham Ryken

NUMBERS:
God's Presence in the Wilderness
by Iain M. Duguid

ISAIAH:
God Saves Sinners
by Raymond C. Ortlund, Jr.

JEREMIAH AND LAMENTATIONS:
From Sorrow to Hope
by Philip Graham Ryken

DANIEL:
The Triumph of God's Kingdom
by Rodney D. Stortz

MARK, VOLUME ONE:
Jesus, Servant and Savior

MARK, VOLUME TWO:
Jesus, Servant and Savior

LUKE, VOLUME ONE:
That You May Know the Truth

LUKE, VOLUME TWO:
That You May Know the Truth

JOHN:
That You May Believe

ACTS:
The Church Afire

ROMANS:
Righteousness from Heaven

2 CORINTHIANS:
Power in Weakness

EPHESIANS:
The Mystery of the Body of Christ

COLOSSIANS AND PHILEMON:
The Supremacy of Christ

1 & 2 TIMOTHY AND TITUS:
To Guard the Deposit
by R. Kent Hughes and Bryan Chapell

HEBREWS, VOLUME ONE:
An Anchor for the Soul

HEBREWS, VOLUME TWO:
An Anchor for the Soul

JAMES:
Faith That Works

THE SERMON ON THE MOUNT:
The Message of the Kingdom

EPHESIANS

The Mystery of the Body of Christ

R. Kent Hughes

CROSSWAY

WHEATON, ILLINOIS

Ephesians

Copyright © 1990 by R. Kent Hughes

Published by Crossway
1300 Crescent Street
Wheaton, Illinois 60187

Cover banner: Marge Gieser

First printing, 1990

Printed in the United States of America

Library of Congress Catalog Number 89-50324

Unless otherwise noted, all Bible quotations are taken from *The Holy Bible: New International Version*, copyright © 1978 by the New York International Bible Society. Used by permission of Zondervan Bible Publishers.

Library of Congress Cataloging-in-Publication Data

Hughes, R. Kent
   Ephesians : the mystery of the body of Christ / R. Kent Hughes.
     p.   cm. — (Preaching the word)
   Includes bibliographical references and indexes.
   ISBN 13: 978-0-89107-581-3 (hc)
   ISBN 10: 0-89107-581-X
   1. Bible. N.T. Ephesians—Commentaries. I. Title. II. Series: Hughes,
R. Kent. Preaching the word.
BS2595.4.H84
227'.506—dc20   90-80622

Crossway is a publishing ministry of Good News Publishers.

TS		19	18	17	16	15	14	13	12	11	10
18	17	16	15	14	13	12	11	10	9	8	7

To Verl and Lois Lindley
who taught me the mystery of the Church

*"Praise be to the God and Father
of our Lord Jesus Christ,
who has blessed us in the heavenly realms
with every spiritual blessing in Christ."*

(*Ephesians 1:3*)

Table of Contents

Acknowledgments   ix

A Word to Those Who Preach the Word   xi

1   Celebration of Blessing   15
     (EPHESIANS 1:1-3)

2   Celebration of Election   23
     (EPHESIANS 1:3-6)

3   Celebration of Redemption   31
     (EPHESIANS 1:7-10)

4   Celebration of Salvation   41
     (EPHESIANS 1:11-14)

5   A Prayer for Enlightenment   49
     (EPHESIANS 1:15-19)

6   The Fullness of Him   57
     (EPHESIANS 1:18-23)

7   From Death to Life   65
     (EPHESIANS 2:1-7)

8   All of Grace   73
     (EPHESIANS 2:8-10)

9   God's Amazing Work   81
     (EPHESIANS 2:10)

10   Alienation to Reconciliation   89
      (EPHESIANS 2:11-18)

11   The Third Race   97
      (EPHESIANS 2:19-22)

12   Mystery of Christ   105
      (EPHESIANS 3:1-13)

13   A Prayer for the Third Race   113
      (EPHESIANS 3:14-21)

14   Building the Church's Unity   121
     (EPHESIANS 4:1-6)

15   Growing the Church   131
     (EPHESIANS 4:7-16)

16   The Divine Wardrobe   139
     (EPHESIANS 4:17-24)

17   Living Under the Smile   147
     (EPHESIANS 4:25-32)

18   The Cookie Jar Syndrome   155
     (EPHESIANS 5:1-7)

19   Shades of Life   163
     (EPHESIANS 5:8-14)

20   The Fullness of the Spirit   171
     (EPHESIANS 5:15-21)

21   The Mystery of Marriage (I)   181
     (EPHESIANS 5:21-24)

22   The Mystery of Marriage (II)   189
     (EPHESIANS 5:25-33)

23   Instructions to Children and Parents   197
     (EPHESIANS 6:1-4)

24   Slaves and Masters   205
     (EPHESIANS 6:5-9)

25   The View for Victory   213
     (EPHESIANS 6:10-12)

26   Armed for Battle (I)   223
     (EPHESIANS 6:13, 14)

27   Armed for Battle (II)   231
     (EPHESIANS 6:15, 16)

28   Armed for Battle (III)   239
     (EPHESIANS 6:17)

29   Armed for Battle (IV)   249
     (EPHESIANS 6:18-20)

30   Glad Benedictions   261
     (EPHESIANS 6:21-24)

     Notes   269

     Scripture Index   287

     General Index   295

     Index of Sermon Illustrations   299

     About the Book Jacket   304

Acknowledgments

Special thanks are due to Mrs. Sharon Fritz for her professional expertise and attention to detail in the preparation of this manuscript, to Mr. Herb Carlburg for the painstaking checking of the Scripture references and to Mr. Ted Griffin, Managing Editor of Crossway Books, for his wise and intelligent editing.

A Word to Those Who Preach the Word

There are times when I am preaching that I have especially sensed the pleasure of God. I usually become aware of it through the unnatural silence. The ever-present coughing ceases and the pews stop creaking, bringing an almost physical quiet to the sanctuary — through which my words sail like arrows. I experience a heightened eloquence, so that the cadence and volume of my voice intensify the truth I am preaching.

There is nothing quite like it — the Holy Spirit filling one's sails, the sense of his pleasure, and the awareness that something is happening among one's hearers. This experience is, of course, not unique, for thousands of preachers have similar experiences, even greater ones.

What has happened when this takes place? How do we account for this sense of his smile? The answer for me has come from the ancient rhetorical categories of *logos*, *ethos*, and *pathos*.

The first reason for his smile is the *logos* — in terms of preaching, God's Word. This means that as we stand before God's people to proclaim his Word, we have done our homework. We have exegeted the passage, mined the significance of its words in their context, and applied sound hermeneutical principles in interpreting the text so that we understand what its words meant to its hearers. And it means that we have labored long until we can express in a sentence what the theme of the text is — so that our outline springs from the text. Then our preparation will be such that as we preach, we will not be preaching our own thoughts about God's Word, but God's actual Word, his *logos*. This is fundamental to pleasing him in preaching.

The second element in knowing God's smile in preaching is *ethos* — what you are as a person. There is a danger endemic to preaching, which is having your hands and heart cauterized by holy things. Phillips Brooks illustrated it by the analogy of a train conductor who comes to believe that he has been to the places he announces because of his long and loud heralding of them. And that is why Brooks insisted that preaching must be "the bringing of truth through personality." Though we can never *perfectly* embody the truth we preach, we must be subject to it, long for it, and make it as much a part of our ethos as possible. As the Puritan William Ames said, "Next to the Scriptures, nothing makes a sermon more to pierce, than when it comes out of the inward affection of the heart without any affectation." When a preacher's ethos backs up his logos, there will be the pleasure of God.

Last, there is *pathos* — personal passion and conviction. David Hume, the Scottish philosopher and skeptic, was once challenged as he was seen going to hear George Whitefield preach: "I thought you do not believe in the gospel." Hume replied, "I don't, but *he does*." Just so! When a preacher believes what he preaches, there will be passion. And this belief and requisite passion will know the smile of God.

The pleasure of God is a matter of *logos* (the Word), *ethos* (what you are), and *pathos* (your passion). As you *preach the Word* may you experience his smile — the Holy Spirit in your sails!

R. Kent Hughes
Wheaton, Illinois

EPHESIANS

Paul, an apostle of Christ Jesus by the will of God, To the saints in Ephesus, the faithful in Christ Jesus: Grace and peace to you from God our Father and the Lord Jesus Christ. Praise be to the God and Father of our Lord Jesus Christ, who has blessed us in the heavenly realms with every spiritual blessing in Christ. (1:1-3)

1

Celebration of Blessing

EPHESIANS 1:1-3

W hen one takes up the study of
Ephesians, he finds that commentators and preachers outdo themselves in
lavish encomiums. It has been called "[t]he crown and climax of Pauline theology,"[1] "[t]he sublimest communication ever made to men,"[2] "the
quintessence of Paulinism,"[3] "the consummate and most comprehensive
statement which even the New Testament contains of the meaning of the
Christian religion. It is certainly the final statement of Pauline theology."[4]
Samuel Taylor Coleridge called it "the divinest composition of man."[5] John
A. Mackay, past president of Princeton Theological Seminary, waxed eloquent as well: "Never . . . was the reality of Revelation more obvious and the
reflective powers of the Apostle's mind more transfigured than in the great
book which is known by the title, *The Epistle to the Ephesians.*"[6]

These eloquent recommendations alone are sufficient reasons to be
enthused about the prospect of study, but there is furthermore the grand
theme of Ephesians and its dual focus on *Christ* and on the *Church* — the
"mystery" of "Christ and the church" (5:32). The theme is clarified when
we compare it to that of Colossians. Colossians explains Christ's person
and work in relation to the whole universe — *the cosmic Christ*; whereas
Ephesians explains what *the Church's cosmic role* is as the Body of the cosmic Christ. Ephesians reveals the position and job description of the Church
in effecting God's new order. It answers the question, *what does it mean to
be in Christ, and what does this demand of us?*

Because Ephesians has such a magisterial theme and because it is so
practical, it is also immensely powerful. John Mackay, in his book *God's
Order*, recounts how he became spiritually alive as a fifteen-year-old. One
Saturday about noon in the month of July 1903, young Mackay was attending
a "preparation" service for an old-time Scottish Communion in the open air,

among the hills in the Highland parish of Rogart, in Sutherlandshire. A minister was preaching from a wooden pulpit to several hundred people sitting under the shade of trees in the glen. Though Mackay could never remember what was said, he was quickened that halcyon day and knew he was called to preach. For the rest of the summer he lived in the pages of a tiny New Testament which he had purchased for a penny. Most of his time was spent in Paul's letters — especially Ephesians, which became his favorite book of the Bible.[7] Mackay later wrote:

> From the first, my imagination began to glow with the cosmic significance of Jesus Christ. It was the cosmic Christ that fascinated me, the living Lord Jesus Christ who was the center of a great drama of unity, in which everything in Heaven and on earth was to become one in him. I did not understand what it all meant, but the tendency to think of everything in terms of Jesus Christ and a longing to contribute to a unity in Christ became the passion of my life. It became natural then, and it has remained natural ever since, to say "Lord Jesus."[8]

Ephesians — carefully, reverently, prayerfully considered — will change our lives. It is not so much a question of what we will do with the epistle, but what it will do with us.

We should also note that the Letter to the Ephesians is compellingly ecumenical and catholic in the primary sense of these words. The designation "in Ephesus" is not in the earliest manuscripts, and we conclude that it was a circular letter meant for *all* the churches in Asia Minor.[9] Thus, its ecumenical message is for the Church everywhere and in every age: namely, that Christ reconciles all races and cultures by bringing them to himself and making them one with him and with one another. It is a message of unity, a message for the Church, and a message for a fragmented, war-torn world.

The structure of the book is typically Pauline: first Paul states the *doctrine* (chapters 1 — 3), then he states the *duty* (chapters 4 — 6). The duty section ends with a description of spiritual battle, so some like to divide it in two. Thus the book can be given an easy-to-remember division such as:

The *wealth* (1-3), *walk* (4-5), *warfare* (6:10f)[10]

Or,

sit (1-3), *walk* (4-5), *stand* (6:10f)[11]

The opening verses of Ephesians are a "Celebration of Blessing." The mood is exuberant joy. Paul buoyantly begins a song (modeled on the

Hebrew *berakhah* or blessing song) celebrating God's work in bringing us salvation. In quick order Paul celebrates *himself*, the *saints*, *their God*, and *their blessings*.

CELEBRATING SELF (v. 1a)

Paul's personal celebration is centered in the fact that he is "an apostle of Christ [Messiah] Jesus by the will of God" (v. 1a). This certainly was not due to his own will. At the onset of Christianity he had been a militant opponent of Christ, even an accessory to the murders of believers (Acts 7). But then on the Damascus off-ramp he met the Lion of the Tribe of Judah and heard his call: "Saul, Saul, why do you persecute me? . . . I am Jesus, whom you are persecuting" (Acts 9:4, 5). The effect was radical conversion, so radical that in a few days Saul "baffled the Jews living in Damascus by proving that Jesus is the Christ" (Acts 9:22). It was a *miracle*, and nothing else, that made him one with the Twelve!

As an *apostolos*, one sent, Paul's authority was not self-generated, but was ordained of God. He therefore could not help but preach Jesus. "I cannot boast," he said, "for I am compelled to preach. Woe to me if I do not preach the gospel!" (1 Corinthians 9:16). This was something to celebrate!

But it was not a cause for selfish vanity. Before he met Christ he was "Saul," named after the tallest (and vainest) of the Benjamites, King Saul, from whom he was descended (Philippians 3:4-6). But now, after coming to know Christ, he takes the name "Paul" — *small*. The Lion had cut him down to size. Now he humbly says, "But we have this treasure in jars of clay to show that this all-surpassing power is from God and not from us" (2 Corinthians 4:7). Paul's smallness became the medium for God's bigness, his weakness a channel for God's power.

Paul's opening words celebrate a self which had been liberated from the crushing bondage of ego, included (by God's sovereign decision) in the apostolic band, and imbued with divine authority and purpose. And so, writing from prison, Paul's song went forth, just as later would that of St. John of the Cross from his Toledo cell, and John Bunyan from the Bedford jail, and Charles Colson from a modern prison.

Paul's song is ours in a less dramatic, perhaps, but equally significant way. For in Christ, every one of us has been delivered from self and has been given position and purpose and authority in him. And that is something to continually celebrate.

CELEBRATING THE SAINTS (vv. 1b, 2)

Paul's celebration moves from self to others with his simple designation, "To the saints . . . the faithful in Christ Jesus" (v. 1b), for the designation is a celebration in itself. Why? Because in the Greek translation of the Old Testament the people of Israel, and sometimes even the angels, were given the honored title "saints." Therefore, as Marcus Barth explains, "By using the same designation . . . the author of Ephesians bestows upon all his pagan-born hearers a privilege formerly reserved for Israel, for special (especially priestly) servants of God, or for angels."[12] Applying the privileged word "saints" to pagan Greeks was mind-boggling to those with a Jewish background. Hebrew detractors considered it a rape of sacred vocabulary. But from the Christian perspective it was a fitting word to celebrate the miracle of God's grace.

"Saints" means "holy ones, those set apart and consecrated." The word was descriptive of what had happened in their hearts. They were saints though living under the shadow of pagan temples amidst the moral decay of Asia Minor. They were saints while going about their lives — shopkeeping, sailing, building, raising children.

Paul also adds that they were "faithful" — they were actively believing and trusting God. Their saintliness grew out of their believing. As Calvin said, "No man is . . . a believer who is not also a saint; and, on the other hand, no man is a saint who is not a believer."[13] This was all because they were "in Christ Jesus" — they were personally and intimately in him, as appendages are part of the body or branches are part of the tree.

"Saints" — "faithful" — "in Christ Jesus" — what a cause for celebration! And how does he celebrate it? "Grace and peace to you from God our Father and the Lord Jesus Christ" (v. 2). This greeting bears the poetry of redemption, for the regular Greek greeting was "Rejoice!" (*chaire*), and the regular Jewish greeting was "Peace" (Hebrew *shalom*, Greek *eiriene*). But here Paul combines the two, and then replaces rejoice (*chaire*) with the similar sounding but far richer *charis* — "grace."[14] He in effect combines the greetings of the Eastern and Western worlds, then modifies the Western and gives the whole world the sublime Christian greeting, "Grace and peace." This greeting celebrates how the gospel works. *Grace* comes first, and as it fills our lives through the Holy Spirit, it brings *shalom* — peace, reconciliation, wholeness.

This is a huge Christian greeting! There never had been anything like it in the world. This "Grace and peace" has enabled thousands to lift up God even when the world is falling in. Consider H. P. Spafford, who composed one of the Church's great hymns as he sailed over the watery grave of his family, drowned on the *Ville du Havre*:

> *When peace like a river attendeth my way,*
> *When sorrows like sea billows roll;*
> *Whatever my lot, Thou hast taught me to say,*
> *"It is well, it is well with my soul."*

This is what we have to offer to others — a brand-new greeting from another world: "Grace and peace." All who truly want this can have it through Jesus Christ.

CELEBRATING THEIR BLESSINGS (v. 3)

Paul has celebrated *himself*: his calling, his mission, his deliverance from self. He has also celebrated the *saints*. Now he celebrates their mutual *blessings*: "Praise be to the God and Father of our Lord Jesus Christ, who has blessed us in the heavenly realms with every spiritual blessing in Christ" (v. 3). This is a dramatic, introductory prelude to a song which extends to the end of verse 14, one long rhapsodic sentence.

At the root of Paul's celebration here is the idea that both he and the Ephesians, by virtue of their being in Christ, have been elevated to "the heavenly realms." That is, they occupy the place where Christ is now enthroned, seated at the Father's right hand (1:20). This is also where *all* of us who are united to him through faith are seated: "And God raised us up with Christ and seated us with him in the heavenly realms in Christ Jesus" (2:6). "The heavenly realms" are "the immaterial reign, the 'unseen universe' which lies behind the world of sense"[15] — the place of Christ's throne, where we are enthroned with him! *Temporally* we live here on earth; but *spiritually* we live in the heavenly realms where Christ lives. Paul calls us to immerse ourselves in this truth and to celebrate.

But there is more. We have been blessed "with every spiritual blessing in Christ." Under the Old Covenant, God's promised blessings were largely material, such as those promised to obedient Israel in Deuteronomy 28:1-14 — fruitful wombs, flourishing crops, abundant flocks, bread in every basket, prosperity, and world influence. Likewise, under the New Covenant Jesus takes care of his own materially and charges them not to worry about their needs (Matthew 6:25-34). As Spurgeon once said, "He that gives us heaven will surely give us all that is needful on the road thither."[16] And, "We shall have enough spending money on the road to glory; for he who has guaranteed to bring us there will not starve us along the way."[17]

But in addition to this, the overwhelming promises of the New Covenant are *spiritual* (cf. Jeremiah 31:31-34). The song, the *berakhah*, in verses 3-14 includes five dynamic spiritual elements: 1) holiness, 2) adoption, 3) redemption and forgiveness, 4) the Holy Spirit, and 5) the hope of glory. The fact is, we receive thousands of blessings under these headings, all crowned with "love, joy, peace, patience, kindness, goodness, faithfulness, gentleness and self-control" (Galatians 5:22).

We have been and are now blessed "with every spiritual blessing in Christ." "To be in Christ . . . is to partake of all that Christ has done, all He is, and all that He ever will be."[18] Of course, it remains for us to grow and thus claim more and more of these blessings which are now ours. What a wonderful pursuit! The Devil may curse us, but if God blesses us, what does it matter?

Paul's stupendous assertion about our status of blessedness demands our careful attention. *First, we must believe it.* Paul's statement in 1:20 that Christ is seated at the right hand of God in "the heavenly realms" is fairly easy for believing hearts to accept. But it is not so easy for the same believers to truly embrace the fact that they themselves are seated in "the heavenly realms," as 2:6 asserts. "After all, we've never been there," they object, "and we've had no heavenly experiences like Paul claimed to have had. Perhaps Paul was speaking symbolically or metaphorically." This seems to be plausible reasoning, but it is absolutely wrong! For if we are merely there metaphorically, it must be the same for Christ.

The truth is: Christ is in the heavenly realms and so are we! He is there *literally*, and we are there *representatively*, as members of his Body. He is there as our Head and brings our actual presence with him because we are in him. Believing this will greatly elevate our Christian living. Paul's massive conception of the heavenlies and his present relation to them which we see here in Ephesians, and in such passages as 2 Corinthians 12:1-6, Colossians 3:1-4, and Philippians 3:20, 21, endowed him with noble motivation and great energy for his earthly ministry.

We *are seated* in the heavenly realms. We *do have* every spiritual blessing. Belief is the beginning.

Second, we must focus on this truth. Paul calls us to be spiritual extraterrestrials — to live in the supra-mundane. We must reject the deadly notion that this is mystical, incomprehensible, and beyond our ability to practice. Paul says, "Since, then, you have been raised with Christ, set your hearts on things above, where Christ is seated at the right hand of God. Set your minds on things above, not on earthly things" (Colossians 3:1, 2). What is our mind set on? Position? A new car? A promotion? Our wardrobe? Paul says, Stop! Rather, keep on seeking the things which are above. This is our divinely-given responsibility.

Third, we must ask for the blessings. Jesus says in Luke 11:13, ". . . how much more will your Father in heaven give the Holy Spirit to those who ask him!" What does Jesus mean? Isn't the Holy Spirit already given to believers? The answer is explicit in the Greek grammar, which means *the operation of the Holy Spirit.*[19] Prayer brings increased fullness and power of the Holy Spirit. *We must ask!* As we ask for more holiness — a greater sense of adoption, more peace, more love, more patience, more power from the Spirit — we will receive it all.

CELEBRATING GOD (v. 3)

In all of this Paul celebrates God. "Praise be to the God and Father of our Lord Jesus Christ, who has blessed us in the heavenly realms with every spiritual blessing in Christ."

Our highest response to all this must be to hold our gifts up to God and sing the boundless praise of him who reigns above! *Our theology must become doxology.*

Late in his life Dr. Mackay reflected on his Ephesians-experience with Christ:

> Fifty years almost have passed since that boyish rapture in the Highland hills. . . . The sun of life is westering, and this mortal pilgrimage must, in the nature of things, be entering the last lap before sunset. Life has been throughout an adventure, a movement from one frontier to another. For me, as I reflect upon the passage of the years . . . A subjective fact, an experience of quickening by God's Holy Spirit in the classical tradition of Christian conversion, moulded my being in such a way that I began to live in Christ and for Christ, and 'for His Body's sake which is the Church.' My personal interest in God's Order began when the only way in which life could make sense to me was upon the basis of an inner certainty that I myself, through the operation of a power which the Ephesian Letter taught me to call 'grace,' had become part of that Order, and that I must henceforth devote my energies to its unfolding and fulfillment.[20]

May the Ephesian letter do the same for us!

Praise be to the God and Father of our Lord Jesus Christ, who has blessed us in the heavenly realms with every spiritual blessing in Christ. For he chose us in him before the creation of the world to be holy and blameless in his sight. In love he predestined us to be adopted as his sons through Jesus Christ, in accordance with his pleasure and will — to the praise of his glorious grace, which he has freely given us in the One he loves. (1:3-6)

2

Celebration of Election

EPHESIANS 1:3-6

W e are indeed seated with Christ in the heavenly realms. Why? We are his people. How? He chose us!

Commentators agree that verses 4-14 amplify the thoughts of verse 3, and this being so, the first thing Paul wants to expand is the truth of divine election.

THE FACT OF ELECTION (v. 4)

He does this with very specific statements in verses 4-6. "For he chose us in him before the creation of the world" (v. 4a). Later in that long sentence, verse 11, he neatly summarizes it again: "In him we were also chosen, having been predestined according to the plan of him who works out everything in conformity with the purpose of his will." From these statements we cull several points.

First, the choosing was before time as we know it — "before the creation of the world," to use Paul's words. God's choosing antedated human need — indeed, human existence! As Calvin says, "The very time of election shows it to be free; for what could we have deserved, or in what did our merit consist, before the world was made?"[1] (Cf. Romans 9:11.)

Second, the reasons for God's choosing were only in himself. Verses 4, 5 reveal that it was "In love he predestined us." His choosing cannot be separated from love. God did not do his choosing with a roulette wheel or a throw of celestial dice, because "Where love is supreme there is no place for fate or caprice."[2] Verse 5 expands on this by stating that this was "in accordance with his pleasure and will." "His pleasure" bears the idea of his *good* pleasure or *good* desire. Marcus Barth says, "Far from any idea of arbitrariness it has warm and personal connotations. When God's good pleasure is mentioned, his willingness and joy in doing good are indicated."[3]

God's eternal choice is warm and smiling — far from the dispassionate stereotype so often thought of. Again, the ground of his choice is his love and good pleasure, not man's or woman's goodness.

Third, the choice was made "in him" — that is, in Jesus. How absolutely fitting this is, for creation itself exists *in him*, as is taught so beautifully in the great Colossian Hymn of the Incarnation:

> For by Him all things were created, both in the heavens and on earth, visible and invisible, whether thrones or dominions or rulers or authorities — all things have been created by Him and for Him. And He is before all things, and in Him all things hold together. He is also head of the body, the church; and He is the beginning, the first-born from the dead; so that He Himself might come to have first place in everything. (Colossians 1:16-18, NASB)

Everything in creation comes from Christ, sings the Colossian Hymn. And here in the overture to Ephesians, everything is subject to his sovereign election. "He is foundation, origin, and executor: all that is involved in election and its fruits depends on him."[4] Jesus, who became sin for us on the cross (2 Corinthians 5:21) and a curse (Galatians 3:13), bearing the inconceivable pain of separation from the Father for us, is the agent and facilitator of the Father's choice. *In Christ* we were chosen.

This is primary truth, and as John Stott, a man known for measured sensibility, says: *"The doctrine of election is a divine revelation, not a human speculation."*[5] It was not dreamed up by Martin Luther or John Calvin or St. Augustine, or by the Apostle Paul for that matter. It is not to be set aside as the imagination of some overactive religious minds, but rather humbly accepted as revelation (however mysterious it may be) from God. We must never allow our subjective experience of choosing Christ water down the fact that we would not have chosen him if he had not first chosen us. (Cf. John 6:44, John 15:16, 2 Thessalonians 2:13, 1 Peter 1:2, 1 Thessalonians 1:4-7.) The doctrine of election presents us with a God who defies finite analysis. It is a doctrine which lets God be God.

It also forms a bedrock of confidence for the believer. A God who chose you before time, when only he existed, will not leave you victim to the time and tides of life. As a sixteen-year-old I read Arthur W. Pink's *The Sovereignty of God*, through which I was made to see the transcendent holiness of God, my own utter sinfulness, and his sovereign working in bringing men and women to himself. The effect of this was to increase my trust in him.

In view of this, there can be no room for pride or imagined merit, but rather profound humility and thanksgiving. It is not by accident that as Paul begins his overture of blessing, he opens with celebrating the blessing of being chosen. Paul could never get over it. And neither should we!

THE PURPOSES OF ELECTION (vv. 4-6)

Sanctification. The first purpose of election which Paul notes is sanctification: "For he chose us in him before the creation of the world to be holy and blameless in his sight" (v. 4). One of the false charges made against the doctrine of election is that it is morally debilitating — "If we are chosen, then we can do as we like." Nothing could be further from the truth! Rather, election is morally elevating because it is election to a dynamic two-sided sanctification. *Positively* it is "to be holy" — that is, set apart from the world, separate, different. And *negatively* it is to be "blameless" — literally, without spot or blemish, a sacrifice to be presented to God. Election demands and promotes the radical moral excellence of Romans 12 — the offering of believers' "bodies as living sacrifices, holy and pleasing to God" (Romans 12:1).

That is why the telltale evidence of one's election is holiness. Harold Ockenga, pastor of Park Street Church and founding president of Fuller Seminary and Gordon-Conwell Seminary, put it in no uncertain terms:

> If God has elected us He has not elected us to remain sinners but to become holy. It is an anomaly or an error to speak of the elect living in sin. God never chose us to continue in sin. We are created in Christ Jesus unto good works which God hath before ordained that we should walk in them. Therefore, the test of our election is the holiness of our lives. Christ "gave himself for us, that he might redeem us from all iniquity, and purify unto himself a peculiar people, zealous of good works." We ought not to delude ourselves into believing that we belong to the elect of God if we are not living holy lives before Him. . . . The proof of this is that we become holy, that we approximate the character of our Lord Jesus Christ. Thus John was able to say, "Whosoever sinneth hath not seen him, neither known him. . . . He that committeth sin is of the devil. . . . Whosoever is born of God doth not commit [practice] sin."[6]

I cannot agree more! If your life is characterized by a pattern of conscious sin, you very likely are not a Christian. If some of your most cherished thoughts are hatreds, if you are determined not to forgive, you may not be a true believer. If you are a committed materialist who finds that your greatest joys are self-indulgence — clothing your body with lavish outfits, having all your waking thoughts devoted to house, cars, clothing, and comforts — you may not be a Christian. If you are a sensualist who is addicted to pornography, if your mind is a twenty-four-hour bordello — *and you think it's okay* — you may very well not be a Christian, regardless of how many times you have "gone forward" and mouthed the evangelical shibboleths. Election ultimately results in holiness, but the process begins *now*. Are you concerned for holiness? Are you growing in holiness?

Adoption. The next grand purpose of election which the apostle celebrates is adoption — "he predestined us to be adopted as his sons through Jesus Christ, in accordance with his pleasure and will," sings Paul (v. 5). This is an especially lyrical chord — and for good reason. The writers of the Old Testament only referred to God as Father fourteen times in the huge corpus of its thirty-nine books — and these rather impersonally. In those fourteen occurrences of "Father," the term was always used with reference to the nation and not individuals. But when Jesus came on the scene, he addressed God only as Father. The Gospels record Jesus using "Father" more than sixty times in reference to God. He never used any other term except when quoting Psalm 22 on the cross. No one in the entire history of Israel had spoken or prayed like Jesus. No one! But this amazing fact is only part of the story, because the word Jesus used for *Father* was not a formal word. It was the common Aramaic word with which a child would address his or her father — "Abba." This was astounding!

Even more astounding, it became the subconscious and conscious refrain of the elect, who were "adopted as his sons through Jesus Christ." Paul says of this, "For you did not receive a spirit that makes you a slave again to fear, but you received the Spirit of sonship. And by him we cry, '*Abba*, Father.' The Spirit himself testifies with our spirit that we are God's children" (Romans 8:15, 16). "Because you are sons, God sent the Spirit of his Son into our hearts, the Spirit who calls out, '*Abba*, Father.' So you are no longer a slave, but a son; and since you are a son, God has made you also an heir" (Galatians 4:6, 7).

Do we have a "spirit of adoption"? Do we sense that God is our Father? Do we think of him and address him as our "Dear Father"? If we cannot answer in the affirmative, it may be because he is not our spiritual Father, and therefore we need to heed the words of Scripture and receive him. "Yet to all who received him, to those who believed in his name, he gave the right to become children of God" (John 1:12).

Dr. J. I. Packer considers our grasp of God's Fatherhood and our adoption as sons or daughters as of essential importance to our spiritual life. He says:

> If you want to judge how well a person understands Christianity,
> find out how much he makes of the thought of being God's child,

and having God as his father. If this is not the thought that prompts and controls his worship and prayers and his whole outlook on life, it means that he does not understand Christianity very well at all. For everything that Christ taught, everything that makes the New Testament new, and better than the Old, everything that is distinctively Christian as opposed to merely Jewish, is summed up in the knowledge of the Fatherhood of God. "Father" is the Christian name for God.[7]

That name testifies to the reality of our adoption. The richness of our adoption will also be revealed in a future public recognition. Paul says, "The creation waits in eager expectation for the sons of God to be revealed" (Romans 8:19). The day of our investiture as sons and daughters is coming, and he is our loving Father right now.

A young mother wrote:
"I stayed with my parents for several days after the birth of our first child. One afternoon, I remarked to my mother that it was surprising our baby had dark hair, since both my husband and I are fair.
"She said, 'Well, your daddy has black hair.'
"'But, Mama, that doesn't matter because I'm adopted.'
"With an embarrassed smile, she said the most wonderful words I've ever heard: 'I always forget.'"[8]

Our adoption is complete, and we are eternally God's sons and daughters. We were predestined for this before the foundation of the world, "In love . . . in accordance with his pleasure and will." This ought to be the the the melody of our hearts continually.

Praise. The last stated purpose of our election is praise — "to the praise of his glorious grace, which he has freely given us in the One he loves" (v. 6). His "glorious grace" is the undeserved riches which are ours in Christ. The emphasis here is on the bounty of it, for the words "which he has freely given" are literally "begraced."[9] So Paul's words memorably read, "to the praise of his glorious grace, which he has begraced us with, in the One he loves." This is an abundant overflow of grace, like the "fullness of his grace" of John 1:16.[10]

Paul has let himself go, throwing his heart into grand jubilation over the greatness of salvation. Clause tumbles after clause in his grand poem of praise. We are actually seated "in the heavenly realms" in Christ. Our position in the heavenlies opens us to "every spiritual blessing in Christ." We have been chosen before time began because of his love and good pleasure. The choice was not due to anything in us, but because of Jesus. He is everything.

27

This choice gives us great reason to rejoice, for it brings: *sanctification* — a holiness in conformity with that of God; *adoption* — we become the actual sons and daughters of God, so that we cry in our heart of hearts, "Abba, Father"; and *praise* in our hearts for "his glorious grace with which he has begraced us" — "fullness of grace."

In him we have redemption through his blood, the forgiveness of sins, in accordance with the riches of God's grace that he lavished on us with all wisdom and understanding. And he made known to us the mystery of his will according to his good pleasure, which he purposed in Christ, to be put into effect when the times will have reached their fulfillment — to bring all things in heaven and on earth together under one head, even Christ. (1:7-10)

3

Celebration of Redemption

EPHESIANS 1:7-10

The song of celebration with which Paul begins the letter to the Ephesians strains analysis, because in his exultant spirit one great thought presses upon another. The doxology runs on and on in one colossal (some would say monstrous) sentence filled with prepositional phrases: "in Christ . . . in him . . . in the One he loves . . . in him . . . in Christ . . . in him . . . in him . . ."[1] Nevertheless, as we carefully examine it, we find that it does have a kind of structure. After the initial burst of praise in verse 3, Paul celebrates (in vv. 4-6) the blessings of God's eternal *election* of us to *adoption* and *sanctification* and a life of *benediction*. The doctrine of election is singularly refreshing and sweet to the believing heart!

Now in verse 7 the thought structure abruptly switches from the blessings of election *past* to a celebration of *present* redemption and its *future* effects. This is a proper celebration for all who truly know Christ.

CELEBRATION OF THE PRESENT BLESSINGS OF REDEMPTION (vv. 7, 8)

Paul memorably celebrates our present blessings in verses 7 and 8: "In him we have redemption through his blood, the forgiveness of sins, in accordance with the riches of God's grace that he lavished on us with all wisdom and understanding." Here Paul emphasizes four elements: first, *redemption*, and then the three attendant blessings of *forgiveness*, *overflowing grace*, and *spiritual discernment*.

Redemption. Paul is explicit regarding the fact of redemption: "In him we have redemption through his blood" (v. 7a). What does he mean?

31

A story which has captured and informed young imaginations for years is helpful here. In a city on the shore of a great lake lived a small boy who loved the water and sailing. So deep was his fascination that he, with the help of his father, spent months making a beautiful model boat, which he began to sail at the water's edge. One day a sudden gust of wind caught the tiny boat and carried it far out into the lake and out of sight. Distraught, the boy returned home inconsolable. Day after day he would walk the shores in search of his treasure, but always in vain. Then one day as he was walking through town he saw his beautiful boat — in a store window! He approached the proprietor and announced his ownership, only to be told that it was not his, for the owner had paid a local fisherman good money for the boat. If the boy wanted the boat, he would have to pay the price. And so the lad set himself to work doing anything and everything until finally he returned to the store with the money. At last, holding his precious boat in his arms, he said with great joy, "You are twice mine now — because I made you, and because I bought you."

Just so! Redemption is payment of a price or ransom. The price was Christ's own blood, and the object was our souls. All humanity was in the slave market of sin and thus powerless to affect self-deliverance, but Christ has purchased his Church with an infinite price as the Scriptures repeatedly attest:

> For you know that it was not with perishable things such as silver or gold that you were redeemed from the empty way of life handed down to you from your forefathers, but with the precious blood of Christ, a lamb without blemish or defect. (1 Peter 1:18, 19)

> [Jesus] entered the Most Holy Place once for all by his own blood, having obtained eternal redemption. (Hebrews 9:12b)

> [Jesus came] "to give his life as a ransom for many." (Mark 10:45)

Our redemption cost the whole life of Christ — an astounding mystery which the prophets puzzled over and which angels "long to look into" (cf. 1 Peter 1:10-12).

This too is cause for great celebration, and that is why it is so prominent in Paul's song of praise. In fact, it is such a source of cosmic wonder that in eternity men and angels will join together to sing a new song, as Revelation records:

> And they sang a new song: "You are worthy to take the scroll and to open its seals, because you were slain, and with your blood you purchased men for God from every tribe and language and people

and nation. You have made them to be a kingdom and priests to serve our God, and they will reign on the earth." Then I looked and heard the voice of many angels, numbering thousands upon thousands, and ten thousand times ten thousand. They encircled the throne and the living creatures and the elders. In a loud voice they sang: "Worthy is the Lamb, who was slain, to receive power and wealth and wisdom and strength and honor and glory and praise!" (Revelation 5:9-12)

We will sing this song with the angels, but the best part is ours because we are "twice his," having been created by him and then being redeemed by his blood!

Forgiveness. Concomitant with redemption is forgiveness — "the forgiveness of sins" (v. 7). As a believer, the Apostle Paul remained profoundly aware of his sinful life apart from Christ and that he was still a sinner — "the chief of sinners," to use his own words. But along with this was the profound knowledge that he was forgiven.

Ancient man was aware of his sin. The brilliant Roman philosopher Seneca called himself a *homo non tolerabilis*, "a man not to be tolerated."[2] (Our wives no doubt sometimes think this would be a perfect title for us, with the addition of some adjectives like *maximus*!) What humankind needed, said Seneca in despair, was a hand to lift them up.

Charles Colson tells of watching Albert Speer being interviewed on "Good Morning, America." Speer was the Hitler confidant whose technological genius kept the Nazi factories running throughout World War II. He was *the only one* of the twenty-four war criminals tried at Nuremburg to admit his guilt, and he had served twenty years in a Spandau prison. The interviewer referred to a passage in one of Speer's earlier writings: "You have said the guilt can never be forgiven or shouldn't be. Do you still feel that way?" Colson says he will never forget the look of pathos on Speer's face as he responded, "I served a sentence of twenty years, and I could say, 'I'm a free man, my conscience has been cleared by serving the whole time as punishment.' But I can't get rid of it. This new book is part of my atoning, of clearing my conscience." The interviewer pressed the point: "You really don't think you'll be able to clear it totally?" Speer shook his head. "I don't think it will be possible." Colson says:

> For thirty-five years Speer had accepted complete responsibility for his crime. His writings were filled with contrition and warnings to others to avoid his moral sin. He desperately sought expiation. All to no avail. I wanted to write Speer, to tell him about Jesus and his death on the cross, about God's forgiveness. But there wasn't time. The ABC interview was his last public statement; he died shortly after.[3]

The tragedy for both Seneca and Speer is that there was, and is, a hand to lift them up — complete forgiveness of sins — though they didn't know it.

John Calvin said, in preaching on this very text in Geneva in 1558, "God puts our sins out of his remembrance and drowns them in the depths of the sea, and, moreover, receives the payment that was offered him in the person of his only Son."

The Scriptures sing in glorious harmony about the fullness of forgiveness:

... as far as the east is from the west, so far has he removed our transgressions from us. (Psalm 103:12)

"I have swept away your offenses like a cloud, your sins like the morning mist. Return to me, for I have redeemed you." (Isaiah 44:22)

"For I will forgive their wickedness and will remember their sins no more." (Jeremiah 31:34b)

You will . . . hurl all our iniquities into the depths of the sea. (Micah 7:19)

[At the Last Supper, Jesus commanded his own to drink, saying] "This is my blood of the covenant, which is poured out for many for the forgiveness of sins." (Matthew 26:28)

If we confess our sins, he is faithful and just and will forgive us our sins and purify us from all unrighteousness. (1 John 1:9)

It is because of this massive Scriptural affirmation that we conclude the Apostles' Creed by saying, "I believe in . . . the forgiveness of sins, the resurrection of the body, and the life everlasting. Amen."

Total forgiveness is something to celebrate. It is beyond anything positive thinking, therapy, or hypnosis can provide. It is complete, extending to the conscious and unconscious sins in our lives, because God knows all things and because Jesus' blood is infinite. I remember my first experience of God's forgiveness and how his Holy Spirit gave me the assurance that my sins were totally forgiven. The burden was so consciously lifted that I felt as if I could float. And anyone can be forgiven, no matter what their sin is, whether they are the commandant of Auschwitz or John Wayne Gacy or the most immoral (or even the most moral) person in America. Total forgiveness is possible through Christ. And having that, we are compelled to sing as Paul does here.

Grace. Paul's song goes on to the inevitable mention of grace. Our redemption and forgiveness, he says, are "in accordance with the riches of God's grace that he lavished on us . . . " (vv. 7b, 8a).

Think of it this way: John D. Rockefeller was the richest man in the world, the richest man America had ever produced. If Rockefeller wished to give of his riches there were two ways he could — *according to* his riches, or *from* his riches. History records that he most often did the latter, giving from his riches. The most famous picture of Rockefeller shows him as a wizened old man, dressed in a top hat and cut-away coat giving a dime to some little waif. Rockefeller reportedly did this again and again for the press to dutifully photograph. One wonders how many boys were truly set on the road to wealth and moral excellence by a wonderful gift *from* Rockefeller's fortune.

But think what it would have been like had he given *according to* his riches. If he had done that, he would have perhaps given a grand home, say the famous greystone Kykiut on the family estate Pocantico, and for the living room a Gilbert Stuart or George Washington, a Rodin for the lawn, and a forest, and a Dusenberg for the carriage house.

When God gives "in accordance with the riches of [his] grace" he gives from his unlimited treasure-house. Grace is unmerited favor — "an overflowing abundance of unmerited love, inexhaustible in God and freely accessible through Christ," says Charles Hodge.[4]

In addition to being redeemed and forgiven, we are now eternal objects of his divine favor in accordance with his riches which he lavished on us and will continue to lavish! As believers with Paul, we are wealthy beyond the dreams of avarice, for God gives not *from* the riches of his grace, but *according to* the riches of his grace! We are going to be lavished with favor for eternity. This ought to bring music to our souls.

> *When we've been there ten thousand years,*
> *Bright shining as the sun,*
> *We've no less days to sing God's praise*
> *Than when we first begun.*
>
> (John Newton)

Discernment. Paul's final thought regarding our present blessings is that our redemption brings spiritual discernment — "wisdom and understanding." Our English text here leads us to think that in God's own wisdom and understanding he decided to lavish us. That is not the idea at all. What is meant is that along with "redemption" and "forgiveness" and "grace" he has given us "wisdom and understanding."[5] University of Chicago professor Allan Bloom, in his book *The Closing of the American*

Mind, describes how his "uneducated" grandparents lived on a wise and noble level because of the influence of the Bible. Then he says this:

> I do not believe that my generation, my cousins who have been educated in the American way, all of whom are M.D.s or Ph.D.s, have any comparable learning. When they talk about heaven and earth, the relations between men and women, parents and children, the human condition, I hear nothing but clichés, superficialities, the material of satire. I am not saying anything so trite as that life is fuller when people have myths to live by. I mean rather that a life based on the Book is closer to the truth, that it provides the material for deeper research in and access to the real nature of things.[6]

What Professor Bloom says is eminently true. But there is still more, for when one's life is steeped in God's Word, and through God's grace one has been given "wisdom and understanding," one is equipped with the spiritual discernment to face whatever comes in life. "Wisdom is the knowledge which sees to the heart of things, which knows them as they really are . . . understanding [is that] which leads to right action."[7] Those so equipped can discern the spirit of the times and stand tall and confident.

Now put all the present blessings together as they flow out of redemption. There is *redemption* itself — we are twice-owned by God! There is absolute, total, comprehensive *forgiveness* and the freedom it brings. There is the fact that it is not from the riches of his *grace,* but in accordance with the riches of his grace that he lavishes grace on us — a veritable flood of undeserved favor that will go on for eternity. And there is the wonderful gift of *spiritual discernment.* Each of these notes comes together to produce a remarkable song in the heart of the redeemed which will only be amplified in eternity.

CELEBRATING THE FUTURE BLESSINGS OF REDEMPTION (vv. 9, 10)

Paul's emphasis on the blessing of wisdom and understanding prepares the way for the next focus of celebration, the *future* blessings of redemption. Paul continues, "And he made known to us the mystery of his will according to his good pleasure, which he purposed in Christ, to be put into effect when the times will have reached their fulfillment — to bring all things in heaven and on earth together under one head, even Christ" (vv. 9, 10).

The redeemed see that a new order is coming. It was a "mystery," a secret, in times past, not because it was incomprehensible, but because it was undiscoverable by human reason.[8] It could only be known through divine revelation. What is "the mystery"? Simply this: "when the times will have reached their fulfillment" (in other words, at the appropriate time), God will "bring all things in heaven and on earth together under one head, even Christ."

As believers, we know this to be true. We do not share the pessimism and despair of the world, like that of G. N. Clark in his inaugural lecture at Cambridge when he said, "There is no secret and no plan in history to be discovered. I do not believe that any future consummation could make sense of the irrationalities of preceding ages."[9] But the redeemed know otherwise. History is going somewhere. All will make sense when everything is brought under the headship of Christ.[10]

What do the "all things in heaven and on earth" encompass? 1) Regenerated souls, and 2) the created universe. The work has begun with God's children. Believers are presently united in the Body of Christ over which he is the Head. This brings believing Jews and Gentiles together — a major miracle in Paul's eyes, as we will later see (chapter 2). A solidarity between the Church Triumphant in Heaven and the Church Militant on earth is a reality. Whether here or there, we all share blessing, election, adoption, grace, redemption, forgiveness, and spiritual wisdom — and we will all be brought together in him. As Calvin says, "Man has been lost, but angels were not out of danger. By uniting together both into His own Body, Christ has conjoined them to God the Father, that He might establish a true harmony in heaven and on earth"[11] (cf. 3:10, 15). This is the new order.

Along with this, the cosmos, which Christ created and sustains (Hebrews 1:2, 3; Colossians 1:15-18), will be ordered under Christ. Paul says in Colossians 1:16 that "all things were created by him and for him" — or *toward Him*, as some have it.[12] He is the Alpha and Omega, the beginning and the end. All things came out of him, and all things will return to him. Thus all creation is moving toward its consummation in him, as described in Romans 8:19-21 — "The creation waits in eager expectation for the sons of God to be revealed . . . the creation itself will be liberated from its bondage to decay and brought into the glorious freedom of the children of God" (cf. 2 Peter 3:10-13; Matthew 19:28). Thus all redeemed souls, all the universe, and all the faithful angelic hosts — literally everything in Heaven and on earth — everything material, everything spiritual, everything within, without, above, and below — will be united in Christ. This is the blessing of the universe!

Paul's torrent of blessing is difficult to analyze, but as we look closely there is an order to his tumbling words. After his initial burst of blessing in verse 3, "Praise be to the God and Father of our Lord Jesus Christ, who has blessed us in the heavenly realms with every spiritual blessing in Christ," he celebrates blessings originating in the *past* in verses 4-6: election, sanctification, adoption, and benediction/praise. Then in verses 7, 8 he celebrates the *present* blessings: redemption, forgiveness, grace, spiritual discernment. And finally, in verses 9, 10, he celebrates the *future* order as everything is brought under Christ's headship. These blessings rooted in the past, being experienced in the present, and waiting in the future are reason to sing — and the best part does not belong to the angels, but to us, for *we are the redeemed!*

Paul's mind lived in the past, present, and future. His heart inhabited eternity. We need to look up — that's doctrine! And we need to sing — that's doxology! And we need to fight — that's duty!

In him we were also chosen, having been predestined according to the plan of him who works out everything in conformity with the purpose of his will, in order that we, who were the first to hope in Christ, might be for the praise of his glory. And you also were included in Christ when you heard the word of truth, the gospel of your salvation. Having believed, you were marked in him with a seal, the promised Holy Spirit, who is a deposit guaranteeing our inheritance until the redemption of those who are God's possession — to the praise of his glory. (1:11-14)

4

Celebration of Salvation

EPHESIANS 1:11-14

We now come to the end of Paul's song of celebration, which, as we have seen, is one long, sublime sentence extending from verse 3 through verse 14. As Paul begins this new section, he again sounds the chord of election, as he had in verses 4-6, and again launches into its celebration: "In him we were also chosen, having been predestined according to the plan of him who works out everything in conformity with the purpose of his will, in order that we, who were the first to hope in Christ, might be for the praise of his glory" (vv. 11, 12). Evidently, for Paul the doctrine of election was immensely comforting, just as it was centuries later for Jonathan Edwards, who wrote that "The doctrine has often appeared exceedingly pleasant, bright, and sweet. Absolute sovereignty is what I love to ascribe to God."[1]

But what arrests our attention here is that up to this point in his song Paul had been speaking of all the elect in general, but now begins to make distinctions to emphasize the inclusion of Gentiles in salvation. We see this emphasis in the change of pronouns: "In him we [*Jews*] were also chosen, having been predestined according to the plan of him who works out everything in conformity with the purpose of his will, in order that we [*Jews*], who were the first to hope in Christ, might be for the praise of his glory. And you [*Gentiles*] also were included in Christ when you heard the word of truth, the gospel of your salvation. Having believed, you [*Gentiles*] were marked in him with a seal, the promised Holy Spirit, who is a deposit guaranteeing our [*Jews' and Gentiles'*] inheritance until the redemption of those who are God's possession — to the praise of his glory." Paul is celebrating the miracle of the salvation and union in Christ which Jews and Gentiles share. This is a miracle to which he will give full exposition in 2:11-22.

How was it that this miraculous inclusion of Gentiles in election and salvation took place? What are the dynamics of it?

INCLUDED THROUGH THE WONDER OF BECOMING "IN CHRIST" (v. 13a)

To begin with, Paul is very clear that at the root of the miracle is the wonder of their becoming "in Christ." As verse 13 says, "And you also were included in Christ when you heard the word of truth, the gospel of your salvation." We must stop to think about this term because it is by far one of the most important theological concepts in the New Testament. In Paul's present song he uses it or its equivalent nine times. Experts on Pauline theology as diverse as Adolf Deissmann and Albert Schweitzer agree that the term "in Christ" is the central category in Paul's thinking. The term "in Christ" or "in Christ Jesus" is used in Paul's letters, according to Deissman's calculation, some 169 times.[2] The terms are not found prior to Paul and are rare outside his writings.[3] What does the term signify?

First, it indicates *radical transformation*. Paul delineates this in 2 Corinthians 5:17 — "Therefore, if anyone is in Christ, he is a new creation; the old has gone, the new has come!" This is a dynamic assertion which is even more powerful in the Greek because there are no verbs in the original: "If any man in Christ — new creation!" He is radically, fundamentally new. Not only that, but "the new *has come*!" and, as the Greek perfect tense stresses, will continue to remain.

Being "in Christ" is nothing less than being made alive. ". . . so in Christ all will be made alive," says Paul (1 Corinthians 15:22; cf. 2:5). This is a total spiritual change. "He becomes the soil in which they grow, the atmosphere which they breathe, the source and goal of their entire existence as men."[4]

Being in Christ brings a radical reorientation — a movement from external righteousness to inward righteousness which radicalizes our conduct. As a result, though the world hates, those in Christ forgive; while the world lusts for more, those in Christ are content.

From my perspective, "in Christ" far outstrips the term "Christian" in describing Christianity. Aside from the fact that "Christian" is only used three times in the New Testament (Acts 11:26; Acts 26:28; and 1 Peter 4:16), that title allows for an ambiguous interpretation. It can mean one who has a specific cultural affinity, or the "western tradition," or one who lives on one side of barbed wire and is killing those on the other side. But "in Christ" invites no such abuse, because it demands reflection on a dynamic, living relationship. No wonder Paul loved it. "For to me, to live is Christ," said Paul (Philippians 1:21). *Christianity is Christ!* Those who are not "in

Christ" are not Christians, and if and when they become real Christians they will be *in Christ* — and thus radically transformed and alive!

Secondly, being in Christ brings a *dynamic unity of cosmic dimensions*. The heart of our unity is that we become members of the Body of Christ. Spiritually there is organic relationship with him. We are seated in the "heavenly realms" with him (2:6) — we are there because we are in him. Through this union we also enter into a profound oneness with other believers. "There is neither Jew nor Greek, slave nor free, male nor female, for you are all one in Christ Jesus" (Galatians 3:28). It was this dynamic unity which astounded the ancient world. As Alexander Maclaren so eloquently said:

> When these words were spoken, the then-known civilized world was cleft by great, deep gulfs of separation, like the crevasses in a glacier, by the side of which our racial animosities and class differences are merely superficial cracks on the surface. Language, religion, national animosities, differences of condition, and saddest of all, difference of sex, split the world up into alien fragments. A "stranger" and an "enemy" were expressed in one language, by the same word. The learned and the unlearned, the slave and his master, the barbarian and the Greek, the man and the woman, stood on opposite sides of the gulfs, flinging hostility across. Then the benefits of the Gospel came! Then "the Barbarian, Scythian, bond and free, male and female, Jew and Greek, learned and ignorant," clasped hands and sat down at one table, and felt themselves "all one in Christ Jesus." They were ready to break all bonds.[5]

The "in Christ" is what conquers the world. There is much in professing Christianity which seems to deny the dynamic unity which Christ brings. The sixth edition of the *Handbook of Denominations in the United States* lists no less than twenty-eight Baptist and nineteen Methodist denominations — not to mention the thousands of independent Baptist churches. Let me name some denominational choices the *Handbook* offers:

The Duck River (and Kindred) Associations of Baptists
The Two-Seed-in-the-Spirit Predestinarian Baptists
The River Brethren
The (Original) Church of God, Inc.,
The Churches of the New Jerusalem
The Fire Baptized Holiness Church
The Pillar of Fire Church
The Schwenkfelder Church
The Triumph of the Church and Kingdom of God in Christ Church.[6]

If that isn't enough, all we have to do is lift our eyes to Northern Ireland where "Christians" of the two great ecumenical traditions are killing each other, or to South Africa's support of apartheid. But having said this, the fact remains that those truly in Christ really do have profound sharing and true ecumenicity. Those truly in Christ can experience a friendship which surpasses all others in its understanding, commitment, and comfort. And that ought to be the norm for the Church, as Jesus prayed in his High Priestly prayer on the eve of his death: "Holy Father, protect them by the power of your name — the name you gave me — so that they may be one as we are one" (John 17:11). What a balm to the soul this spiritual unity is!

Thirdly, our being in Christ brings *deep satisfaction*. The simple fact is, it is not possible to be fulfilled outside of Christ. John Stott once shared this old Chinese proverb when speaking at the Union League Club in Chicago:

> You want to be happy for one hour — get drunk.
> You want to be happy for three days — get married.
> You want to be happy for eight days — kill your pig and eat it.
> You want to be happy forever, become a gardener.

This is something less than a sure-fire formula for fulfillment! The pleasure which the world offers is very much like a Chinese dinner. No matter how good it is, you'll be hungry again in two hours! It is in Christ, and in Christ only, that lasting fulfillment, deep human satisfaction, is found. "Jesus declared, 'I am the bread of life. He who comes to me will never go hungry, and he who believes in me will never be thirsty'" (John 6:35).

Shortly after Malcolm Muggeridge became a Christian he delivered a sermon in Queen's Cross Church, Aberdeen (Sunday, May 26, 1968) in which he made this confession:

> I may, I suppose, regard myself, or pass for being, a relatively successful man. People occasionally stare at me in the streets — that's fame. I can fairly easily earn enough to qualify for admission to the higher slopes of the Inland Revenue — that's success. Furnished with money and a little fame even the elderly, if they care to, may partake of trendy diversions — that's pleasure. It might happen once in a while that something I said or wrote was sufficiently heeded for me to persuade myself that it represented a serious impact on our time — that's fulfillment. Yet I say to you, and I beg you to believe me, multiply these tiny triumphs by a million, add them all together, and they are nothing — less than nothing — a positive impediment — measured against one draught of that living water Christ offers to

the spiritually thirsty — irrespective of who or what they are. What, I ask myself, does life hold, what is there in the works of time, in the past, now and to come, which could possibly be put in the balance against the refreshment of drinking that water?[7]

To this we hear Christ's eternal offer: "On the last and greatest day of the Feast, Jesus stood and said in a loud voice, 'If a man is thirsty, let him come to me and drink. Whoever believes in me, as the Scripture has said, streams of living water will flow from within him.' By this he meant the Spirit . . ." (John 7:37-39).

It is in Christ that there comes radical transformation, "new creation," and resurrection life. It is in Christ that we experience union with him and oneness with one another. And it is in Christ only that one finds satisfaction and fulfillment. Could there be a more enticing menu — transformation, union, satisfaction? This fare meets every need.

How does it come to us? Humanly speaking it comes through believing, as Paul says in verse 13 — "And you also were included in Christ when you heard the word of truth, the gospel of your salvation. Having believed . . ." Believing in Christ is the path to being in Christ! This worked for me and millions of others, and it will most surely work for all who come to Christ.

THE AMAZING WORK OF THE HOLY SPIRIT (vv. 13b, 14a)

None of this could happen without the astounding work of the Holy Spirit in bringing about this union and our inclusion in the Body of Christ. Paul describes the Spirit's work in the final sentence of verse 13 and in the first part of verse 14: "Having believed, you were marked in him with a seal, the promised[8] Holy Spirit, who is a deposit guaranteeing our inheritance . . ."

We must answer two questions in order to mine these riches: 1) What does it mean to be "marked in him with a seal"? 2) How is the Holy Spirit "a deposit guaranteeing our inheritance"?

In regard to sealing, in the ancient world the owner announced his ownership by attaching his seal to his possessions. That is what God has done for us. He has tagged us, he has left his mark on us in our hearts, and we who have the seal know it. "The Spirit himself," says Paul in Romans 8:16, 17, "testifies with our spirit that we are God's children. Now if we are children, then we are heirs — heirs of God and co-heirs with Christ." The seal not only assures us that we are his — it also assures us of his protection. Later in Ephesians we find the same word as we read that with the Holy Spirit of God we are "sealed for the day of redemption" (4:30). We are owned by our Lord and are under his protection until the great day of redemption.

Along with his mark or seal, the Holy Spirit serves as a deposit guaranteeing our inheritance. We understand from the Greek and Roman culture of that day that it was customary to make a deposit, an *arrabon* as they called it, on the purchase of a possession. The *arrabon* was a down payment which announced that more of the same would be coming — the first installment. Today we often call it "earnest money." Thus we understand that the spiritual life given to us by the Holy Spirit is an *arrabon* of what is to come. The celebrated Greek scholar Bishop Lightfoot of Cambridge says, "The actual spiritual life of the Christian is the same in kind as his future glorified life."[9] It is the same in kind, though immeasurably less in degree.[10] It is a true foretaste.

Imagine the sublimest, most treasured experiences of the Holy Spirit we have ever had and then realize they are only a foretaste, the tip of the tongue on the spoon, of what is to come. Remember the release in coming to Christ and knowing you were forgiven? Remember that time when in worship you were smitten with awe? Remember the time you followed the Spirit's leading and were wonderfully used? Remember the satisfaction of finding the fruits of the Spirit surprising you with goodness where you once responded wickedly? Think of all this and then multiply it a millionfold. Here on earth we have experienced the first dollar of a million celestial dollars — the earnest. We have the dawning of knowledge, but then we will have the midday sun. "'No eye has seen, no ear has heard, no mind has conceived what God has prepared for those who love him' — but God has revealed it to us by his Spirit" — the *arrabon* (1 Corinthians 2:9, 10).

Do you have the *arrabon* of the Holy Spirit? It is the real thing, but nevertheless just a taste! What will the first five minutes be like when we come into the fullness of our inheritance? The first fifteen minutes? The first hour? The first day — week — month — year — thousand years?

The end of all of this is sounded in the concluding words of the song which tell us that the *arrabon*, the deposit, guarantees "the redemption of those who are God's possession — to the praise of his glory" (v. 14b).

We are "God's possession." The huge significance of this statement can only be seen when we understand that in the Old Testament Israel, and only Israel, is called God's possession. Malachi, the very final book in the Old Testament, testifies to this: "'They will be mine,' says the Lord Almighty, 'in the day when I make up my treasured possession'" (Malachi 3:17; cf. the same word in the LXX of Exodus 19:5; Deuteronomy 6:7; cf. also Deuteronomy 14:2; 26:18; Isaiah 43:21). To have these words applied now to Gentiles is one of the most stupendous things in the New Testament (cf. 1 Peter 2:9; Acts 20:28). This places Jews and Gentiles on equal footing in regard to the benefits of election and salvation.

Jews and Gentiles are to live, as the final phrase of the song says, "to the praise of his glory." Take a final look at Paul's song. It begins with praise in verse 3: "*Praise* be to the God and Father of our Lord Jesus Christ, who has blessed us in the heavenly realms with every spiritual blessing in Christ." Then in verse 6 we are again called "to the *praise* of his glorious grace," and again in verse 12, "for the *praise* of his glory," and finally in verse 14, "to the *praise* of his glory." I think he is trying to tell us something! We are to celebrate being "in Christ" and the radical transformation that brings, the dynamic union with God and his people and the fulfillment which comes. We must celebrate our seal or *arrabon* as his Spirit bears witness with our spirit because that foretaste is going to multiply a million-fold.

Let us live "to the praise of his glory."

> Praise the Lord.
> Praise God in his sanctuary;
>   praise him in his mighty heavens.
> Praise him for his acts of power;
>   praise him for his surpassing greatness.
> Praise him with the sounding of the trumpet,
>   praise him with the harp and lyre,
> praise him with tambourine and dancing,
>   praise him with the strings and flute,
> praise him with the clash of cymbals,
>   praise him with resounding cymbals.
> Let everything that has breath praise the Lord.
> Praise the Lord.
>
> (Psalm 150)

For this reason, ever since I heard about your faith in the Lord Jesus and your love for all the saints, I have not stopped giving thanks for you, remembering you in my prayers. I keep asking that the God of our Lord Jesus Christ, the glorious Father, may give you the Spirit of wisdom and revelation, so that you may know him better. I pray also that the eyes of your heart may be enlightened in order that you may know the hope to which he has called you, the riches of his glorious inheritance in the saints, and his incomparably great power for us who believe. That power is like the working of his mighty strength. . . . (1:15-19)

5

A Prayer for Enlightenment

Ephesians 1:15-19

As we come to this section of
Ephesians Paul has completed his song of celebration — a record-setting
203-word sentence in which he has successively celebrated their mutual
blessing and *redemption* and, finally, *salvation*. But though the song has
ended, he has not stopped celebrating, because he now goes on to praise
God for the practical outworking of the blessings he has been singing about,
as evidenced by the Ephesians' *faith* and *love*. "For this reason, ever since
I heard about your *faith* in the Lord Jesus and your *love* for all the saints, I
have not stopped giving thanks for you, remembering you in my prayers"
(vv. 15, 16, italics added).

In thanking God for their faith in Jesus, Paul is, of course, praising
God for their *saving faith*. They had been saved by grace through faith and
not by their own hand. Their boast was in Christ alone (2:8, 9), and that was
something to thank God for! But Paul was also giving thanks for their *practical faith*. The Ephesian church not only rested its salvation but also its
everyday life on Christ. The Ephesians believed Christ would take care of
them through thick and thin. Their faith was not like the man who was
attempting to cross the frozen St. Lawrence River in Canada. Unsure
whether the ice would hold, the man first tested it by laying one hand on it.
Then he got down on his knees and gingerly began making his way across.
When he got to the middle of the frozen river trembling with fear, he heard
a noise behind him. Looking back, to his horror he saw a team of horses
pulling a carriage down the road toward the river. And upon reaching the
river they didn't stop, but bolted right onto the ice and past him, while he
crouched there on all fours, turning a deep crimson. If only he had known

how firm the ice really was that day . . . The Ephesians knew Christ had saved them and could hold them up, and as a result they were charging straight ahead. For this, Paul thanked God.

Paired with their exemplary faith was their "love for all the saints." Significant here is the word *all*; they loved *all* their fellow Christians! The reason this is so striking, of course, is that this is often not true in Christian circles. As Jonathan Swift (himself a clergyman) so rightly observed: "We have just enough religion to make us hate, but not enough to make us love one another."[1] Our surface Christianity arms us with what we think are proper prejudices and a rationale for criticizing those who fall short, keeping them at arm's length. Not so with the Ephesians! That is why the word for "love" here is *agape* — a thoughtful, volitional, purposeful love that wills to love even the unlovely — the very love of God himself.

The Ephesians had this love in their hearts through the work of the Holy Spirit (Romans 5:5), and they chose to exercise it toward one another. The attitude among the Ephesians was, "my life for your life." I once saw a picture of Hell. It showed several obviously selfish, unhappy people seated around a table for a meal. Each held a long-handled spoon with which it was impossible to feed themselves — they could only feed each other. But no one was willing to do that. Of course, that meal was "Hell." There was none of this in Ephesus. They looked out for each other, bearing each other's inadequacies and eccentricities and sins in love. They lived out Jesus' new commandment: "'A new commandment I give you: Love one another. As I have loved you, so you must love one another. All men will know that you are my disciples if you love one another'" (John 13:34, 35). The city of Ephesus knew this, and as a result many had turned to Christ.

Calvin says: "Observe here, that under faith and love Paul sums up the whole perfection of Christians."[2] Thus, when faith and love are paired together in a church we have something for which to thank God. This is what Paul was doing *par excellence*: "I have not stopped giving thanks for you, remembering you in my prayers" (v. 16). His thanksgiving went on and on, and this apostolic effervescence is a beautiful thing. This attitude is so typical of Paul, and it ought to typify us (Romans 1:9; 1 Corinthians 1:4; Philippians 1:3, 4; Colossians 1:3; 1 Thessalonians 1:2; 2 Thessalonians 1:3; Philemon 4).

Do we thrill at hearing of the faith and love of others? Do we rejoice in others' spiritual attainments? Especially revealing, do we praise God when this is happening in places we are not present? Other churches? Other organizations? St. John of the Cross put it this way: "As far as everyone is concerned, many experience displeasure when they see others in possession of spiritual goods. They feel sensibly hurt because others surpass them on this road and they resent it when others are praised."[3] Paul's attitude calls us upward. His is a heart to be emulated.

It is a fact that only those who are thankful for the spiritual achieve-ment of others can truly pray for them.[4] So Paul's celebrating heart moves from a preamble of praise to powerful petition. How should we pray for those we love — our brothers and sisters in Christ? This is beautifully answered by Paul's fervent example.

PAUL PRAYS FOR A BETTER KNOWLEDGE OF CHRIST (v. 17)

To begin with, Paul prays that the Ephesians will develop a deeper knowl-edge of Christ: "I keep asking that the God of our Lord Jesus Christ, the glorious Father, may give you the Spirit of wisdom and revelation, so that you may know him better" (v. 17).

Knowing Christ is one of the New Testament's ways of describing saving faith. Jesus himself said in his High Priestly prayer, "Now this is eternal life: that they might *know* you, the only true God, and Jesus Christ, whom you have sent" (John 17:3, italics added). Those who know Christ have eternal life; those who do not know him are without it.

What does knowing Christ involve? It involves knowing more than facts about Christ. I know a lot about President Bush. I know where he went to school. I know what sports he played. I know his chronological his-tory. I know some of his weaknesses and strengths. But I do not know George Bush. The facts are helpful, but they are not enough. Knowing Christ involves more than a passing acquaintance.

I once met a famous movie star (Dick Van Dyke) at a party. I shook hands with him, stood next to him, sized him up (he's shorter and skinnier than I expected — the magic of the silver screen). I chatted with him. But I do not know Dick Van Dyke — and he certainly does not know me!

To truly know another, there must be mutual knowledge and a mutual exchange. And knowing Christ goes even beyond this. The word "know" here has an Old Testament heritage behind it in which the word *yada* often expressed sexual intimacy — "Adam knew Eve his wife; and she con-ceived, and bore Cain" (Genesis 4:1, KJV). It is the spiritual parallel of this that Jesus has in mind in describing those who have eternal life.

Tragically, there are many religious people who believe they are Christians and yet do not know Christ. Jesus warns, "Many will say to me on that day, 'Lord, Lord, did we not prophesy in your name, and in your name drive out demons and perform many miracles?' Then I will tell them plainly, 'I never knew you. Away from me, you evildoers!'" (Matthew 7:22, 23).

So the question which must be asked is: Do we really know Christ? Are we in him? Is he in us? Does he know us? (See Galatians 4:9; 1 Corinthians 8:3.) Is there an intimate exchange between him and us?

Of course the Ephesians knew Christ, but Paul is praying that they might "know him better." The regular Greek word for personal knowing is *gnosis*, but here the word is intensified with the preposition *epi*. Paul is asking for an *epignosis* — a "real, deep, full knowledge" [5] — a "thorough knowledge"[6] (cf. Romans 3:20 and 1 Corinthians 13:12). Paul wants his beloved Ephesians, who are so full of faith and love, to go deeper and deeper in their knowledge of Christ.

Here Paul puts his emphasis on the great need of the Church. The wisdom and focus of the world is summed up in two words: "know yourself," and the focus of many, perhaps most, Christians is very often the same. They are occupied with getting a knowledge of self, improving their Gestalt, rather than knowing Christ! As a result they are stunted in their growth. As E. W. Bullinger said: "Instead of breathing this life-giving air of heaven, their windows are closed, and their doors are shut, and they are asphyxiated with their own exhalation. They are breathing over again and again their own breath, from which all vitality is gone."[7]

The great need of any church, whether it is healthy or not, is knowing Christ — an *epignosis* — a better, deeper, fuller knowledge of Christ. I have memorized only a few verses in the Greek, but Philippians 3:10 is one, and it begins *tou gnonai auton* — "that I may know Him" (NASB). That is the key to all of life. We ought to read the Scriptures with an eye to knowing him. We ought to listen to preaching with this in mind. We ought to pray this for the Church and ourselves, for it is an apostolic, Spirit-ordained prayer.

We should note before moving to the next verses that Paul prays for the Holy Spirit to do this — "the Spirit of wisdom and revelation." Deep knowledge of Christ can only come as the Holy Spirit ministers it. "The Spirit searches all things, even the deep things of God . . . no one knows the thoughts of God except the Spirit of God" (1 Corinthians 2:10, 11). Ask for the Spirit to build your *epignosis* of Christ, who said, ". . . how much more will your Father in heaven give the Holy Spirit to those who ask him!" (Luke 11:13).

PAUL PRAYS FOR BETTER SPIRITUAL VISION (vv. 18, 19)

From asking for a better knowledge of Christ, Paul moves on to request better spiritual vision: "I pray also that the eyes of your heart may be enlightened" (v. 18a). In Scripture, the heart is the fulcrum of man's being, the seat of his intelligence and will. Paul asks, therefore, that our spiritual center will be given spiritual vision.

As in our physical life, so it is with our soul — virtually everything depends on our sight. King Zedekiah had his eyes gouged out by the king of Babylon. He was taken to the fabled city, but saw nothing of her tiled palaces and hanging gardens and brass gates. We don't need more truth or better truth (impossible!). We simply need our spiritual eyes opened to the truths that surround us.

Specifically, Paul asks that we would have our vision bettered regarding three things: *hope*, *riches*, and *power*. Observe the words in this prayer: "I pray also that the eyes of your heart may be enlightened in order that you may know the hope to which he has called you, the *riches* of his glorious inheritance in the saints, and his incomparably great *power* for us who believe" (vv. 18, 19a).

First, *hope*. Paul wants us to have a better vision of "the hope to which he has called you." Our hope has its source in our election, which took place before the creation of the world (1:4). It is sealed in us by the Holy Spirit, given as a sweet down payment, an *arrabon*, of what is to come. This hope is the grand hope of being manifested with Christ in glory — "the hope of the glory of God" (Romans 5:2). "Now if we are children, then we are heirs — heirs of God and co-heirs with Christ, if indeed we share in his sufferings in order that we may also share in his glory" (Romans 8:17). "When Christ, who is your life, appears, then you also will appear with him in glory" (Colossians 3:4). Paul prays that we will take hold of this gigantic hope.

Hope is the opposite of despair — it breathes a massive optimism! We are going to stand with Christ at the final press conference of the universe, and our photograph is going to be taken with him, and we are going to look *like* him. "Dear friends, now we are children of God, and what we will be has not yet been made known. But we know that when he appears, we shall be like him, for we shall see him as he is" (1 John 3:2).

Second, *riches*. Paul prays that our eyes will be opened as to "the riches of his glorious inheritance in the saints." What he wants us to see is that *we are God's riches* — "his possession," as verse 14 also previously mentioned! F. F. Bruce says regarding this:

> Paul prays here that his readers will appreciate the value which God places on them, his plan to accomplish his eternal purpose through them as the first fruits of the reconciled universe of the future, in order that their lives may be in keeping with the high calling and that they may accept in grateful humility the grace and glory thus lavished on them.[8]

Think of it: he owns all the heavens and numberless worlds, but *we* are his treasures. The redeemed are worth more than the universe. We ought to be delirious with this truth! Paul prays that we will see this with our heart's eyes.

Third, *power*. Here Paul outdoes himself as he stacks synonym upon synonym in an attempt to describe it. With the Greek synonyms inserted, verse 19 reads like this: ". . . and his incomparably great power [*dunamis*] for us who believe. That power [*kratos*] is like the working [*energia*] of his mighty strength [*ischus*]." Paul has layered these synonyms to express as best he can the highest power possible. He exhausted his language describing this power of the resurrection (see v. 20). What we must see is that the power that raised Jesus from the dead can bear directly on our lives now and at his appearing. This stupendous power changes us from children of Hell to children of God and gives us practical victory over sin in our lives. We will see it visibly someday in the resurrection of our bodies, for no created power in the universe can do that. Only through the "great power" — "That power . . . the working . . . his mighty strength" — is it possible! Yet, this same power is operating in and for those of us who believe right now! Paul would ask, "Do you see it?"

The great celebration of spiritual blessing of verses 3-14 led Paul to the preamble of praise in verses 15 and 16 for the practical outworking of faith and love in the Ephesian church. This preamble gave way to his two-pronged prayer. First (v. 17) he prayed that we would have a better knowledge of Christ — that we would "know him better." The more we see of Jesus, the more we will be drawn to him, and then become like him. Are we making this part of our personal and corporate prayers?

Second, (vv. 18, 19) Paul prayed that we would have better spiritual vision regarding three things: 1) the great "hope to which he has called" us — that we will share in his glory; 2) that our eyes would be opened to "the riches of his glorious inheritance in the saints" — that we are his treasured inheritance; 3) that his all-surpassing power is on us and will continue on to our glorification.

We need to see this! Some years ago I read a quotation from Armitage Robinson, the greatest of all Ephesians scholars, who said Paul's spiritual vision made him the foremost of apostles. Since that time I have come to believe this with deeper and deeper conviction. We need to have our eyes opened, like Elisha's servant (2 Kings 6:15-17). We need to pray for "the [Holy] Spirit of wisdom and revelation," that we might see Christ more and more. If we pray this apostolic prayer we will not be the same.

I pray also that the eyes of your heart may be enlightened in order that you may know the hope to which he has called you, the riches of his glorious inheritance in the saints, and his incomparably great power for us who believe. That power is like the working of his mighty strength, which he exerted in Christ when he raised him from the dead and seated him at his right hand in the heavenly realms, far above all rule and authority, power and dominion, and every title that can be given, not only in the present age but also in the one to come. And God placed all things under his feet and appointed him to be head over everything for the church, which is his body, the fullness of him who fills everything in every way. (1:18-23)

6

The Fullness of Him

EPHESIANS 1:18-23

Just before World War II in the town of Itasca, Texas, a school fire took the lives of 263 children. There was scarcely a family in town which was not touched by this horrifying tragedy. During the war Itasca remained without school facilities. But when the war ended, the town, like many others, began to expand and in fact built a new school which featured what was called "the finest sprinkler system in the world." Civic pride ran high. Honor students were selected to guide citizens and visitors on tours of the new facility to show them the finest, most advanced sprinkler system technology could supply and money could buy. Never again would Itasca be visited by such a tragedy. With the postwar boom the town continued to grow, and seven years later it was necessary to enlarge the school — and in adding the new wing it was discovered that the sprinkler system had never been connected.[1]

What an incredible story! Its folly strains our belief. Yet, alas, it is a parable of what has happened in so many Christian lives. There is untold power available for every believer in Christ, but so many never hook up, and their lives are thus impotent and shamefully useless.

That is why Paul stacked all those power synonyms upon one another in verses 19 and 20 as he prayed that we might experience "his [God's] incomparably *great power* for us who believe. That *power* is like the *working* of his *mighty strength*, which he exerted in Christ when he raised him from the dead" (italics added). The stupendous power Paul is describing can be glimpsed in the nuances of the synonyms he used: 1) "[P]ower." *Dunamis* is the word we get *dynamite* from and is used over 100 times in the New Testament. It indicates raw power or strength. 2) "[W]orking." *Energeia*, from which we derive our word *energy*, means "inworking" and suggests the inward propulsion of power. 3) "[M]ighty" (*kratos*) means "ability to conquer," as when Caesar conquered Cleopatra. *Autocrat* comes from this word. 4) "[S]trength" (*ischus*) refers to physical force.[2] These graphic synonyms in the Pauline bouquet depict the awesome extent of God's power.

The greatest display of this power was seen "when [God] raised [Christ] from the dead." Just as the cross is the highest display of God's love, so the Resurrection is the ultimate display of his power. No created force could ever do this! But what Paul wants us to see personally and practically is that "his incomparably great power [is] *for us* who believe." How so?

First as *saving power*. Paul says in the opening verses of Romans, "I am not ashamed of the gospel, because it is the power of God for the salvation of everyone who believes: first for the Jew, then for the Gentile" (Romans 1:16). The limitless power of God is brought to bear on souls who are being brought to Christ. This is why no one is beyond his grace. This is why we can confidently offer it to all. Some may say, "You have no idea what I've done. My perversions, my betrayals, my deceptions are beyond your sheltered imagination." But God says his power is adequate — and it is.

Second, this "incomparably great power" comes to us as *sanctifying power* — that is, power to help us live godly lives. Later in Ephesians Paul asserts that "[God] is able to do immeasurably more than all we ask or imagine, according to his power that is at work within us" (3:20). We have, in fact, resurrection power within us. "Or don't you know," says Paul, "that all of us who were baptized into Christ Jesus were baptized into his death? We were therefore buried with him through baptism into death in order that, just as Christ was raised from the dead through the glory of the Father, we too may live a new life" (Romans 6:3, 4). That is why Paul prays, "I want to know Christ and the power of his resurrection" (Philippians 3:10). Christ, by his Spirit, gives "his incomparably great power for us who believe," so we can live life as we ought. This is resurrection power!

The problem is, many never hook up. The system is in place, but it is dysfunctional because of ignorance or sin or disbelief. If you are not experiencing his power as you ought to be, Paul's prayer is that "the eyes of your heart may be enlightened in order that you may know . . . his incomparably great power for us who believe." This is Paul's underlying motivation in verses 18-23.

Having looked at the display of his power in the Resurrection, we want now to focus in these verses on his power as it is seen in his *Exaltation* and in his *Lordship* — and how it affects us.

GOD'S POWER WROUGHT CHRIST'S GLORIOUS EXALTATION (vv. 20, 21)

Christ's glorious exaltation is detailed in verses 20, 21 in this way: when the Father raised Jesus from the dead he "seated him at his right hand in the heavenly realms, far above all rule and authority, power and dominion, and every title that can be given, not only in the present age but also in the one to come."

After Jesus' triumphant resurrection he ministered over a period of forty days, appearing to groups large and small, teaching them regarding his Kingdom. But at the end of the forty days he gathered them at Jerusalem and charged them with this task: "But you will receive power when the Holy Spirit comes on you; and you will be my witnesses in Jerusalem, and in all Judea and Samaria, and to the ends of the earth" (Acts 1:8). As the echo of his words faded away, there appeared a luminous cloud, the Shekinah Glory, and Jesus began to slowly[3] be elevated before their awestruck eyes and was engulfed in the shimmering cloud as he ascended to Heaven (Acts 1:9-11; Luke 24:50-53; cf. Revelation 12:1-6). Theologians all agree that this was the official Ascension of Christ. But some theologians believe there had already been a secret ascension on Easter morning, so that Jesus' appearances during the forty days before his public ascension occurred as he returned intermittently from Heaven to encourage people.[4]

Whatever the case, all joyously concur that Christ's exaltation at the Father's "right hand in the heavenly realms" was unutterably glorious! The "right hand" is a metaphor for the position of highest honor and bliss and glory and authority and power. The writer of Hebrews alludes to Psalm 110:1, which is also in view here, as he sings in wonder, "To which of the angels did God ever say, 'Sit at my right hand until I make your enemies a footstool for your feet'?" (Hebrews 1:13). The image we have of this exaltation in Ephesians is that of a victory parade (4:7-10). Imagine the music, the perpetual starbursts of color, and the shouting of myriads and myriads of angels at Jesus' enthronement! Paul puts it in song to Timothy as a confessional statement for the church:

> Beyond all question, the mystery of godliness is great:
> He appeared in a body,
>   was vindicated by the Spirit,
> was seen by angels,
>   was preached among the nations,
> was believed on in the world,
>   was taken up in glory.
>
> (1 Timothy 3:16)

The Ascension of our Lord Jesus Christ does at least five things:

1) It *completes the Resurrection*. The body which Christ took on in Bethlehem, and died in, and was resurrected in was removed gloriously to Heaven in the Ascension. This has wonderful implications for us, because his body was like ours. A body like ours is in Heaven!

2) He became the *firstfruits of his people*, for as the first in the harvest he guarantees the final redemption and exaltation of those in union with him (1 Corinthians 15:15, 20, 23; Colossians 1:15, 18).

3) Jesus ascended to begin his *ministry of intercession* for his people. Thus the worship and prayer of his people is offered through him, the High Priest, to God the Father (see Hebrews generally, especially 4:15; also Romans 8:34).

4) From his position at the Father's right hand, he is *dispenser of the Holy Spirit*. With the Spirit are given spiritual gifts for the enrichment and mission of the Church (John 14 — 16; Acts 2). With Jesus' ascension *the real "new age"* began, the age of the Spirit, experienced by those who are in Christ.

5) But most of all, the Ascension of our Lord speaks of his super-exaltation above everything![5]

Again Paul stacks up words to make his point (v. 21): "far above all rule and authority, power and dominion, and every title that can be given, not only in the present age but also in the one to come." Christ is exalted above every conceivable intelligence — angelic, demonic, or human. Armitage Robinson says, "Above all that anywhere is, anywhere can be — above all grades of dignity, real or imagined, good or evil, present or to come — the mighty power of God has exalted and enthroned the Christ."[6]

The heart application for all of us is this: if we want to know Christ better and have the *epignosis* that Paul prays for in verse 17, we must understand the glory of his exaltation — and believe it. This is our Jesus today! Do we *see* it? Do we believe it? If so, there is something else — which ought to give us spiritual goose bumps — and that is, he wants us to be there with him! In his High Priestly prayer Jesus prayed, "Father, I want those you have given me to be with me where I am, and to see my glory, the glory you have given me because you loved me before the creation of the world" (John 17:24).

I personally find this astounding. Jesus wants me and you to be with him, to see his glory, and to share in it (cf. Romans 8:18-30)!

GOD'S POWER DISPLAYS CHRIST'S ABSOLUTE LORDSHIP (v. 22)

Christ's unparalleled exaltation anticipates and demands his absolute, sovereign Lordship, which receives unequivocal statement next in verse 22: "And God placed all things under his feet and appointed him to be head over everything for the church." As we attempt to think about this, we must keep in mind that Christ was already Creator of everything, as the parallel Colossians hymn so explicitly states. The entire universe had been created and set in motion by Jesus (Colossians 1:15-18)!

Sir Isaac Newton, it is said, had an exact replica of our solar system made in miniature. At its center was a large golden ball representing the sun, and revolving around it were smaller spheres attached at the ends of rods of varying lengths. They represented Mercury, Venus, Earth, Mars, and the other known planets. These were all geared together by cogs and belts to make them move around the "sun" in perfect harmony.

One day as Newton was studying the model, a friend who did not believe in God stopped by for a visit. Marveling at the device, and watching as the scientist made the heavenly bodies move in their orbits, the man exclaimed, "My, Newton, what an exquisite thing! Who made it for you?" Without looking up Sir Isaac replied, "Nobody." "Nobody?" his friend asked. "That's right! I said nobody! All of these balls and cogs and belts and gears just happened to come together, and wonder of wonders, by chance they began revolving in their set orbits and with perfect timing." His friend got the message. The Scriptures proclaim that Jesus is the Creator! By virtue of his Creatorship and then his Saviorhood, everything is twice his because he made it and bought it.

What does this mean to us? Simply this: man was made to have dominion over the earth — "You made him ruler over the works of your hands; you put everything under his feet" (Psalm 8:3-9, esp. v. 6). But mankind failed, except for one, and that was the last Adam, Jesus. But those of us who are in him will fulfill this Psalm with him in his Kingdom. We are going to reign with him — rule the earth — be all we are meant to be!

Jesus is absolute, sovereign Lord of the universe — a dizzying thought in itself. But perhaps even more mind-boggling is that God also "appointed him to be head over everything for the church" (v. 22b). That the Father has given such a glorious One *to* the Church seems incredible.

John Owen, the great Puritan theologian and onetime chaplain to Oliver Cromwell, made a sublime comment on this matter of Christ's exaltation and Lordship and headship over the Church, listing eleven glories entailed in all that. In part Owen said:

> Thus is he glorious in his *throne*, which is at "the right hand of the Majesty on high," glorious in his *commission*, which is "all power in heaven and earth;" glorious in his *name*, a name above every name, — "Lord of lords, and King of kings;" glorious in his *sceptre*, — "a sceptre of righteousness is the sceptre of his kingdom;" glorious in his *attendants*, — "his chariots are twenty thousand, even thousands of angels," among them he rideth on the heavens, and sendeth out the voice of his strength, attended with ten thousand times ten thousand of his holy ones; glorious in his *subjects*, — all creatures in heaven and in earth, nothing is left that is not put in subjection to him; glorious in his *way of rule*, and the adminis-

tration of his kingdom — full of sweetness, efficacy, power, seren-
ity, holiness, righteousness, and grace, in and towards his elect, —
of terror, vengeance, and certain destruction towards the rebellious
angels and men; glorious in the *issue of his kingdom,* when every
knee shall bow before him, and all shall stand before his judgment-
seat. And what a little portion of his glory is it that we have pointed
to! This is the Beloved of the church, — its head, its husband; this
is he with whom we have communion. . . .[7]

Jesus Christ our Savior is absolute, imperial Lord, the Head of all creation, and he has been given to the Church as such. How he loves the
Church — you and me!

THE SIGNIFICANCE OF HIS RESURRECTION, EXALTATION, AND LORDSHIP FOR THE CHURCH (v. 23)

The ultimate significance of all we have been saying lies in the final verses
of this section, which describe us as "the church, which is his body, the fullness of him who fills everything in every way" (vv. 22b, 23). From this we
observe two wondrous things.

First, we are the Body — which complements the Head. This means
there is a subtle and vital union between Christ and us. Thinking of our
union in terms of an actual human body, we realize that the body is not a
bunch of loose parts somehow attached to each other. The marvel of the
body is that all of its parts are really one. My fingers are not joined to the
palms of my hands loosely. Nor are they tied on. There is a living connection, a vital union. "They are parts of one another; the connection is intimate and organic and vital and living."[8] We, the Body of Christ, actually do
share and will share in the Resurrection, Exaltation, and Lordship of the
Head of the universe and the Church, Jesus Christ!

The second thing we observe is that as the Body we are "the fullness
of him who fills everything in every way." What does this mean? To begin
with, we must understand that it is paradoxical language, which is typical of
Paul when he wants to state a deep truth. The meaning is: the Church is "the
fullness [that is, the *complement,* or *that which fills*] of him who fills everything [*the entire universe*] in every way." *The Church is that which fills up
Christ, who fills the universe in every way!*[9]

How can this be? How can Jesus, who created the universe and is its
Head and who fills it in every way, be filled by the Church? After all, as
God he is totally without need and independent of anything. The answer to
this paradox lies in the metaphor of the head and body: A head is incomplete without the body. As Martyn Lloyd-Jones says: "A body needs a head,
and you cannot think of a head without a body. So the body and the head

are one in a mystical sense."[10] Thus we, as the Body, are part of that which fills up Christ.

Various metaphors help our understanding: As the bridegroom is not complete without the bride, as the vine is not complete without the branches (cf. John 15), as the shepherd is incomplete without the sheep, as the head is not complete without the body, so the Church is the complement of Christ![11]

This is an astounding wonder which caused Calvin to exclaim:

This is the highest honor of the church that, unless He is united to us, the Son of God reckons Himself in some measure imperfect. What an encouragement it is for us to hear, that not until He has us as one with Himself is He complete in all His parts, or does He wish to be regarded as whole![12]

Our Lord Jesus Christ has an inexplicable, unfathomable love for us so that he sees himself, as a groom, incomplete without us! What a lofty position this gives to the Church. Even in eternity we will never get to the bottom of this. Those who are hurting in ways no one else can understand must conclude from this that *Jesus does understand and care!*

As we run our eyes back up this text, we begin to understand why Paul prayed that the eyes of our hearts would be opened so that we might glimpse "his incomparably great power for us who believe" — that power which brought about Jesus' resurrection, ascension, and exaltation, displaying his Lordship. Seeing this, we must understand that because we are his Body, because he loves us so much that he considers himself incomplete without us, that power is operable on our behalf right now!

There is only one thing necessary, and that is belief. Are we hooked up? If not, we can be by saying with our heart, "I see the power for us who believe. It is resurrection and ascension and sovereign power. And I believe it is for me because I am in 'his body, the fullness of him who fills everything in every way.'"

Can we believe it? Can we rest in it? Can we say, "Jesus, I believe"? Let us each tell him now.

As for you, you were dead in your trangressions and sins, in which you used to live when you followed the ways of this world and of the ruler of the kingdom of the air, the spirit who is now at work in those who are disobedient. All of us also lived among them at one time, gratifying the cravings of our sinful nature and following its desires and thoughts. Like the rest, we were by nature objects of wrath. But because of his great love for us, God, who is rich in mercy, made us alive with Christ even when we were dead in transgressions — it is by grace you have been saved. And God raised us up with Christ and seated us with him in the heavenly realms in Christ Jesus, in order that in the coming ages he might show the incomparable riches of his grace, expressed in his kindness to us in Christ Jesus. (2:1-7)

7

From Death to Life

Some years ago as a youth pastor I hiked with some of my high schoolers to the top of Mt. Whitney in California, the highest spot in the continental United States (14,495 feet). We exulted over the wonderful panorama of the Sierra Nevadas and the Mojave Desert. What a spot, with its rarefied, crystal-clear air, its indigo and turquoise lakes — vista giving way to vista as far as one could see. As we gazed together from what seemed to be the top of the world, one of our party pointed out that only eighty miles to the southeast was Death Valley, the lowest spot in the United States at 280 feet below sea level and the hottest place in the country with a record 134 degrees in the shade!

What a contrast! One place is the top of the world, the other the bottom. One place is perpetually cool, the other relentlessly hot. From Mt. Whitney you look down on all of life. From Death Valley you can only look up to the rest of the world.

In Ephesians 2 Paul takes us down to the Death Valley of the Soul (vv. 1-3) and then up to "the heavenly realms in Christ Jesus" (vv. 4-7). His method is contrast: from death to life, from Hell to Heaven, from bondage to freedom, from pessimism to optimism. The journey's contrast will enhance our appreciation for what we have in Christ and will influence the way we live.

DEATH VALLEY (vv. 1-3)

Paul begins at the very bottom of Death Valley: "As for you, you were dead in your transgressions and sins" (v. 1). This is an *absolute* statement. He doesn't mean that they were merely in danger of death, but that they were in a state of "real and present death."[1] Death is not a figure of speech. *Paul means they were absolutely dead.* Moreover, though Paul speaks of Gentiles in verse 1, he includes his fellow Jews in verse 3. This state of spiritual death is universal. He is not describing some decadent, drugged-out segment of society, but *all humanity*, from top to bottom. All people are dead apart from Christ.

The bottom line here is, when Paul says "dead" he means it to have *universal* and *absolute* application — no exceptions. I have in my file a photograph of the corpse of the philosopher Jeremy Bentham, father of utilitarianism. The photo shows his body sitting in a chair, dressed and hatted in early nineteenth-century gentleman's wear. The whole thing is a result of his dark humor, for when he died he gave orders that his entire estate be given to the University College Hospital in London on the condition that his body be preserved and placed in attendance at all the hospital's board meetings. This was duly carried out, and every year to this day Bentham is wheeled up to the board table and the chairman says, "Jeremy Bentham, present but not voting." This is, of course, a great joke on his utilitarianism. Jeremy Bentham will never raise his hand in response, he will never submit a motion — because he has been dead for nearly a hundred and sixty years.

The fact is, dead people can't do anything, and that is what Paul is talking to us about — the spiritual state of those apart from Christ.

How can this be, some wonder, when so many around us, unlike Jeremy Bentham, are so very much alive? Their bodies are virile and robust, they have quick, active intellects, they are brimming with personality. The answer is this: in the area which matters most, the soul, they have no life. They are blind to the reality, demands, and glory of Christ — and they do not love him. They are as deaf to the Holy Spirit as a corpse. "Abba, Father!" has no part in their vocabulary. Because of this, John Stott says, "We should not hesitate to reaffirm that a life without God (however physically fit and mentally alert the person may be) is a living death, and that those who live it are dead even while they are living."[2] Those without Christ are in Death Valley!

These are hard, hard words. How does Paul support his thesis? Those who are spiritually dead are under the sway of the *world*, the *Devil*, and the *flesh*, and Paul names them in this order in verses 2 and 3.

World. Regarding their domination by the world, he says in the first part of verse 2, "in which you used to live when you followed the ways of this world." The word translated "world" (*kosmos*) is used 186 times in the Greek New Testament, and virtually every instance has an evil connotation. Linked with the word "way" or *age* this phrase means, "the present evil age" (cf. Galatians 1:4). Those without Christ are captive to the social and value system of the present evil age, which is hostile to Christ. They are willing slaves to the pop culture of the media, the "group think" of the talk shows, post-Christian mores, and man-centered religious fads. The spiritually dead are dominated by the world!

The Devil. Paul describes the Devil as "the ruler of the kingdom of the air, the spirit who is now at work in those who are disobedient" (v. 2). Satan is described in Scripture as "the prince of this world" (John 12:31), "the prince of demons" (Matthew 9:34), and, a sobering title, "the god of this age" (2 Corinthians 4:4). As "the ruler of the kingdom of the air," he commands innumerable hosts in the unseen world and thus creates a spirit of the age, a *cosmos diabolicus* in which he knits just enough good with evil to achieve his purposes. This Devil dominates and energizes the spiritually dead!

The flesh. "All of us also lived among them at one time, gratifying the cravings of our sinful nature [*the flesh*] and following its desires and thoughts. Like the rest, we were by nature objects of wrath" (v. 3). The dead are corrupted from within too. Take, for example, the little girl who was disciplined by her mother for kicking her brother in the shins and then pulling his hair. "Sally," said her mother, "why did you let the Devil make you kick your little brother and pull his hair?" To which she answered, "The Devil made me kick him, but pulling his hair was my idea!" Yes, people sin under the Devil's influence, but they also sin on their own.

The dead, those without Christ, are dominated by the *world*, the *Devil*, and the *flesh*. The world dominates from *without*, the flesh from *within*, and the Devil from *beyond*. These are the terrible dynamics of spiritual death!

Paul concludes, "Like the rest, we were by nature objects of wrath" (v. 3b). Everyone, Jews and Gentiles, were (and are) sinners "by nature." They all sinned in and with Adam and are therefore guilty (Romans 5:12-14), objects of God's settled wrath. As John the Baptist said, "Whoever believes in the Son has eternal life, but whoever rejects the Son will not see life, for God's wrath remains on him" (John 3:36).

It has been often noted that these verses in Ephesians are a three-verse summary of the first three chapters of the Book of Romans, which teach the total *depravity* and *death* of humankind. The Biblical doctrine of depravity means that every part of the human person is tainted by sin.[3] It does not mean that all humans are equally depraved, for most do not go near the depths they could go. As John Gerstner says, there is always room for "deprovement." Nor does it mean that humans are not capable of any good (cf. Luke 11:13), or that there is no dignity in man, for there certainly is — he is the imperfect bearer of the divine image (Genesis 1:27). Rather, the meaning is that no part of the human being (mind, emotions, heart, will) is unaffected by the Fall. All of us are depraved — totally!

Because of this, apart from Christ we are totally lost. So profound is human depravity that near the end of his argument in Romans 3 Paul says, "There is no one righteous, not even one; there is no one who understands, no one who seeks God" (3:10, 11). We often hear people say, "Such and such a person is seeking after God." Indeed, it may be true that he or she is seeking the peace or hope that salvation brings, but if we are to believe God's Word and not our sentiment, it is the Holy Spirit who is prompting them. The Biblical doctrine of depravity demands an acceptance of man's absolute spiritual death.

A pastor friend of mine once told me that when he was working in a mortuary (while attending college and seminary) one night he walked into the darkened mortuary chapel and saw an eerie sight — an open casket at the front of the chapel with a body lying in it. He crept slowly to the casket and then slowly elevated himself so he could see the tip of the corpse's nose — and then shouted, "*Boo!*" It didn't move an eyelash! The Jeremy Bentham principle is still intact. *Dead men cannot respond.*

The uniqueness of the Biblical position can be seen when we note that in the long history of the human race there have been (and are) three basic views of human nature: man is *well*, man is *sick*, or man is *dead*. Supporters of the first view argue that all he needs is a good diet, exercise, and some vitamins. "I'm alright and you're alright" is their motto. Proponents of the second view agree that man is sick, maybe even mortally sick, but his situation is certainly not hopeless. The Biblical view is that man is not well or sick, but dead — "dead in [his] transgressions and sins." All man's self-help will avail nothing![4] You can play reveille in the Arlington National Cemetery for a whole year, but you will get no response from the dead soldiers there.

Every soul outside of Christ is in the Death Valley of the Soul. This is a desolate image, almost exactly like that which Ezekiel gives in the thirty-seventh chapter of his prophecy:

> The hand of the Lord was upon me, and he brought me out by the Spirit of the Lord and set me in the middle of a valley; it was full of bones. He led me back and forth among them, and I saw a great many bones on the floor of the valley, bones that were very dry. He asked me, "Son of man, can these bones live?" I said, "O Sovereign Lord, you alone know." (Ezekiel 37:1-3)

Everyone without Christ is dead. Most people do not want to hear this today, and many pulpits are silent about this doctrine. But it is a crucial truth because Christ's atoning death does not make any sense without it. A view of the Death Valley of the Soul is necessary for a proper view of the heavenlies.

THE HEIGHTS OF LIFE (vv. 4-7)

Resurrection. The journey from Death Valley to the spiritual heights of life is accomplished only by resurrection! "But because of his great love for us,

God, who is rich in mercy, made us alive with Christ even when we were dead in transgressions — it is by grace you have been saved" (vv. 4, 5). The eminent New Testament scholar Marcus Barth says that "in the majority of occurrences in the New Testament, the verb 'to make alive' is a synonym of 'to raise' from the dead."[5] Man is radically dead, and he can be saved only by the radicalness of resurrection!

If you are a Christian you have experienced resurrection power, for as Paul earlier said of God's power in the believer in 1:19, 20: "That power is like the working of his mighty strength . . . when he raised him from the dead." Humanity is divided into two groups: those who are resurrected, and those who are dead. Self-help will not save those who are "dead in [their] transgressions and sins." No one can crawl from the casket. He or she must be "made . . . alive with Christ."

When we were dead in our sins, we were depraved in every area. But having been made alive, his life now touches every area. Instead of deprovement, there has come improvement. The archives of the Billy Graham Center contain a letter which the soon-to-be-great evangelist Charles Fuller wrote to his wife the night of his conversion, July 16, 1916:

> There has been a complete change in my life. Sunday I went up to Los Angeles and heard Paul Rader preach. I never heard such a sermon in all my life. Ephesians 1:18. Now my whole life and aims and ambitions are changed. I feel now that I want to serve God if he can use me instead of making the goal of life the making of money.[6]

Charles Fuller experienced a spiritual resurrection that warm July night, and the change was so radical that he became a mighty instrument of God.

Ascension. With spiritual resurrection comes ascension to the heights of Heaven: "And God raised us up with Christ and seated us with him in the heavenly realms in Christ Jesus" (v. 6). Though not yet there physically, we Christians are already in the heavenlies by virtue of our union with Christ. Spiritually we are seated on the throne along with other believers. The powers of the spiritual realm have been brought to bear on our present life.

Riches. And what will be the end of all this? Actually there will be no end, because as verse 7 concludes, "in the coming ages he [will] show the incomparable riches of his grace, expressed in his kindness to us in Christ Jesus." A Roman matron was once asked, "Where are your jewels?" She responded by calling her two sons and, pointing to them, said, "These are my jewels."[7] So it is with Christ and his Church. He is going to show the all-surpassing riches of his grace to his children in the "limitless future, as age succeeds age."[8] He will show his grace and kindness before his return, at his return, after his return, and in all ages.[9]

On that beautiful day as my friends and I stood on the pinnacle of Mt. Whitney rejoicing at the beauty of the scene, a navy jet buzzed over us, breaking the sound barrier as it crossed the summit about 100 feet over our heads. Then he did barrel rolls off into the horizon, only to come back from the opposite direction and do the same thing. He was having a good time, but his thrill didn't compare to ours. He was just an observer passing by in a plastic bubble. We were *there* — standing on the summit, breathing alpine freshness, feeling God's creation. Only one thing would have made it better — rising from Death Valley that very morning, from the lowest to the highest.

We Christians have done that very thing in Christ. We were all in the Death Valley of the Soul, in desolation, lost, hopeless. But through his resurrection we have been raised to the highest heaven! We are fully alive!

Where are our friends and loved ones right now — "dead in [their] transgressions and sins" or "made alive with Christ"? There is resurrection power available for all who are without life, even among the parched bones of Death Valley.

> The hand of the Lord was upon me, and he brought me out by the Spirit of the Lord and set me in the middle of a valley; it was full of bones. He led me back and forth among them, and I saw a great many bones on the floor of the valley, bones that were very dry. He asked me, "Son of man, can these bones live?" I said, "O Sovereign Lord, you alone know." Then he said to me, "Prophesy to these bones and say to them, 'Dry bones, hear the word of the Lord! This is what the Sovereign Lord says to these bones: I will make breath enter you, and you will come to life. I will attach tendons to you and make flesh come upon you and cover you with skin; I will put breath in you, and you will come to life. Then you will know that I am the Lord.'" So I prophesied as I was commanded. And as I was prophesying, there was a noise, a rattling sound, and the bones came together, bone to bone. I looked, and tendons and flesh appeared on them and skin covered them, but there was no breath in them. Then he said to me, "Prophesy to the breath; prophesy, son of man, and say to it, 'This is what the Sovereign Lord says: Come from the four winds, O breath, and breathe into these slain, that they may live.'" So I prophesied as he commanded me, and breath entered them; they came to life and stood up on their feet — a vast army. (Ezekiel 37:1-10)

As men or women realize the need of new life and ask God for his grace, they will be saved. Hallelujah!

For it is by grace you have been saved, through faith
— and this not from yourselves, it is the gift of God
— not by works, so that no one can boast. For we are
God's workmanship, created in Christ Jesus to do
good works, which God prepared in advance for us to
do. (2:8-10)

8

All of Grace

EPHESIANS 2:8-10

As we have seen, those without Christ are spiritually dead and so cannot respond to the witness of the Holy Spirit or understand the glories of Christ. On the other hand, those in Christ are actually animated by God's Spirit and "walk in newness of life" (Romans 6:4, NASB). Paul has taken us on a dreary walk through the Death Valley of the Soul (vv. 1-3) and then on an exuberant ascent to the pinnacle of salvation and life in the heavenly places in Christ (vv. 4-7). He has taken us from:

> *Hell to Heaven*
> *Bondage to freedom*
> *Gloom to light*
> *Despair to hope*
> *Wrath to glory*
> *Death to life*

Now Paul is at the magnificent pinnacle of spiritual life, where he pauses to catch his breath and then recapitulates in these brief but immortal words from the mountaintop: "For it is by grace you have been saved, through faith — and this not from yourselves, it is the gift of God — not by works, so that no one can boast" (vv. 8, 9). This is the gospel in a nutshell — the most cogent summary of the dynamics of salvation to be found in Scripture. As such, it is a text which the Holy Spirit often uses to bring life to those without Christ. All who have not been saved, or who are not sure of their status, would do well to shut out all distractions and give attention to these words of life.

NOT BY WORKS

How is one saved? We answer first with Paul's negative affirmation in verse 9: "not by works, so that no one can boast." It is absolutely essential to understand and believe this if one is to be saved. *Salvation does not come by works!*

To accept the Bible's teaching that salvation is "not by works" means to go against the notions of our culture. I recall hearing an unbelieving preacher illustrate his philosophy by telling of a frog which fell into a large milk can. Try as it would, it could not get out. There was nothing to do but keep paddling, which it did until it churned a pad of butter and presto! saved itself by leaping from its self-made launching pad. Personally, if I fell into a pail of milk I would keep paddling as long as I could too, but I would not make that my philosophy of achieving eternal salvation. To think like that is to fall into the ancient Pelagian heresy which St. Augustine fought so passionately.

The sad truth is, the frog is an apt symbol of American folk religion. "Just keep on keeping on and you'll be all right" — "I'm a good person, not perfect, but there are a whole lot of people worse than I" — "God knows I'm not perfect, but I'm doing my best." That may be okay for Kermit the Frog, but it is not the language of salvation.

Our text gives us one reason salvation is not by works — "so that no one can boast." If salvation came by works, eternity would spawn a fraternity of rung-dropping, chest-thumping boasters — an endless line of celestial Pharisees: "God, I thank you that I am not like all other men — robbers, evildoers, adulterers" (Luke 18:11). In Jesus' parable of the sheep and the goats in Matthew 25, the goats on his left do all the boasting and are sent to judgment (Matthew 25:46; cf. 7:22). The sheep on his right (the saved, who go on to their heavenly reward) cannot even recall their good deeds (Matthew 25:37-39; cf. vv. 40-46), *for salvation does not come by works.* No one who is saved will have grounds to boast before God — or will even want to.

Important as this reason is, there are even deeper reasons why salvation is not by works — namely, the utter sinfulness of humanity contrasted with God's transcending standard of righteousness. God is radically righteous (Romans 1:17; 3:21). His righteousness of being is his standard, and no human can attain this because we are all radically sinful beings. The word *radical* comes from the Latin word *radix*, which means "root." The very root of our being, every part of our person, is tainted with sin. This is the foundation of the Apostle Paul's devastating litany of condemnation in Romans 3:10-18 where Paul employs the rabbinical technique of *charaz* (Hebrew for "string of pearls") in putting together an overwhelming list of evidences which prove the universally corrupt *character* (vv. 10-12) and *conduct* (vv. 13-18) of man. He concludes there that the entire human race

— Jews and Gentiles, religious and irreligious, pious and pagan — suffers from a radical inner corruption. Even our very best works are colored by sin and can never approach the radical righteousness which God demands. No matter how high we climb our moral ladder, it is not high enough. Salvation is "not by works."

Imagine that an airplane flies over the South Atlantic and crashes a thousand miles from any coast. In the plane there are three individuals: a great Olympic swimmer, an average swimmer, and someone who cannot swim at all. The Olympic star calls out, "Follow me — I'll get you out of this!" and takes off with an impressive crawl, heading for the tip of South America a thousand miles away. The other two jump after him. In about thirty seconds the non-swimmer goes down to Davy Jones' Locker. It takes about thirty minutes for the average swimmer to be deep-sixed. But the champion swimmer churns away for twenty-five hours, covering an impressive fifty miles. Terrific! Only 475 more hours to go! He'll be there in nineteen days if he doesn't slow down.

The truth is, despite our popular folk religion, our paddling will never do, no matter how "good" we are. The distance is too far, and we are too flawed. We can try, but all our works will be no more beneficial than rearranging the deck chairs on the *Titanic*. The Bible says, "not by works," and that is the truth.

Suppose I went to a close personal friend and said, "You are a terrific person, but I don't believe a thing you say." How would he feel? Yet this is the way some people treat God. "God, I believe you are great. I believe that Jesus is real. I simply can't believe your Word that salvation is *not by works*."

No one has that option. Whoever truly believes salvation is not by works is right at the door, for Jesus says, "Blessed are those who realize that they have nothing within themselves to commend them to God, for theirs is the Kingdom of Heaven" (author's paraphrase of Matthew 5:3).

BY GRACE

If we are not saved by works, how are we saved? The answer from the Bible is, by *grace*: "For it is by grace you have been saved, through faith — and this not from yourselves, it is the gift of God" (v. 8).

What is grace? *It is unmerited favor — the love of God going out toward the utterly undeserving.* It has reference here to forgiveness of sin and the riches which Christ brings. It is a lavish, sumptuous, joyous word. But the great and transcending emphasis of our text is that grace is a free gift. The idea of, "and this not from yourselves" is that "By God's grace you are people who have been saved through faith, and this whole event and experience is . . . God's free gift to you."[1]

A large prestigious church had three mission churches under its care. On the first Sunday of the New Year all the members of the mission churches came to the big city church for a combined Communion service. In those mission churches, which were located in the slums of the city, were some outstanding cases of conversions — thieves, burglars, and so on — but all knelt side by side at the Communion rail.

On one such occasion the pastor saw a former burglar kneeling beside a judge of the Supreme Court of England — the very judge who had sent him to jail where he had served seven years. After his release this burglar had been converted and become a Christian worker. Yet, as they knelt there, the judge and the former convict, neither one seemed to be aware of the other.

After the service, the judge was walking out with the pastor and said to him, "Did you notice who was kneeling beside me at the Communion rail this morning?" The pastor replied, "Yes, but I didn't know that you noticed." The two walked along in silence for a few more moments, and then the judge said, "What a miracle of grace." The pastor nodded in agreement. "Yes, what a marvelous miracle of grace." Then the judge said, "But to whom do you refer?" And the pastor said, "Why, to the conversion of that convict." The judge said, "But I was not referring to him. I was thinking of myself." The pastor, surprised, replied: "You were thinking of yourself? I don't understand." "Yes," the judge replied, "it was natural for the burglar to receive God's grace when he came out of jail. He had nothing but a history of crime behind him, and when he saw Jesus as his Savior he knew there was salvation and hope and joy for him. And he knew how much he needed that help.

"But look at me. I was taught from earliest infancy to live as a gentleman; that my word was to be my bond; that I was to say my prayers, to go to church, take Communion and so on. I went through Oxford, took my degrees, was called to the bar and eventually became a judge. Pastor, it was God's grace that drew me; it was God's grace that opened my heart to receive it. I'm a greater miracle of his grace."

Perhaps there is something to the judge's insistence upon his life being the greater miracle. But in both cases it was God's free, unearned grace and certainly not works which brought salvation.

Again, how contrary to the spirit of our age this is — especially American culture ("We make our money the old-fashioned way. We earn it!"). Such a mentality is proper to its realm, but in regard to salvation it is deadly! "For it is by grace you have been saved, through faith — and this not from yourselves, it is the gift of God" (v. 8). It is all of grace.

Paul reinforces this in Romans 11:6 — "And if by grace, then it is no longer by works; if it were, grace would no longer be grace." The fact is, as soon as there is a mixture of even the smallest percentage of works, grace is debased and perverted. No one will be saved except for God's unmerited grace.

Pascal said, "Grace is indeed required to turn a man into a saint; and he who doubts this does not know what either a man or a saint is."[2] He is so right.

The reason the judge saw his own salvation as a greater miracle than that of the thief is that his position had made him proud and hardly the kind of man to humble himself enough to receive God's free gift. But this is what we must do.

> *But in this world of sin*
> *Where meek souls will*
> *Receive Him still*
> *The dear Christ enters in.*

Men and women must be meek enough to receive his grace, to admit they cannot save themselves or earn their own admittance into Heaven. They must listen with all they have to Paul's third point, that salvation comes "through faith."

THROUGH FAITH

For it is by grace you have been saved, through faith — and this not from yourselves, it is the gift of God. (v. 8).

If there is no faith there is no grace and no salvation. In Scripture, faith/belief is the thing that God honors more than any single quality: "'*Believe* in the Lord Jesus, and you will be saved'" (Acts 16:31). "Yet to all who received him, to those who *believed* in his name, he gave the right to become children of God" (John 1:12). "'Through him everyone who *believes* is justified from everything you could not be justified from by the law of Moses'" (Acts 13:39). "[T]o the man who does not work but *trusts* God who justifies the wicked, his faith is credited as righteousness" (Romans 4:5). No one has sins forgiven, no one goes to Heaven, no one has peace until there is faith in Jesus Christ.

What, then, is faith? Faith is not the mere intellectual reception of Christian truth, nor is it belief alone. *True faith is belief plus trust.*

A story which comes from the last century makes this clear. During the 1900s Jean Francois Gravalet, better known by his stage name, Blondin, was a world-famous acrobat. Born in France in 1824, Blondin became well-known while still a child. As he grew older, his skill and showmanship brought him fame throughout Europe and America. Once in London he played the violin on a tightrope 170 feet off the ground and then did a somersault wearing stilts. His most spectacular feats were the crossings of Niagara Falls on a tightrope 1,100 feet long and 160 feet above the water. On one occasion he took a stove onto the tightrope and cooked an omelette above the roaring falls. "*Bon appétit!*" On another occasion he pushed a wheelbarrow across while blindfolded. On still another he stood on his head on the precarious wire. That is why today in London there are Niagara and Blondin Avenues.

Once, in an unusual demonstration of skill, Blondin carried a man across Niagara Falls on his back. After putting his rider down he turned to the large crowd and asked a man close by, "Do you believe I could do that with you?" "Of course," the man answered, "I've just seen you do it." "Hop on," said Blondin, "I'll carry you across." "Not on your life!" the man called back. *There is no real faith without trust.*

To be truthful, I would not have hopped onto Blondin's back either. In fact, I would not do it if the rope was more than ten feet off the ground, for three reasons: There is the *me factor*. What if I "lost it"? Down we would go. There is the *chance factor*. What if the rope broke? There is the *Blondin factor*. What if the only time he made a mistake in his whole life was with me? I *believe* with all my heart he could do it, but I just would not *trust* him with my life!

But it is a universe of difference between the tightrope walker and Jesus! He cannot drop me. I cannot even drop myself. And there is no such thing as chance. Do we *believe* Jesus is who he says he is? Do we *believe* he died for our sins? Do we *believe* he was resurrected and lives today? Have we *trusted* him to save us?

The only way to go from the Death Valley of the Soul to the highest heavens of spiritual life is to be carried there by Jesus. And for this to happen there are some things we must understand and believe, for they are the gospel in a nutshell.

First, salvation is not "by works." Do we believe that what the Bible says is true? Do we see that our best will never get us there because we are radically sinful and God is radically righteous? Do we see that our works are nothing more than rearranging the chairs on a sinking ship or a frog paddling in a sea of infinity?

Second, we must see and believe that salvation is only "by grace" — it is a completely free gift. "For it is by grace you have been saved, through faith — and this not from yourselves, it is the gift of God" (v. 8). We must understand and believe that we cannot mix works and grace in respect to eternal salvation.

Where meek souls will
Receive Him still
The dear Christ enters in.

Third, we must understand that salvation is "through faith" and must trust him alone for our salvation. Have we stepped out onto Jesus and received the gift of eternal life? Can we trust him now? The Bible says, "Believe in the Lord Jesus, and you will be saved" (Acts 16:31).

For we are God's workmanship, created in Christ
Jesus to do good works, which God prepared in
advance for us to do. (2:10)

9

God's Amazing Work

EPHESIANS 2:10

The remarkable flow of thought in the second chapter of Ephesians, leading up to the magnificent statement of verse 10, begins with *Amazing Depths* (vv. 1-3) as Paul takes us down to the Death Valley of the Soul where all are seen to be dead in their transgressions and sins. Then (vv. 4-7) we are taken up, up and away to *Amazing Heights*, to the very pinnacle of life as we are seated in the heavenly realms with Christ. This incredible journey from the amazing depths to the amazing heights is capsulized in the *Amazing Grace* described in verses 8 and 9 — "For it is by grace you have been saved, through faith — and this not from yourselves, it is the gift of God — not by works, so that no one can boast." *Amazing Depths, Amazing Heights, Amazing Grace,* and now we come to verse 10 — God's *Amazing Work*: "For we are God's workmanship, created in Christ Jesus to do good works, which God prepared in advance for us to do."

In this great statement we see: 1) God's role in salvation, and 2) man's responsibility to God. In regard to the first we will answer the question, what does it mean to be "God's workmanship"? And in regard to our responsibility, what does our being "God's workmanship" require of us?

WHAT DOES IT MEAN TO BE GOD'S WORKMANSHIP?

The word "workmanship" comes from the Greek word *poiema*, from which we derive our English word *poem*. The Greek literally means, "that which has been made — a work — a making," and sometimes it is even translated as "poem." In one of Sir Walter Scott's novels he has one of his characters say to another who has just given a beautiful description of a city, "Aha, so thou can'st play the maker yet?" Then Scott adds a footnote explaining that the ancient Scottish word for "poet" is the word "maker," which is the literal translation of the original Greek.[1] Because of this some have tried to replace "workmanship" (as the NIV renders it) with "poem" — "we are His poem." But the result is misleading because the Greek *poiema* meant any work of art. It could mean a statue or a song or architecture or a poem or a painting.

The best translation by far is that given by F. F. Bruce: "his work of art, his masterpiece."[2] *We are God's works of art.* I do not think there is any more exalted description of a believer in all of Scripture. You and I are God's works of art — his masterpieces!

God is the Creator. Nothing exists apart from him. He brought everything into being. "The heavens declare the glory of God; the skies proclaim the work of his hands" (Psalm 19:1). The galaxies, the stars, our solar system are his handiwork. Yet as wonderful as the cosmos is, it is not his masterwork.

Nature radiates the glory of God. The very trees on our streets do this if we take time to notice. Perhaps you have *really looked* and had an experience like that of Annie Dillard and have seen your backyard tree for what it is: full of lights, "each cell buzzing with flame," and you were "knocked breathless" and your heart went up in wonder to God.[3] Nature breathes the glory of God.

I remember fishing at Cabo San Lucas at the mouth of the Sea of Cortez — the cloudless, windless day, the perfect sunlight dancing rhythmically on the water in platinum and blue. I recall gliding into an emerald cove surrounded by a cactus desert, donning a snorkel, and slipping over the side into a world of green and turquoise and yellow and pink — and another world of slower, gentler rhythm. I remember too the sunset with its Pacific fire as we sat on the sand gazing at the summer stars. There I saw God through his handiwork. *But in all those wonders I did not see his chief work!* That same day I marveled at his animate creation: the ever-present gulls in flight, a sea of yellow-fin tuna and porpoise I could not see across, a striped marlin walking on its tail and crashing back into the water like a fallen horse. It was all so beautiful, *but it was not his ultimate workmanship.*

Consider something far beyond that: a newborn human baby, eyes and mouth wide-open, arms reaching for life — the apex of God's creation. Why do we say this? The baby is, of course, a physical wonder. Its mind is an amazing computer recording virtually everything it experiences. Its eyes pass on incredible amounts of data — first through the cornea, then through the focusing lens where the image strikes the retina, stimulating 125 million nerve endings simultaneously. This is processed by millions of microswitches and funneled down the optic nerve, which contains one million separate insulated fibers (so there are no short circuits). When the information reaches the brain, an equally complex process begins — all of which takes place in a millisecond! Likewise, the infant's ears are so tuned to the vibrating around her that one day she will make music.

But far beyond this wonder is the fact that the baby is made in the image of God. "So God created man in his own image, in the image of God he created him; male and female he created them" (Genesis 1:27). He or she not only has a body but an eternal soul. That newborn child has, despite its sin nature, a delicate moral sensibility and mind-boggling possibilities of achievement. St. Augustine said:

> Men go abroad to wonder at the height of mountains, at the huge waves of the sea, at the long courses of the rivers, at the vast compass of the season, at the circular motion of the stars; and they pass by themselves without wondering.

Man is without a doubt the apex of God's creation. No angel can rival him, for no angel is made in the image of God.

Yet, as wondrous as man is, he is not the masterwork spoken of in our text as "God's workmanship, created in Christ Jesus." The ultimate workmanship of God is a human being who, despite being dead in his transgressions and sins, has been made alive in Christ. We say this because *he is the subject of two creations by Christ.* His very existence is due to the work of Christ. "For by him all things were created: things in heaven and on earth, visible and invisible, whether thrones or powers or rulers or authorities; all things were created by him and for him. He is before all things, and in him all things hold together" (Colossians 1:16, 17; cf. Proverbs 8:22-31). Every human being is created and held together by Christ.

But the masterwork here has undergone a second creation "in Christ Jesus." Christ, Lord of creation, is also the executor of salvation. Paul describes this elsewhere as well: "Therefore, if anyone is in Christ, he is a new creation; the old has gone, the new has come!" (2 Corinthians 5:17). This is a greater work than the Sea of Cortez and the summer stars because it cost the Son, the Father, and the Spirit everything, and because it involved the unparalleled power of the Resurrection! To quote Jonathan Edwards, the supreme mind on conversion, the "spiritual life which is reached in the work of conversion, is a far greater and more glorious effect than mere being and life."[4] God's most stupendous creation is man made alive! As the subject of Christ's two creations, we are his ultimate workmanship, his masterwork!

"[I]n Christ" we are of untold worth. This great truth may be hard to actually take hold of as we exist in frail human bodies carried along in the rush of modern-day busyness. Some of us have had things happen which make us doubt our worth. But we are his "workmanship" — his work of art. Moreover, we are in process.

Michelangelo was once asked what he was doing as he chipped away at a shapeless rock. He replied, "I'm liberating an angel from this stone." That's what God is doing with us. We are in the hands of the great Maker, the ultimate sculptor who created the universe out of nothing, and he has never yet thrown away a rock on which he has begun a masterwork.

His tools are Jesus Christ and the Holy Spirit, his Word, and the preaching of the Word. Very often he uses difficulties and difficult people, like David's Shimei, to sculpt our character. Other times it is a great saint with which God carves his impression upon us.

WHAT DOES BEING HIS WORKMANSHIP REQUIRE OF US?

Having established the grand truth that we are His "workmanship" — his masterwork — the question is, What does this privileged position ask of us? Two things are required. One is to *believe* it, for simple belief that this is true will lift us from the prison of despair. The other is to *hold still*. Our tendency is to be like a two-year-old in the barber's chair — squirming so much that we really never get the care we need. We must submit to the authority of his Word and the shaping influences he brings to our lives!

We must keep in mind that Paul is very clear in verses 8, 9 that no one is saved by works, "so that no one can boast." There is an old story from the Middle East which speaks to this issue. A man was traveling on his donkey when he came upon a small fuzzy object lying in the road. He dismounted to look more closely and found a sparrow lying on its back with its scrawny legs thrust skyward. At first he thought the bird was dead, but close investigation proved it to be very much alive. The man asked the sparrow if he was all right. The sparrow replied, "Yes." The man said, "What are you doing lying on your back with your legs pointed toward the sky?" The sparrow responded that he had heard a rumor that the sky was falling, and so he was holding his legs up in support. The man replied, "You surely don't think you're going to hold it up with those two scrawny legs, do you?" The sparrow, with a very solemn look, retorted, "One does the best he can." The little bird's self-deceit and futile works were obvious.

In the same way man's condition is so desperate that his works are no more effective than a bird's legs in the air or putting makeup on a corpse. No one will ever be saved by works.

But once we are saved and become his "workmanship," we must work. "For we are God's workmanship, created in Christ Jesus to do good works, which God prepared in advance for us to do" (v. 10). Works are a sign that we are his workmanship! "No one more wholeheartedly than Paul repudiated good works as a ground of salvation; no one more strongly insisted on good works as a fruit of salvation."[5] Authentic believers, those made by God's hand, work for him.

In the last century a famous Scottish clergyman foolishly wrote that from what was to him "the highest of all authority, the authority of his own experience," he concluded that the ministry required only two days a week, leaving the other five days to pursue higher interests such as mathematics and science. He insisted that "There is almost no consumption of intellectual effort in the peculiar employment of a minister." What was needed was a friendly disposition which enjoyed comforting others and an open air of honesty.[6]

In 1911 this Scottish divine, Thomas Chalmers, was converted, and with his conversion came the greatest outpouring of energy the Scottish church has ever seen (apart from John Knox) as Chalmers mixed his evangelism with social action and turned the city of Glasgow upside down.[7] From a leisured ministerial dilettante, Chalmers became a man on fire, mourning, in his own words, "the littleness of time." He lived out Luther's dictum that "Justification is by faith alone, but not by faith that is alone" — for where there is faith, there are works!

This truth is echoed by the prayers of the New Testament again and again: "May our Lord Jesus Christ himself . . . encourage your hearts and strengthen you in every good deed and word" (2 Thessalonians 2:16, 17). "And we pray this in order that you may live a life worthy of the Lord and may please him in every way: bearing fruit in every good work, growing in the knowledge of God" (Colossians 1:10). "Now the God of peace . . . equip you in every good thing to do His will, working in us that which is pleasing in His sight, through Jesus Christ, to whom be the glory forever and ever, Amen" (Hebrews 13:20, 21, NASB).

Not only are we, as God's workmanship, to work, says Paul, but we are to realize that we are "to do good works, which God prepared in advance for us to do" (v. 10). Each of us has an eternally-designed job description which includes the task, the ability, and the place to serve. You may prefer Jerusalem, but you will glorify him more in Babylon if he has called you there. And whatever the task to which he has called you, you will be equipped for it as surely as a bird is capable of flight. And in doing the works he has called you to do, you will be both more and more his workmanship and more and more your true self.

Sometimes as I have been preaching I have become aware of an unnatural silence. The ever-present coughing ceases and the pews stop creaking, bringing an almost physical silence to the sanctuary through which my words sail like arrows. A heightened eloquence invades my speech so that the cadence and volume of my voice intensify the truth I am preaching. Though I know that I am speaking, I have thought at these times, "What is going on here? Is this me?" And then, seeing it for what it is, my heart has cried, "Lord, help me!"

Thousands of preachers have had like experiences, even greater ones.

But what makes it so amazing to me is the fact that during the early years of my preaching there was little to indicate I would ever experience this. Though I had the nerve to attempt to preach when I was just sixteen years old, it was a painful experience for both me and my hearers because of my obvious discomfort. Though I made other attempts during the following years and eagerly sought leadership positions in church and school, public speaking remained very painful. Some today probably think I am in the ministry because I pursued my natural strength of public speaking. Not so! It never ceases to amaze me that I am able to stand and preach in the pulpit of any church. And at those times when the sanctuary assumes that telltale hush, I feel like pinching myself.[8]

What is the point of all this? All of us are "God's workmanship," and as such we have been given "good works" to do which were appointed before our existence. And when we do them, he gives us the necessary power and a marvelous sense of the Holy Spirit in our sails.

There is nothing more beautiful than his workmanship working for him. Are we doing this?

Therefore, remember that formerly you who are Gentiles by birth and called "uncircumcised" by those who call themselves "the circumcision" (that done in the body by the hands of men) — remember that at that time you were separate from Christ, excluded from citizenship in Israel and foreigners to the covenants of the promise, without hope and without God in the world. But now in Christ Jesus you who once were far away have been brought near through the blood of Christ. For he himself is our peace, who has made the two one and has destroyed the barrier, the dividing wall of hostility, by abolishing in his flesh the law with its commandments and regulations. His purpose was to create in himself one new man out of the two, thus making peace, and in this one body to reconcile both of them to God through the cross, by which he put to death their hostility. He came and preached peace to you who were far away and peace to those who were near. For through him we both have access to the Father by one Spirit. (2:11-18)

10

Alienation to Reconciliation

EPHESIANS 2:11-18

A study of the history of the ancient world tells us that none of today's social distinctions — none of our racial barriers, our narrow nationalisms, our iron curtains — are more exclusive or unrelenting than the separation between Jews and Gentiles in Biblical times. The Jews believed the Gentiles were created to fuel the fires of Hell. A common motto was, "The best of the serpents crush . . . the best of the Gentiles kill." It was not lawful to aid a Gentile woman in giving birth, for that would bring another heathen into the world.[1]

The Gentiles, even apart from their animosity for Jews, had their own parochial hatreds for anyone not like them. Plato said that the barbarians (anyone non-Greek) were his enemies by nature. The Roman Livy confirmed this in his day, saying, "The Greeks wage a truceless war against people of other races, against barbarians."[2] And of course this was eminently true of the imperialistic Romans.

The collision of Gentile/Jewish exclusiveness was monumental. The Gentiles were dogs in Jewish parlance, and the Jews were homicidal enemies of the human race in Gentile terms. Verse 11 of our text calls this to remembrance: "Therefore, remember that formerly you who are Gentiles by birth and called 'uncircumcised' by those who call themselves 'the circumcision' (that done in the body by the hands of men) . . ."

What was the reason for this alienation? The answer is not social or cultural but spiritual. We must understand that though our text in verses 1-10 has shown that both Jews and Gentiles were spiritually alienated from God, there was in one sense an even greater distance to the Gentiles' alienation. Our text shows how this was overcome in reconciliation.

ALIENATION — "FAR OFF" (vv. 11, 12)

"[R]emember," says Paul in verse 12, "that at that time you were separate from Christ, excluded from citizenship in Israel and foreigners to the covenants of the promise, without hope and without God in the world."

The Gentiles suffered fivefold alienation. They were *Christless* (aliens to the Messiah) — "remember that at that time you were separate from Christ." They were not part of the Messianic people (cf. Romans 9:5). They had no thought or hope of a Messiah. They were *stateless* (alien to God's nation) — "excluded from citizenship in Israel." Israel was a nation under God, a theocracy, but the Gentiles had no part or franchise in this. They were *friendless* (alien to the covenants) — "and foreigners to the covenants of the promise." God had bound himself unconditionally to bring blessing upon and through Israel. But the Gentiles had no such promise. (Cf. Genesis 12:2ff.; 13:14ff.; 15:1ff.; 17:1ff.; and 22:15ff.) They were *hopeless* and *godless* (alien to hope and to God) — "without hope and without God in the world." The pagan world was religious in everything. There were temples and statues everywhere. Similarly, look at the great world religions today. Can the Scriptures be right — is the pagan world then and now godless? Yes, because false gods are *nothing*, and religious ceremonies are *nothing* without the true God. The Christian Church needs to believe its own Scriptures (cf. Romans 3:11). The Gentiles were indeed without hope and without God.

Theognes (c. 500 B.C.) wrote:

> I will try to have a good time while I'm young, because I will lie under the earth for a long time — voiceless as a stone, and I shall leave the sunlight that I loved . . . then I shall see no more.
>
> Have a good time, my soul, while young; soon others will take my place, and I shall be black earth in death.
>
> No mortal is happy under the sun.[3]

The Roman poet Catullus (c. 50 B.C.) wrote:

> *The sun can set and rise again*
> *But once our brief light sets*
> *There is one unending night to be slept through.*[4]

The first century was an age of suicide. Tacitus tells of a man who killed himself in indignation that he had been born.[5] The French philosophers are not so *nouveau* after all! For the Gentiles, history was going nowhere. There was no Messiah, no hope. That is the way it is today also, apart from Christ.

Social Darwinist Herbert Spencer wrote: "My own feeling respecting the ultimate mystery is such that I cannot even try to think of it without some feeling of terror so that I habitually shun the thought."[6]

Those apart from Christ typically wrap their lives around things and refuse to think about ultimate reality. The escape can be very intellectual on one hand, or on the other an eternal Nintendo game. As a believer who has found hope, I cannot imagine living without God.

The word which describes all of this is *alienation*. The Gentile dilemma (which is the world's dilemma) produces alienation from God and alienation from man with all its dehumanizing and debilitating results. This is a root of racism. It is the basis for the great national cleavages in Ireland and Korea and Europe and Africa. It is the reason so many well-intentioned people cannot get along. Take, for instance, a 1986 peace march that largely self-destructed through bickering. It began in Los Angeles only to stall in Barstow, about 120 miles out of L.A., where about half the 1,200 marchers went home. Soon those remaining polarized over those who were real walkers and those who rode in vehicles. They fought over a dress code. They decided to hold an election, but disagreed over who could vote, finally allowing even children to vote. Then the election was declared invalid. Many ended the peace march not speaking to each other.[7]

Sadly, some very similar things can be told about the Church. The answer to this lies in the remedy which our text prescribes for the alienation between Jews and Gentiles. The answer given to them is also the answer for our world.

RECONCILIATION — "BROUGHT NEAR" (vv. 13-18)

The answer is grounded in the sacrificial death of Christ, as verses 13 and 14 inform us: "But now in Christ Jesus you who once were far away have been brought near through the blood of Christ. For he himself is our peace, who has made the two one and has destroyed the barrier, the dividing wall of hostility . . ." Those "far away" were Gentiles, those "near" were God's covenant people (cf. Isaiah 57:17; 49:1; and Psalm 148:14). The blood of Christ makes it possible for regenerated Jews and Gentiles to come profoundly near. Why? Because "he himself is our peace." That is, he is the peacemaker between us and the Godhead. In the Greek "he himself" is powerfully emphatic, and the emphasis is meant to go to our hearts. This is a statement well worth memorizing — "For *he himself* is our peace."

As our peace, he "has made the two one and has destroyed the barrier, the dividing wall of hostility." This again is graphic, emotive language because in Herod's Temple there was a wall which separated the Court of the Gentiles from the rest of the Temple, and on that wall were inscriptions in Latin and Greek forbidding Gentiles to enter. Josephus spoke of these inscriptions,[8] and in excavations made in 1871 and 1934 two of these inscriptions were found. They read: "No foreigner may enter within the barricade which surrounds the sanctuary and enclosure. Anyone who is caught doing so will have himself to blame for his ensuing death."[9] These *Thanatos* (death) inscriptions are now on display in the Archaeological Museum in Istanbul and the Rockefeller Museum in Jerusalem.

Paul says that Christ has ripped this odious barrier down by his death, and thus Jews and Gentiles alike have access to God and have spiritual unity. The ultimate answer to vertical and horizontal alienation is not intellectual or political or social, but *spiritual*! The answer comes when we cross the broken barrier and thus come near to God and then near to each other (cf. 1 John 1:3, 4).

Picture the wall leveled, the *Thanatos* inscriptions lying under the rubble, and the nations (us!) joyfully stepping across as Jewish and Gentile brothers and sisters. How did Christ's death bring down the wall? In three ways, which we see in the main verbal phrases of verses 15 and 16.

First, he *abolished the law* — "abolishing in his flesh the law with its commandments and regulations" (v. 15a). How did he do this, especially since he said in his Sermon on the Mount, "Do not think that I have come to abolish the Law or the Prophets; I have not come to abolish them but to fulfill them" (Matthew 5:17)? Christ fulfilled the *moral* law, keeping all its requirements, but he abolished the Jewish *ceremonial* law. Thus, the requirements of the ceremonial law (the washings, the Sabbath restrictions, etc.) which had been such a barrier were gone. And since he fulfilled the moral law, taking away its condemnation, all have free access through grace (cf. 2 Corinthians 3:6-15). The gospel is now, "For it is by grace you have been saved, through faith — and this not from yourselves, it is the gift of God — not by works, so that no one can boast" (2:8, 9), and because of this we fly across the barrier to God!

So first Christ abolished the impossible ceremonial code, and second, *he created a new humanity* — "His purpose was to create in himself one new man out of the two, thus making peace" (v. 15).

Bishop John Reed tells about driving a school bus in Australia which carried whites and aborigines. Tired of all the squabbling, one day far out in the country he pulled over to the side of the road and said to the white boys, "What color are you?" "White." He told them, "No, you are green. Anyone who rides in my bus is green. Now, what color are you?" The white boys replied, "Green." Then he went to the aborigines and said, "What color are you?" "Black." "No, you are green. Anyone who rides on my bus is green." All the aborigines answered that they were green. The situation seemed resolved until, several miles down the road, he heard a boy in the back of the bus announce, "All right, light green on this side, dark green on that side."

Bishop Reed had the right idea. What was needed was a new race, "the greens," but he couldn't pull it off! Our text says that Jesus created a new man, a new humanity, a new race. Back in the second century Clement of Alexandria wrote: "We who worship God in a new way, as the third race, are Christians." The Epistle of Diogenes calls believers "this new race."[10]

Jesus didn't Christianize the Jews or Judaize the Gentiles. He didn't create a half-breed. He made an entirely new man. "For we are God's workmanship, created in Christ Jesus . . ." (2:10). We are God's masterwork, a new race, in Christ Jesus! This must not be watered down. This is the answer to alienation, to racism, to prejudice, to hatred, to estrangement.

> *In Christ there is no East or West,*
> *In Him no South or North,*
> *But one great fellowship of love*
> *Throughout the whole wide earth.*
> (John Oxenham)

This new race is the subject of the glorious practical chapters 4 — 6 of Ephesians, where we see how members of a new race lives with each other and in the home and in the world.

There is a third aspect of Jesus' destruction of the wall: *he reconciled the new humanity to God* — "and in this one body to reconcile both of them to God through the cross, by which he put to death their hostility" (v. 16). Jesus killed, in his own body on the cross, the hostility of Jews and Gentiles — indeed of all humankind. This is a reality in the hearts and churches where Christ truly reigns, and in the end will be a universal reality.

All of this culminates in Christ's ministry of peace and reconciliation — "He came and preached peace to you who were far away and peace to those who were near. For through him we both have access to the Father by one Spirit" (vv. 17, 18). Remember the fourth gift on God's eternal Christmas list in Isaiah 9:6? — "Prince of Peace." Through him Isaiah prophesied there would be preached "'Peace, peace, to those far and near'" (57:19) — that is, to Gentiles and Jews. When Christ came to earth the angels sang, "'Glory to God in the highest, and on earth peace to men on whom his favor rests'" (Luke 2:14). On the eve of his death he said, "Peace I leave with you; my peace I give you" (John 14:27). After his resurrection Jesus came to his disciples through locked doors and said, "Peace be with you!" (John 20:19, 20). Paul says in our text of reconciliation, "For he himself is our peace" (v.14), and, "He came and preached peace to you who were far away and peace to those who were near" (v. 17). *He is our peace.*

Lastly, of verse 18 John R. W. Stott says: "The highest and fullest achievement of our peacemaking, reconciling Christ is the Trinitarian access of the people of God, as through him by the one Spirit we come boldly to our Father."[11] We see this in verse 18 — "For through *him*

[Christ] we both have access to the *Father* by one *Spirit*" (italics added). When we are in contact with the Father, the Son, and the Holy Spirit, we have peace with all who are in contact with them.

This peace and reconciliation is the peace of the Church, not the peace of the world. Peace between Jew and Gentile, the world's races and ethnic groups, rich and poor, educated and uneducated comes only in Christ. This means that the Church has an immense responsibility to be a pocket of reconciliation and *shalom* in an alienated world.

Robert Louis Stevenson, in his *Picturesque Notes of Edinburgh*, tells the story of two unmarried sisters who shared a single room. As people are apt to do who live in close quarters, the sisters had a falling out, which Stevenson says was "on some point of controversial divinity." In other words, they disagreed over some aspect of theology. The controversy was so bitter that they never spoke again (ever!). There were no words, either kind or spiteful — just silence. Nevertheless, possibly because of a lack of means, or because of the innate Scottish fear of scandal, they continued to keep house together in the single room. A chalk-line was drawn across the floor to separate their two domains. For years they coexisted in hateful silence. Each woman's meals, baths, and family visitors were exposed to the other's unfriendly silence. At night each went to bed listening to the heavy breathing of her enemy. Thus, the two sisters (ostensibly daughters of the Church!) continued the rest of their miserable lives.[12]

They probably were not true Christians, because Christians are not to resist reconciliation and forgiveness. Jesus said, "For if you forgive men when they sin against you, your heavenly Father will also forgive you. But if you do not forgive men their sins, your Father will not forgive your sins" (Matthew. 6:14). Being forgiving is a sign of knowing God's forgiving grace.

Jesus also says to us, "Therefore, if you are offering your gift at the altar and there remember that your brother has something against you, leave your gift there in front of the altar. First go and be reconciled to your brother; then come and offer your gift" (Matthew 5:23, 24). Reconciliation is essential to worship; alienation gives the lie to what the Church is all about.

If this is a problem with us, what are we to do? We must use our Trinitarian access to the fullest. We must spend time in prayer, restoring our fellowship with the Father, Son, and Holy Spirit. We must ask for strength for reconciliation — and do it.

> "Blessed are the peacemakers,
> for they will be called sons of God."
> (Matthew 5:9)

Consequently, you are no longer foreigners and aliens, but fellow citizens with God's people and members of God's household, built on the foundation of the apostles and prophets, with Christ Jesus himself as the chief cornerstone. In him the whole building is joined together and rises to become a holy temple in the Lord. And in him you too are being built together to become a dwelling in which God lives by his Spirit. (2:19-22)

11

The Third Race

The death of Christ has created a new humanity — "a third race" as it has been called from the early centuries. For the Gentiles, the effects of this were immediate and stupendous. Upon believing, these outcasts moved to the very center of God's purpose. Interlopers became insiders, aliens heirs, the lowest class first class.

As Calvin so movingly said:

> Those who were formerly profane and unworthy . . . [have now become] partners with the godly, have now the rights of citizens along with Abraham, with all the holy patriarchs, and prophets, and kings, nay [i.e., *no, better than that!*], with the angels themselves.[1] (italics added)

This was, and is, a great miracle: a new humanity reconciled first to God and then to each other.

Paul's vision of this new third race is one of matchless grandeur, and as he continues to describe it he reaches for three graphic, mind-grabbing images: first, a *city*, then a *family*, and finally a great *building*. Each of the images is elevating, and together they make the believing heart soar.

GOD'S CITY (v. 19a)

Anyone who lives abroad for any length of time begins to miss his or her country. On the last Sunday of May 1987, Barbara and the boys and I had been living in Cambridge, England, for four months, and we missed home. We had attended fine worship services that morning at the Round Church, chatted briefly with our British and Australian friends, found a taxi, and headed for an American cemetery several miles out of town. That cemetery, straddling a low, rolling hilltop, provides a panoramic view of the English countryside. Seemingly endless rows of white crosses are perfectly set in manicured green lawns, marking the remains of most of the American flyers lost in the battle of Britain and many other service personnel. Along with several hundred other Americans we reverently read the names on the wall, recognizing some, like that of Lieutenant Joseph Kennedy, Jr.

Next we gathered around the flagpole and listened to speeches by the Lord Mayor of Cambridge and various military brass. Over fifty wreaths were laid around the flagpole — many by visitors who had traveled from the States to honor their long-dead comrades. Then came the "National Anthem," followed by "Taps" as the American flag was hoisted slowly to the top of the pole. Three jets came toward us from the southeast flying side by side, and when they reached the flag, the middle jet suddenly arched straight up with a deafening roar and rocketed out of sight, reminding me of a soul departing for Heaven. I began to cry, and so did Barbara and many around us. I was thinking of all the boys, my sons' ages, who died in that war. And I thought of our great country and the privileges of living in a democracy which provides so much opportunity. I was, and am, thankful for and proud of my citizenship.

Citizenship was an even greater source of pride in the ancient world. In the Greco-Roman culture to which Paul was writing in Ephesus, citizenship was highly personal. One's city, or *polis*, provided one's identity. The city's laws were a part of one's being, its customs a source of pride. Its inhabitants were one's lifelong friends.[2]

Realizing this, we see in the opening line of verse 19 that Paul was telling the Ephesian Christians something absolutely stupendous — that they were spiritually not naturalized, but *supernaturalized* citizens! They had been "foreigners and aliens" before, but now they had become "fellow citizens with God's people" — *sumpolitai!* They had come to possess a citizenship far superior to any local citizenship and even the coveted Roman citizenship. They were part of a supreme cosmopolitan community, a *third city*.

The implications of their new citizenship were immense. They had lived in alienation, but now having been reconciled to God and to believing Jews and Gentiles they belonged! This is a universal experience for all Christian believers. It was my experience when I came to Christ. The Church was the place where I belonged, where I was understood and loved and could be myself. Believing Jews and Gentiles had become a common people. They had a common language — a language of the heart which they all understood. They had a common heritage and history as part of the community of faith. They had a common allegiance which superseded all loyalties. They had a common goal (glorifying God). They even had the same destination — a place prepared by Christ to which he would take them — the ultimate *polis*, the heavenly city (cf. John 14:1-6). As Paul told the Philippians, "But our citizenship is in heaven. And we eagerly await a Savior from there, the Lord Jesus Christ" (Philippians 3:20; cf. Philippians 1:27).

We can travel throughout the world or even trek among the stars and sojourn in other galaxies. But as believers wherever we go we are free from alienation, for we are reconciled to God and his Church and we belong. And one day we are going to catapult from this life with a force far greater than any ascending jet as we are ineluctably drawn to our city and our people!

GOD'S FAMILY (v. 19b)

The third race has its own citizenship in God's city, and as a reconciled people it is also part of God's family. The whole of verse 19 reads: "Consequently, you are no longer foreigners and aliens, but fellow citizens with God's people and members of God's household . . ." — his family. As wonderful and soul-satisfying as our citizenship is, being "family" — "members of God's household" — represents a far deeper intimacy. All who are part of the reconciled third race have the same Father. Later, in 3:14, 15, Paul will say in recognition of this, "For this reason I kneel before the Father, from whom his whole family in heaven and on earth derives its name." The opening line of the Lord's Prayer also celebrates our mutual paternity: "Our Father in heaven" (Matthew 6:9). As "family" we automatically mouth the same *patronym* — "Abba" — because we have the same "Spirit of sonship" (Romans 8:15; cf. Galatians 4:6). All God's children call him by the same intimate name.

As members of God's household we are in satisfying and tender relationship to one another. Paul tells Timothy that in the Church we are to relate to older men as fathers and says, "Treat younger men as brothers, older women as mothers, and younger women as sisters . . ." (1 Timothy 5:1, 2). Fathers, mothers, sisters, brothers — that is what those in the reconciled third race are. These are terms of endearment. It is profitable to think of fellow members of the Body of Christ and then silently say their names, attaching "brother," "sister," "father," or "mother" in recognition of this eternal truth.

The horizontal relational implications of our being God's family are beautiful. Family is the place where you can be yourself and be assured you are accepted. On Thanksgivings I forgo shaving, put on blue jeans and a flannel shirt, and after dinner lie on the floor and let the grandchildren crawl all over me. Usually I fall asleep. And if things get too hectic, I crawl under our baby grand and sleep where nothing can fall on me. And you know what? Nobody cares! No one says, "What's Dad doing? Where's his tie?" Why? Because we're family, so I can be myself. The Church is the place of reconciliation and acceptance, where you can be your true, redeemed self.

GOD'S TEMPLE (vv. 20-22)

Paul loved to mix metaphors (he never took Freshman English), and we are the richer for it. Now he appropriates the image of a building to illustrate a further dimension of the new humanity. It is a temple "built on the foundation of the apostles and prophets, with Christ Jesus himself as the chief cornerstone" (v. 20). For a thousand years the Jerusalem Temple (first Solomon's, then Zerubbabel's, and then Herod's) had been the official focus of God's presence and of God's people. But now the new race needs a new temple, and a static geographically-grounded one would not be adequate. This new temple would have three elements: a *foundation*, a *cornerstone*, and *building blocks*.

Foundation. It is "built on the foundation of the apostles and prophets." The word order (apostles first, prophets second) suggests that Paul means New Testament apostles and prophets, the prophets being those to whom and through whom the Word of God was proclaimed. In support of this meaning, 3:4, 5 says that the "mystery of Christ . . . has now been revealed by the Spirit to God's holy apostles and prophets" (cf. 4:11).[3] Since both the apostles and prophets had a teaching role, the foundation is teaching. Thus *the foundation of the new temple is God's Word, especially the New Testament Scriptures.* The Church stands or falls in its regard for the New Testament Scriptures. If we tamper with the foundation, the temple will crumble. That is why Paul ordered Timothy to "preach the Word" (2 Timothy 4:2).

Cornerstone. Important as the foundation is, there is another component of even greater importance, and that is the cornerstone — "with Christ Jesus himself as the chief cornerstone." This is immensely rich imagery. For hundreds of years "cornerstone" had been a prophetic designation for the Messiah: "See, I lay a stone in Zion, a tested stone, a precious cornerstone for a sure foundation; the one who trusts will never be dismayed" (Isaiah 28:16; cf. 8:14-16; Psalm 118:22; Matthew 21:42; and Acts 4:11). In addition, virtually every ancient Hebrew understood the importance of the cornerstone, for it determines the stability of the foundation and the character of the entire building. The Jerusalem Temple itself had huge foundation stones, the greatest of which was twenty-nine feet in length — the size of a railroad boxcar![4]

The cornerstone decided the *architectural unity and symmetry.* The lay of the walls, the dimensions of the structure were a result of the chief cornerstone. All other stones had to be adjusted to it. In fact, F. F. Bruce believes that the phrase "a tested stone" in the Isaiah prophecy really means a "stone of testing" — i.e., that it tested the building to show whether it was built to the architect's specifications.[5]

The shape and stability of God's new temple, the third race, is determined by Jesus Christ, the chief cornerstone! How glad I am that our lives, our reconciliation and peace, is built on the infinite Rock, Jesus Christ.

Building blocks. This brings us to the final components of the new temple, the building blocks or stones — *us!* "In him the whole building is joined together and rises to become a holy temple in the Lord. And in him you too are being built together to become a dwelling in which God lives by his Spirit" (vv. 21, 22). The Gentiles were excluded from the Jerusalem Temple by a wall and by signs threatening death. But now, in Christ they actually form the wall of the new temple. God reached down and gathered stones from Death Valley and made them living stones. Peter put it this way: "As you come to him, the living Stone — rejected by men but chosen by God and precious to him — you also, like living stones, are being built into a spiritual house . . ." (1 Peter 2:4, 5a).

What a fabulous image! Picture Jesus Christ as the massive cornerstone, and see his vitality as causing the stone to glow. Next the foundational teaching of the apostles and prophets is laid upon and around him. He gives it its shape and stability, and the whole foundation assumes his glow. Then one by one living stones are set upon it, and they in turn radiate the symmetry of the chief cornerstone, forming a luminous, ever-growing temple.[6]

What is the purpose of this living, growing, moving, radiant temple? ". . . to become a dwelling in which God lives by his Spirit" (v. 22b). Just as God first took up residence in the wilderness Tabernacle, filling it with such glory that Moses could not enter it (Exodus 40:34, 35), and later filling the Jerusalem Temple in the same way (1 Kings 8:10, 11), so now by his Spirit he makes the third race his chosen dwelling-place — a habitat for divinity.

> *The soul wherein God dwells —*
> *What church could holier be? —*
> *Becomes a walking tent*
> *Of heavenly majesty.*
> (Johannes Scheffler)

Paul's vision of the new humanity of reconciled Jews and Gentiles, the third race, is grand indeed. The images used to express its grandeur are unforgettable, and in bouquet they are overpowering.

The city. We are supernaturalized "fellow citizens with God's people." We are a common people with a common language of the heart and common allegiances, goals, and destination. We were aliens, but now we belong. And our citizenship means that we will rise ineluctably upward to our city.

The family. So profound is our reconciliation that we are brothers, sisters, mothers, and fathers — "members of God's household." We have the same Father. There is comfortable love among us.

The temple. Jesus is the chief cornerstone, the teaching of the apostles and prophets is the foundation, and we are the living stones — God lives in us!

For this reason, I, Paul, the prisoner of Christ Jesus for the sake of you Gentiles — Surely you have heard about the administration of God's grace that was given to me for you, that is, the mystery made known to me by revelation, as I have already written briefly. In reading this, then, you will be able to understand my insight into the mystery of Christ, which was not made known to men in other generations as it has now been revealed by the Spirit to God's holy apostles and prophets. This mystery is that through the gospel the Gentiles are heirs together with Israel, members together of one body, and sharers together in the promise in Christ Jesus. I became a servant of this gospel by the gift of God's grace given me through the working of his power. Although I am less than the least of all God's people, this grace was given me: to preach to the Gentiles the unsearchable riches of Christ, and to make plain to everyone the administration of this mystery, which for ages past was kept hidden in God, who created all things. His intent was that now, through the church, the manifold wisdom of God should be made known to the rulers and authorities in the heavenly realms, according to his eternal purpose which he accomplished in Christ Jesus our Lord. In him and through faith in him we may approach God with freedom and confidence. I ask you, therefore, not to be discouraged because of my sufferings for you, which are your glory. (3:1-13)

12

Mystery of Christ

EPHESIANS 3:1-13

In our study of the second chapter of Ephesians we have been observing what Paul describes in chapter 3 with the word "mystery" — a word which conjures in our English-speaking minds names like Agatha Christie or Dorothy Sayers or P. D. James and their sleuths Inspector Pierrot or Lord Peter Wimsey or Inspector Dagleish. These are accurate associations in English, but are misleading in regard to what is meant by Paul. In the New Testament, the Greek word *musterion* means something which is beyond natural knowledge, but has been opened to us by divine revelation through the Holy Spirit.[1] Paul's words in Colossians 1:26 give us the idea: "the mystery that has been kept hidden for ages and generations, but is now disclosed to the saints." It is something previously undreamed of which is now disclosed to believers — an open secret.

Here in Ephesians the mystery was hinted at in 2:10 where Paul says, "For we are God's workmanship" — his masterwork, new spiritual creations "brought near through the blood of Christ" (v. 13). The mystery was further opened in verse 15 where we are told that the nearness (reconciliation) happened through the creation "in himself [of] one new man out of the two" — a new humanity — a third race of humans — the Church. So amazing is the life of this new humanity that he uses three gripping images to describe its life in verses 19-22, and the bouquet of these images further opens the mystery.

This mystery, this now-open secret, dominates Paul's thoughts as he begins chapter 3. In verse 1 he begins to pray: "For this reason I, Paul, the prisoner of Christ Jesus for the sake of you Gentiles . . ." But then he stops because he is still caught up with thoughts of the mystery. So he digresses on the mystery in verses 2-13, and then begins to pray again in verse 14: "For this reason I kneel before the Father . . ." Paul has trouble leaving the marvelous subject of the mystery, but this is the compulsion of a grateful heart.

In verses 2-6 Paul digresses on how the revelation of the mystery came to him, ending the digression with a beautiful capsulization in verse 6 as he employs three parallel terms to describe the dynamic effect of the mystery in the Ephesians' lives. "This mystery," he says, "is that through the gospel the Gentiles are *heirs together* with Israel, *members together* of one body, and *sharers together* in the promise in Christ Jesus" (italics added). The open secret, which was not understood in times past, is that Jews and Gentiles are 1) "heirs together," 2) "members together" (*sussoma*, a new word coined by Paul because no word could adequately describe the mystery of Gentiles being on the same footing with Jews,[2] and 3) "sharers together" — fellow partakers.

This mystery came about from their new double union with Christ and with each other. John wrote about this phenomenon in 1 John 1:3 — "We proclaim to you what we have seen and heard, so that you also may have fellowship with us. And our fellowship is with the Father and with his Son, Jesus Christ." The closer they were to God, the closer they were to each other. No Jew or Gentile had ever conceived of such a mystery in his wildest dreams! And for Paul this remained an abiding wonder and joy throughout his life.

Later in Paul's ministry, he actually delivered Gentile offerings to needy Jews in Jerusalem with the greatest joy, for that act eloquently testified to the working reality of this mystery. Gentiles gave to Jewish brethren and sisters, and, even more miraculous, their Jewish brothers and sisters had the grace and humility to receive from them.

In view of this miraculous togetherness, there is no room at all in the Church of Jesus Christ for separation. There is no room for people who say they believe what Paul says about the mystery, but do not practice it or who rationalize that this mystic togetherness is future and is not to be applied today. Such people see no problem in keeping their church free from people who are "different" because they believe social differences will only be overcome in the eternal state. In addition, I have read of and have been personally told by missionaries about so-called "believers" in South America who have no interest in reaching primitive Indians. These "Christians" even go so far as to say they doubt if the Indians have souls, or if they do, the missionaries can do the work.[3] Those who fall so short of God's sympathies and design had better take a good look at themselves to see where they are in regard to God!

THE MINISTRY OF THE MYSTERY (vv. 7-13)

Having held the mystery of the Church high for all to see, Paul goes on in verses 7 and 8 to exult in the ministry of the mystery: "I became a servant of this gospel by the gift of God's grace given me through the working of his power. Although I am less than the least of all God's people, this grace was given me . . ." Again Paul bends the language. He takes the Greek word for "least" or "smallest" and adds an ending which is impossible linguistically, so that he comes out with the word "leaster." Some think he was playing off his Latin name *Paulus*, which meant "little" or "small," so that the idea is, "I am little by name, little in stature, and morally and spiritually littler than the least of all Christians."[4] *I am Small Paul.*

Was he sincere? Of course! We need to remember that he had been a rabid enemy of the Christians. But even more, as the premier theologian of the Church he had a profound understanding of his own sin. To Timothy he said, "Here is a trustworthy saying that deserves full acceptance: Christ Jesus came into the world to save sinners — of whom I am the worst" (1 Timothy 1:15). To the Corinthians he wrote, "For I am the least of the apostles and do not even deserve to be called an apostle, because I persecuted the church of God. But by the grace of God I am what I am, and his grace to me was not without effect. No, I worked harder than all of them — yet not I, but the grace of God that was with me" (1 Corinthians 15:9, 10). He knew what he was, but he also understood God's grace. Paul simply could not get over the immense privilege he had of ministering for God.

A striking quotation by the great Methodist divine W. E. Sangster is relevant to this point: "Called to preach! . . . commissioned of God to teach the word! A herald of the great King! A witness of the Eternal Gospel! Could any work be more high and holy? To this supreme task God sent his only begotten Son."[5] W. E. Sangster had a Pauline joy in his sense of the privilege of preaching — and thus he had spiritual power.

To whom, and to what end, did Paul focus his message? The text reveals three directions. First, it was *Christ to the Gentiles* — "to preach to the Gentiles the unsearchable riches of Christ" (v. 8b).

The great Toscanini once gave a concert for which the audience was wildly enthusiastic. There were several encores, and still the audience cheered. Finally there was a lull in the din, and Toscanini turned his back to the audience and said so the orchestra could hear, "I am nothing; you are nothing; but Beethoven, he is everything!" Theologically that is where Paul was in his preaching of Christ — Christ was everything. "[B]ut we preach Christ crucified," he told the Corinthians, "a stumbling block to Jews and foolishness to Gentiles, but to those whom God has called, both Jews and Greeks, Christ the power of God and the wisdom of God. For the foolishness of God is wiser than man's wisdom, and the weakness of God is stronger than man's strength" (1 Corinthians 1:23-25). Specifically he preached "the unsearchable riches of Christ" — literally, "the riches that cannot be tracked." The idea is difficult to put into one word, though the translators have attempted with words like inexplorable riches, or untraceable, unfathomable, inexhaustible, illimitable, inscrutable, incalculable, and infinite.[6] What are the unsearchable riches? They are *saving* riches, *sanctifying* riches, *relational* riches, *practical* riches, and *eternal* riches.

What are the implications of this? Primarily, that Christ always enriches life. How mistaken the young man was who rejected the gospel saying, "Don't preach Christ to me. I've got enough problems already." Christ never subtracts from life; he always enriches it with untrackable riches. A corresponding implication for us is that we have a responsibility to share these riches with others.

So the first focus of Paul's preaching was to preach Christ to the Gentiles. His next focus was to *inform the world of the Church* — "to make plain to everyone the administration of this mystery, which for ages past was kept hidden in God, who created all things" (v. 9). Paul was to enlighten all humanity regarding the miracle of Jews and Gentiles becoming a new humanity, a third race.

Several years ago Johanne Lukasse of the Belgian Evangelical Mission came to the realization that evangelism in Belgium was getting nowhere. The nation's long history of traditional Catholicism and the aggression of the cults had left the land seemingly impervious to the gospel. Driven to the Scripture, he came up with a new plan. First, he gathered together a heterogeneous group of believers: Belgian, Dutch, Americans — whoever would come. Second, he had them rent a house and live together for seven months. As is natural, frictions developed among these diverse people. This in turn sent them to prayer and, happily, to victory and love. Following this, they began to see amazing fruit. Outsiders called them "the people who love each other," for they were living out the words and promises of Jesus: "A new commandment I give you: Love one another. As I have loved you, so you must love one another. All men will know that you are my disciples if you love one another" (John 13:34, 35).

It is as we live out the mystery of the third race that we will win the world for Christ. It is to brothers and sisters that the world is drawn. We must realize that dynamic evangelism will take place as we preach and live out two things: Christ and the Church. Paul calls us to the power of the two in concert.

The third purpose for Paul's opening the mystery comes as a surprise: *to inform the angels*: "His [God's] intent was that now, through the church, the manifold wisdom of God should be made known to the rulers and authorities in the heavenly realms, according to his eternal purpose which he accomplished in Christ Jesus our Lord. In him and through faith in him we may approach God with freedom and confidence" (vv. 10-12). Here it will help us to imagine a cosmic drama. The theatre is history. The stage is the world. The actors are the Church. The writer is God, who directs and produces the drama. And the audience? Cosmic beings — "the rulers and authorities in the heavenly realms." The history of the Christian Church is "the graduate school for angels."[7] As John Stott says, "It is through the old creation (the universe) that God reveals his glory to humans; it is through the new creation (the church) that he reveals his wisdom to angels."[8]

The inescapable conclusion is that the angels watch us because we are part of the mystery! This is not the only Scripture which teaches this. First Peter 1:10-12 describes how the prophets searched intently to understand the prophecies regarding Christ which have now been revealed in the gospel, adding at the end of verse 12, "Even angels long to look into these things" (literally, *the angels stoop to look*). This pictures angels bent over and intently observing the teachings and actions of God's people. Then there is that enigmatic line in 1 Corinthians 11:10 which says that "because of the angels, the woman ought to have a sign of authority on her head." We have a far bigger and more observant viewing audience than any of us realize!

The inference of our text and that in 1 Peter is that God has not revealed his complete plan for history and the reconciliation of the universe to the angels, so they observe us to learn about it. Angels, we know, are messengers of God. They also watch over his people. We know too that they gather in innumerable hosts to sing hymns to God and that they delight in beholding the Father's face (Matthew 18:10). We know they were present when each new star was freshly minted and the planets were set to gliding in their courses — "the morning stars [the angels] sang together" (Job 38:7). They have seen the greatness and wisdom of creation. They have navigated the immense distances of space. They have watched God's people from the beginning — Aaron and Moses, the blood-drenched offerings and clouds of smoke in the Tabernacle and the Temple, and on and on. They have seen the advent of Christ — the incarnation, death, and resurrection of their blessed Lord. Yet there still remains much to learn. How will it consummate? they wonder.

And as they watch the Church, God reveals his "manifold wisdom" (literally, *many-colored wisdom*, a rare poetical adjective used in the Septuagint to describe Joseph's coat of many colors — Genesis 37:3, 23, 32). The many-colored fellowship of the Church, the variegated third race of Jews and Gentiles — multicultural and multiracial — shows the many-shaded wisdom of God. Through studying the Church the angelic host observes the reconciling work of Christ, which is the model for the reconciling of the universe when everything on Heaven and earth will be brought together in him (cf. 1:9, 10; Colossians 1:17-22).

All of this demands a view of the Church so high that it challenges belief. The Church, a product of God's reconciling work, will in fact be an agent in the ultimate cosmic reconciliation! This mystery keeps the angels watching.

Our text calls us to recognize and revere the immense centrality of the Church. John Stott has suggested that this includes three grand facts.[9] First, *the Church is central to history.* The open secret is that the Church, the new humanity, a multiracial, multinational third race, will rule in the universe along with Christ and the angels, and that amidst the swirling tides of Marxism, revived militant Islam, and virulent materialism only the Church will survive history.

Second, *the Church is central to the gospel.* Ephesians teaches that the complete gospel involves both the preaching of Christ and the mystery of the Church. Christ died and rose from the dead not only to save us, but to create a single new humanity. That means that the local manifestation of the Church, the church we attend, is very important. It is the third race watched by the world and by angels. When it *preaches Christ* and *lives as the Church*, souls are ineluctably drawn to Christ the Head.

Third, *the Church is central to Christian living.* The text ends with Paul alluding to his suffering: "I ask you, therefore, not to be discouraged because of my sufferings for you, which are your glory" (v. 13). Paul was willing to pay any price to see the Church go forward. As an apostle, he saw his sufferings as the Church's glory.

The bottom line is, the Church is not an option for believers, nor is supporting it an option. I am not saying you have to go to church to be a Christian, but you also do not have to go home to be married. However, if you do not frequent your home, your relationship will be in jeopardy. Attendance and participation in your local church is not an option. Paul's gospel was *Christ and the Church.*

As we all know, the Church on earth is imperfect. Nevertheless, we must be committed to the local manifestation of the universal Church. We must be committed to regular worship and should worship with all we have. As the third race, we must be committed to our church's fellowship as well. If we only attend worship, we are robbing the church and ourselves and Christ. We must be involved in a small group or a Bible school class where we interact and minister to others. Also, since Christ and his Church has the only answer for the world, we must be involved in sharing both. Evangelism is not an option. We must reach out to those who are not like us. When we do, we will be living out one of the supreme glories of the Church.

> *I love Thy kingdom, Lord,*
> *The house of Thine abode,*
> *The Church our blest Redeemer saved*
> *With His own precious blood.*

> *For her my tears shall fall;*
> *For her my prayers ascend;*
> *To her my cares and toils be giv'n,*
> *Till toils and cares shall end.*

The mystery demands ministry. Amen!

For this reason I kneel before the Father, from whom his whole family in heaven and on earth derives its name. I pray that out of his glorious riches he may strengthen you with power through his Spirit in your inner being, so that Christ may dwell in your hearts through faith. And I pray that you, being rooted and established in love, may have power, together with all the saints, to grasp how wide and long and high and deep is the love of Christ, and to know this love that surpasses knowledge — that you may be filled to the measure of all the fullness of God. Now to him who is able to do immeasurably more than all we ask or imagine, according to his power that is at work within us, to him be glory in the church and in Christ Jesus throughout all generations, for ever and ever! Amen. (3:14-21)

13

A Prayer for the Third Race

EPHESIANS 3:14-21

Perhaps you have the same problem I have — my mind sometimes wanders as I pray. As I begin to make petition I pray for my mother, and as I think about her I envision my family home where she still lives. The vision includes my high school hot rod — a gray-primered '41 Ford with racing slicks and the pinstriped epigram *"Swing low, sweet chariot"* just under the driver's window. Next I am behind the wheel heading down Beach Boulevard for Huntington Beach and some bodysurfing! What began so properly and spiritually ends up being a stroll down Memory Lane — or, even worse, a frenetic run through my worries! I need a prayer list!

If you have ever done that, do not be too hard on yourself — it sometimes happens to the very best, even the Apostle Paul. Admittedly his lapse was much more spiritual than mine, but nevertheless it was a lapse. He began to dictate a prayer in verse 1 of chapter 3, only to be sidetracked by his busy mind regarding the mystery of the Church in verses 2-13, and then returned to his prayer in verse 14. This is very apparent if you read verses 1 and 14 together: "For this reason I, Paul, the prisoner of Christ Jesus for the sake of you Gentiles— . . . For this reason I kneel before the Father . . ." (v.14). Perhaps there were times when Paul needed a prayer list too!

Be that as it may, Paul is now fully engaged in a prayer for God's masterwork, the Church, the third race as we have been calling it. This is one of the most beautiful and oft-quoted prayers in Scripture, especially in reference to the *width* and *length* and *height* and *depth* of Christ's love. The incomparable Charles Simeon of Cambridge, the founder of the evangelical movement in the Church of England (and one of my personal heroes), took these "Four Magnitudes" as his life verse and virtually died with them on his lips.[1] The prayer itself has been the text of countless expositions. Alexander Maclaren had six sermons on it. The prayer is uniquely beautiful, but what has made it the subject of so many expositions is that it is a prayer for us, the Church.

The opening statement — "For this reason I kneel before the Father" — may not get our attention, especially if kneeling is part of our normal prayer discipline. But in fact it is remarkable because it was not customary for Jews to kneel in prayer. The ordinary posture was standing, just as we see pious Jews doing today before the Wailing Wall in Jerusalem, rocking back and forth as they intone their prayers.[2] Kneeling indicated an extraordinary event or an unusual passion. For example, when King Solomon prayed at the dedication of the Temple, he knelt on a wooden platform before all the people and lifted his hands to Heaven in prayer (2 Chronicles 6:13). In Gethsemane on the eve of his death Jesus fell to the ground in agonized emotion as he prayed to his father (Mark 14:35, 36). And when Paul made his tearful good-bye to the elders of Ephesus, he knelt with them and prayed (Acts 20:36-38).

Here Paul pens his immortal prayer with unusual emotion, for two discernible reasons. First, because of the stunning impact upon himself of the immense revelation he has been delivering. How beautiful it is to see a man go to his knees because of God's Word. There is a message here for those of us who are preachers of the Word. How easy it is to be like a railroad conductor who after daily shouting out destinations imagines that he has been there, but has no idea what really lies behind his own words. It is also a message for all who listen to Paul's prayer with a ho-hum attitude.

Second, the apostle is on his knees in profound emotion "*before the Father*, from whom his whole family in heaven and on earth derives its name." When my wife, Barbara, and I have time to talk about important things, the first topic we talk about is our children and grandchildren. We discuss what is happening in each of their lives, we relate to each other the conversations we have had with them, we do some paternal and maternal bragging, we congratulate each other on how brilliant our grandchildren are, and we mention our prayer concerns. We especially love our own. They are our joy — and they know it. So it was with Paul's realization of his relationship with his Father, the Father of the third race. Paul knew he was loved, and that put him on his knees!

Paul had fallen to his knees because of two realities: first, the sublime truths of God's Word, and second, the soul-healing Fatherhood under which he rested. This realization now springs forth in three major petitions for the new humanity: for *strength*, for *love*, for *fullness*.

A PRAYER FOR STRENGTH (vv. 16, 17a)

First, he prays for their strength: "I pray that out of his glorious riches he may strengthen you with power through his Spirit in your inner being, so that Christ may dwell in your hearts through faith" (vv. 16, 17a). The main idea is this: just as the ill or infirm need to be strengthened so they can take in all that life has to offer, so also God's children need to be inwardly strengthened to receive all the blessings God desires for them. Paper bags are not fit containers for valuables.

This is all so logical if you have been following Paul's exposition of the wonderful things God wants to do for his own. Their immensity makes us see our inadequacy. As Stuart Briscoe has remarked, we need to be like the little boy who was heard to say when he fell into a barrel of molasses, "Lord, make my capacity equal to this opportunity."[3]

There are two elements here. One is derived from God's wealth. Notice that Paul says, "I pray that out of [literally, *according to*] his glorious riches he may strengthen you with power" (v. 16a). It is futile to come to a pauper with our requests, no matter how moving and passionate the appeal may be. But to come before the One from whom are all things and to whom are all things (Romans 11:36) makes for great optimism, especially when he is no mere John D. Rockefeller who sometimes gave *from* his riches, but is rather the One who gives *according to* his riches — "on the scale and in the style of the wealth of his glory."[4] Such are the resources from which he strengthens us.

The other element in our strengthening is the agency of the Holy Spirit in our inner being: "I pray that out of his glorious riches he may strengthen you with power through his Spirit in your inner being, so that Christ may dwell in your hearts through faith" (vv. 16, 17a). Paul speaks of this in 2 Corinthians 4:16 — "Therefore we do not lose heart. Though outwardly we are wasting away, yet inwardly we are being renewed day by day." The Holy Spirit orchestrates the endowment of the strength which is freely given to us according to the scale of his riches. We are renewed and empowered for life, and we grow stronger and stronger even while our bodies grow old. We are frail containers pulsating with divine power!

In this way we become full of Christ. He "dwells in [our] hearts through faith." This is a beautiful upward spiral: our capacity is strengthened according to his riches so we can appropriate more of his life; his life thus fills us and thus enlarges our capacity so can we hold more of him within. And so it goes onward and upward with Christ.

This prayer for inner strengthening was not a mere wish, but the petition of the Apostle Paul for the Church. It is my prayer for myself and my church too.

A PRAYER FOR LOVE (vv. 17b-19a)

Paul goes on to pray for love: "And I pray that you, being rooted and established in love, may have power, together with all the saints, to grasp how wide and long and high and deep is the love of Christ, and to know this love that surpasses knowledge . . ." (vv. 17b-19a).

The opening expression, "And I pray that you, being rooted and established in love . . ." (v. 17b), is a prayer for a lifestyle of love. Again Paul mixes his metaphors. "[R]ooted" is agricultural, and "established" (literally, *founded*) is architectural, but their significance is perfectly parallel. Like trees, our lives are to send down roots deep and wide into the soil of love. Like buildings, the edifices of our lives here on earth are to have deep, solid foundations of love. If we are properly rooted and properly constructed on a foundation of love, nothing will be able to shake us.

Years ago Dr. Barnhouse pointed out that love is intrinsic to all the fruits of the Spirit listed in Galatians 5:22. He said, "*Love* is the key. *Joy* is love singing. *Peace* is love resting. *Long-suffering* is love enduring. *Kindness* is love's touch. *Goodness* is love's character. *Faithfulness* is love's habit. *Gentleness* is love's self-forgetfulness. *Self-control* is love holding the reins."[5] There are no fruits of the Spirit without love! We must be rooted and founded in love with all the depth and profundity of these metaphors.

Paul prays this because relational love is absolutely crucial to the viability and ministry of the third race. His call is to go beyond superficialities. We must send our roots down, down, down and far out into love. There is nothing static here. Love must grow on until the grave when, of course, it will fully bloom.

Having prayed for a lifestyle of love, Paul turns his focus upward to the vertical love of Christ, praying for the believers' mental comprehension of its dimensions. "And I pray that you, being rooted and established in love, may have power, together with all the saints, to grasp how wide and long and high and deep is the love of Christ" (vv. 17b, 18).

Twenty-nine years ago when I met my wife to be, I immediately fell "head over heels" in love. I was crazy about her. I loved the way she looked, the tone of her voice, her laugh, her aroma, her attitudes, her *joi de vivre*, her devotion — everything. And that love grew. When I married her almost twenty-eight years ago I felt I could not love her more, but I was wrong. The soul-exchange of all those years, the joys and woes of parenting, our mutual love for our children, our ministry together has fostered a love which continues to grow deeper and deeper. I know now that there is even greater love ahead. I have an incalculable love for my wife. It is finite and flawed, but nevertheless there is no instrument on earth that can measure it.

I say this for contrast, because what our text calls us to consider is the infinite love of Christ. The Four Magnitudes — *width, length, height,* and *depth* — are poetic expressions for the infinitude of God's love. We must be careful not to be too fanciful about these, as Augustine and Ambrose have been.[6] Nevertheless, these dimensions can be said to suggest:

1) A love which is *wide* enough to embrace the world. John 3:16 tells us, "For God so loved the world that he gave his one and only Son, that whoever believes in him shall not perish but have eternal life."

2) A love which is *long* enough to last forever (1 Corinthians 13:8). As Spurgeon said, "It is so long that your old age cannot wear it out, so long your continual tribulation cannot exhaust it, your successive temptations shall not drain it dry; like eternity itself it knows no bounds."[7]

3) A love which is *high* enough to take sinners to Heaven (1 John 3:1, 2).

4) A love which is *deep* enough to take Christ to the very depths to reach the lowest sinner (Philippians 2:8).

The Four Magnitudes describe an infinite, incomprehensible love. In A. W. Tozer's words,

> . . . because God is self-existent, His love had no beginning, because he is eternal, his love can have no end, because he is infinite it has no limit, because he is holy it is the quintessence of all spotless purity, because he is immense, his love is an incomprehensibly vast, bottomless, shoreless sea. . . .[8]

Christ's love is indeed incomprehensible, but Paul prays for our comprehension, that we "may have power, together with all the saints, to grasp" its dimensions — literally, to take hold of them, to seize them.[9] He knows this is impossible, but he calls us to this grand spiritual exercise for the health of our souls. It is to be our life's occupation. Have we seriously devoted time to thinking about and trying to understand his love? Have we contemplated his love in, say, the Incarnation? — the cross? — great passages such as this one which extol his love? If not, we have failed in our duty.

But — and here is the key — this is not to be our solitary, individualistic, isolated occupation, for we are to do it "together with all the saints." We can only come to a better, fuller understanding of his love in community! This happens when we sit under the preaching of his Word. It happens when we study it together and discuss it. It happens when we share our knowledge of God's love with each other. It happens when we observe it in our brothers and sisters. It happens as our hearts go upward in the worship of him. We need each other in order to comprehend his Word.

There is one last request by Paul regarding love, and that is for an experiential love of Christ: "and to know this love that surpasses knowledge" (v. 19a). Again this is confusing language because you cannot personally know what is beyond knowledge. However, you can *experience* it. This knowing is not just in the intellect but in the heart. Samuel Rutherford wrote from prison in Aberdeen, "Love, love (I mean Christ's love), is the hottest coal that ever I felt. Oh, but the smoke of it be hot! Cast all the salt sea on it, it will flame; hell cannot quench it; many, many waters will not quench love."[10] For those who have not experienced this love, no words will suffice. For those who have experienced it, no words will quite do.

A PRAYER FOR FULLNESS (v. 19b)

Paul's final petition is that the third race "be filled to the measure of all the fullness of God" (v. 19b). This is a staggering thought, for this fullness is the fullness with which God fills himself. How can we understand this? Some parallel Scriptures come to our rescue — for example, "For God was pleased to have all his fullness dwell in him [Christ]" (Colossians 1:19), and "For in Christ all the fullness of the Deity lives in bodily form, and you have been given fullness in Christ" (Colossians 2:9, 10). How does this work? The answer can be best understood by way of illustration. Several years ago my wife and I stood on the shore of the vast Pacific Ocean — two finite dots alongside a seemingly infinite expanse. And as we stood there we reflected that if I were to take a pint jar and allow the ocean to rush into it, in an instant my little jar would be filled with the fullness of the Pacific. But of course I could never put the fullness of the Pacific Ocean into my jar! Because Christ is infinite, he can hold all the fullness of Deity. But whenever one of us finite creatures dips the tiny vessel of our life into him, we instantly become full of his fullness. We can always open to hold more and more of his fullness. And the more we receive of his fullness, the more we can yet receive! This will be our experience in eternity — the ultimate elevation of our souls. We will be loaded with the fullness of God, integrated more and more into his fullness.

What a prayer! Within this amazing torrent of devotion Paul has prayed for our *strength*, our *love*, and our *fullness*. This is high theology. And this is typical of Paul's thoughts and prayers. But there is one more thing which is also characteristic — and that is that his high theology always becomes doxology, high praise. "Now to him who is able to do immeasurably more than all we ask or imagine, according to his power that is at work within us, to him be glory in the church and in Christ Jesus throughout all generations, for ever and ever! Amen" (v. 20, 21). The God whom Paul makes these requests to has a capacity which exceeds the people's capacity of asking — or even imagining!

To this great God Paul invokes glory: "to him be glory in the church and in Christ Jesus throughout all generations, for ever and ever! Amen" (v. 21). Paul piles synonym upon synonym to emphasize an eternity of glorifying God — "One age supervening upon another into remotest infinity"[11] — literally, "unto all the generation of the age of the ages. Amen." We the Church (though remaining finite) will keep on expanding in our capacity to bring glory to him for all eternity.

With this exultant note the first section of Ephesians ends, and the "Amen!" may well be the congregation's loud affirmation as it was read to them.[12]

We have learned that there are three things the third race must put on its prayer list: 1) prayer for an *inner strengthening* so as to enhance our capacity to hold what he has for us, 2) prayer for *love* so our practical lives will be rooted in love and so we will further understand and experience his unfathomable love, and, 3) prayer for ever-growing *fullness* in this life and in eternity.

If we pray this list, there is ample cause for optimism because of the Scriptural promise in 1 John 5:14, 15 — "This is the assurance we have in approaching God: that if we ask anything according to his will, he hears us. And if we know that he hears us — whatever we ask — we know that we have what we asked of him." Our optimism comes because Paul's Ephesian prayer is God's revealed will. Therefore, if we pray for its three grand emphases, we will receive them!

As a prisoner for the Lord, then, I urge you to live a life worthy of the calling you have received. Be completely humble and gentle; be patient, bearing with one another in love. Make every effort to keep the unity of the Spirit through the bond of peace. There is one body and one Spirit — just as you were called to one hope when you were called — one Lord, one faith, one baptism; one God and Father of all, who is over all and through all and in all. (4:1-6)

14

Building the Church's Unity

EPHESIANS 4:1-6

T he opening sentence of chapter 4, where Paul says, "As a prisoner for the Lord, then, I urge you to live a life worthy of the calling you have received," marks the turning point in the book of Ephesians. The message moves from *theology* to *practicality*. This is typical of Paul's writing. You can observe the same change in Romans 12:1 and Colossians 3:5.

This shift can be expressed in many ways: from *doctrine* to *duty*; from *creed* to *conduct*; from the Christian's *wealth* to his *walk*; from *exposition* to *exhortation*; from the *indicative* to the *imperative*; from *high society* to a *high life*. Because of the amazing theological realities of chapters 1 through 3, Paul urges the Ephesians (and us) "to live a life worthy of the calling you have received."

The Greek word translated "worthy" is *axios*, which has the root idea of weight.[1] This is the word from which we derive our English word *axiom*, which means, "to be of equal weight." In an equation the axiom indicates doing something to each side of the equation so it remains true. Paul is saying we should try to live lives equal to the great blessings described in chapters 1 through 3.[2] We are to be like the man who said, "Christ has done so much for me, the rest of my life is a P.S. to his great work!"

How are we to walk worthy? That should be our natural response. And the remainder of the book answers this. But the immediate charge in chapter 4 contains two ways of doing this: first by walking in *unity* (vv. 1-16), and then by walking in *purity* (v. 17ff.). We will now take up the theme of unity, which we will explore in two studies (vv. 1-6 and vv. 7-16). The present meditation divides under three headings: 1) *The Character Which*

Brings Christian Unity (v. 2), 2) *The Divine Origin of Christian Unity* (vv. 4-6), and 3) *The Charge to Build Christian Unity* (v. 3).

This subject has a special poignancy today in a world which has so failed in its attempts at unity and is so alienated. I was in my teens during the fifties when ecumenism was the big thing with the mainline denominations. But it all came to naught because it was based on an "eviscerated, spineless" theology instead of a "vertebrate system of Christian belief."[3] Today the World Council of Churches is little more than a "mouse that roared." I was in my twenties in the sixties, and I remember visiting Haight Ashbury in San Francisco and being handed flowers and underground newspapers proclaiming a new day of peace. The bright colors were colors of optimism, the communes wishful microcosms of the new order. But today all that is left are some middle-aged anachronisms — cultural dinosaurs. We live in a cold, fragmented world.

Recently a UPI story told of a wheelchair-bound man who was ticketed for setting fire to his armchair. "I set the chair on fire because I'm here by myself," said John J. Davies, fifty-eight. "I was afraid, but I didn't care. I wanted to get attention. . . . I set the fire so someone would get me out of here." Arson investigators said Davies was ticketed for misdemeanor arson to discourage him from doing it again. "Maybe he'll realize it's something serious," Fire Captain Joseph Napravnik said. Actually John Davies already thought it was serious. Alienation and neglect are like death.

I recently spoke to a young man who is so starved for attention that he has his hair cut once a week just to be touched by another human hand in a nonthreatening manner. Life for so many in this world is like an elevator ride — everyone facing forward, no eye contact, no conversation or interaction — and then everyone rushes off to their faceless endeavors. The world is looking for a new humanity, a third race, which is not only walking in unity, but has open, inviting arms and hearts.

THE CHARACTER WHICH BRINGS CHRISTIAN UNITY (v. 2)

The unity which Paul urges upon us begins with character: "Be completely humble and gentle; be patient, bearing with one another in love" (v. 2).

The people who bring unity are first of all "humble and gentle." Humility was despised in the ancient Greco-Roman world as a slave-like quality. What was admired was the *mega-souled* or "great-souled" man who was complete and self-sufficient.[4] Ernest Hemingway, as he portrayed himself in his prime, would be a good example — brimming with male elan, in control, self-assured, needing nothing. The proud white hunter in *The Snows of Kilimanjaro* to whom his adventurer mistress said, "You're the most complete man I've ever known"[5] — that is the man the Greeks would have applauded.

But here Paul extols humility and couples it with the tandem characteristic of "gentle[ness]" (or *meekness*, as it is more often translated). This meekness/gentleness is not weakness. It is rather strength under control. There is nothing spineless or timid about it.[6] Jesus described himself with both words, saying, "I am gentle [meek] and humble in heart" (Matthew 11:29). We see his steel-like meekness in two ways. First, in respect to himself — his power not to practice retaliation, his ability to forgive. And second, in his fierce defense of others or of the truth. I like John Wycliffe's translation—*mild*.

Pride and self-promoting arrogance sow disunity, but a humble, gentle man or woman is like a caressing breeze. Charles Simeon, the great preacher of Kings' College and Holy Trinity Cambridge, was like this. Hugh Evan Hopkins, his biographer, tells us:

> When in 1808 Simeon's health broke down and he had to spend some eight months recuperating on the Isle of Wight, it fell to Thomason to step into the gap and preach as many as five times on a Sunday in Trinity Church and Stapleford. He surprised himself and everyone else by developing a preaching ability almost equal to his vicar's at which Simeon, totally free from any suggestions of professional jealousy, greatly rejoiced. He quoted the Scripture, "He must increase; but I must decrease," and told a friend, "Now I see why I have been laid aside. I bless God for it."[7]

Those who walk in unity are not only humble and gentle but, as the second couplet says, "patient, bearing with one another in love" (v. 2). J. Dwight Pentecost tells of a church split that was so serious each side filed a lawsuit to dispossess the others from the church, completely disregarding the Biblical injunction not to go to court against fellow believers. The civil courts threw it out, but eventually it came to a church court, where it belonged. The higher judiciary of the church made its decision and awarded the church property to one of the two factions. The losers withdrew and formed another church in the area. In the course of the proceedings the church courts found that the conflict had begun at a church dinner when an elder received a smaller slice of ham than a child seated next to him.[8] The root of the impasse was an absence of patience and forbearing love — not to mention humility and gentleness!

We are to "be patient," not short-tempered, literally *long-tempered*. The twin quality of "bearing with one another in love" means far more than tolerating each other — love is to oil our relationships. The Apostle Peter, who began as a proud, rough, impatient man, says in his first letter: ". . . have sincere love for your brothers, love one another deeply, from the heart" (1:22); "Show proper respect to everyone: Love the brotherhood of believers . . ." (2:17); "Finally, all of you, live in harmony with one another; be sympathetic, love as brothers, be compassionate and humble" (3:8); "Above all, love each other deeply, because love covers over a multitude of sins" (4:8).

The truth which radiates from verse 2 is that Christian unity doesn't begin with an external structure, but rather in the attitudes of the heart — *humility* and *mildness* and *patience* and *loving tolerance* of one another. "The unity of the Spirit" (v. 3) takes people who are *so* different and makes them live in soul-satisfying unity. What diversity there is in the average church! Think of all the body types (*somatypes*): tall, short, round, thin, muscular, unathletic. Then imagine all the mental types (*psychetypes*): nervous, calm, mathematical, unmathematical, artistic, musical, other-than-musical, etc., etc. There are huge differences among us! But when the spiritual fruits of humility and patience reign, there is unity. Christian unity in profound diversity brings great glory to God!

THE DIVINE ORIGIN OF CHRISTIAN UNITY (vv. 4-6)

In verses 4-6 Paul celebrates the origin of our unity: "There is one body and one Spirit — just as you were called to one hope when you were called — one Lord, one faith, one baptism; one God and Father of all, who is over all and through all and in all." Many New Testament scholars believe this was an early Christian confessional hymn, and it may well have been (cf. 1 Corinthians 8:6; 12:4-6). The important thing to see is that it teaches us that our unity is rooted in the Holy Trinity ("Spirit," v. 4; "Lord," v. 5; "God," v. 6). Each of the seven great unities in verses 4-6 is connected with one of the Persons of the Trinity.

First, we see the Person of the Holy Spirit and his work in bringing unity — "There is one body and one Spirit" (v. 4a). The Holy Spirit creates the Body of Christ, of which we are members. "For we were all baptized by one Spirit into one body — whether Jews or Greeks, slave or free — and we were all given the one Spirit to drink" (1 Corinthians 12:13). The Holy Spirit creates, fills, coordinates, orchestrates, and empowers the Body of Christ. This accounts for the delightful serendipities we all experience when meeting other believers so different from us — a brief soul-fellowship with a taxi driver on the way to the airport in Washington, D.C. — the same experience in a jeepney in Manila — an exchange of heart in a village in Switzerland — another on the streets of Cambridge.

Second, there is the Person of Christ and his work in ministering unity — "just as you were called to one hope when you were called — one Lord, one faith, one baptism" (vv. 4b, 5). There is no doubt that the "one Lord" here is Jesus. First Corinthians 8:6 says, "There is but one Lord, Jesus Christ, through whom all things came and through whom we live" (cf. Philippians 2:11 and 1 Corinthians 12:3). As our "one Lord" he creates "one faith" because he is the object and focus of our belief. Because of our "one faith" we all have participated in "one baptism" — "into the name of the Lord Jesus" (Acts 8:16; 19:5; cf. 1 Corinthians 1:13-15). The question of water or Spirit baptism is not in view here. Rather, the passage is presenting one shared baptism.[9] Sharing "one Lord" and "one faith" and "one baptism" brings "one hope," which is, first, the return of Christ. ". . . while we wait for the blessed hope — the glorious appearing of our great God and Savior, Jesus Christ" (Titus 2:13). Second, this is the hope of sharing glory with him (1 John 3:2; cf. 1:18 and Colossians 1:23, 27).

Lastly, there is the Person of the Father and his work in unity — "one God and Father of all, who is over all and through all and in all" (v. 6). Again we have the great Ephesian emphasis on our shared paternity. My younger brother Steve and I could hardly be more different. He is a sky diver, motorcycle racer, mechanic, home builder, custom car builder, cabinetmaker, carpet layer, barber, and professional salmon fishing guide. I have spent my life in the ministry and with books. But despite our great differences we have the same father, we are brothers, and we have a deep, undying love for each other. We are, after all is said and done, *family.*

And so it is with those of us who are brothers and sisters in Christ. After all is said and done, we have the same Father — we are family. Our unity comes from seven grand unities all rooted in the Holy Trinity: "one body . . . one Spirit . . . one hope . . . one Lord . . . one faith . . . one baptism . . . one God and Father of all."

What are the implications of our unity being rooted in the the Holy Trinity? Simply this: our unity is eternal and unbreakable. "The unity of the church is as indestructible as the unity of God himself. It is no more possible to split the church than it is possible to split the Godhead."[10] You and I will never be separated! Our unity is more solid than the Himalayas and more enduring than Venus or Mars.

The obvious question is, If this is so, why are there outward divisions in the Church? Some Christian fellowships will not even speak to each other. How can this be?

THE CHARGE TO BUILD CHRISTIAN UNITY (v. 3)

To begin with, we should note that Paul recognizes this problem in verse 3 by commanding us to "Make every effort to keep the unity of the Spirit through the bond of peace." "Make every effort" comes from a root word which means to *make haste*, and thus gives the idea of zealous effort and diligence. "Do your utmost to keep the unity of the Spirit — this is urgent!"

This has tremendous significance for the local church. There is no room for rivalries or hatreds or factions. This is a call to focus on our Triune

God, the root of our unity. The Apostle John makes a monumental statement in this respect: "We proclaim to you what we have seen and heard, so that you also may have fellowship with us. And our fellowship is with the Father and with his Son, Jesus Christ" (1 John 1:3). This verse informs us that the closer we draw to God, the closer we will be to each other. If we would truly live this principle, not just give a superficial nod to it, there would indeed be unity.

Suppose for a moment that by a miracle we could bring some of the great Christians of the centuries together under one roof. From the fourth century there would come the great intellect Augustine of Hippo; from the tenth century, Bernard of Clairvaux; from the sixteenth, the peerless reformer John Calvin. From the eighteenth century would come John Wesley, the great Methodist advocate of free will, and along with him George Whitefield, the great evangelist. From the nineteenth century comes the Baptist C. H. Spurgeon and D. L. Moody. And finally from the twentieth century Billy Graham. If we gathered all these men under one steeple we would be unable to get a unanimous vote on many matters. But underneath it all would be *unity*. And the more these men lifted up Christ and focused on him, the greater their unity would be.

The other thing suggested by the command in verse 3 ("Make every effort to keep the unity of the Spirit through the bond of peace") is to be peacemakers. To begin with, *a peacemaker is characterized by honesty*. The prophet Ezekiel warned against those who act as if everything is all right when it is not, who say "'Peace,' when there is no peace" (Ezekiel.13:10). Such individuals, according to Ezekiel, are merely plastering over cracked walls, and when the rain comes, the walls fall (vv. 10, 11). Jeremiah, using some of the same phrasing, put it memorably: "They dress the wound of my people as though it were not serious. 'Peace, peace,' they say, when there is no peace" (Jeremiah 6:14). The peacemaker is painfully honest about the absence of peace in the world, in the society in which he moves, and in his own personal relationships. He admits when he is at odds with others. He does not pretend that things are OK when they are not.

How this speaks to our condition. All of us tend to putty over the cracks. (I think this is particularly a male tendency.) Even in our most intimate relationships, we tend to act as if everything is fine when it is not. But our avoidance heals the wound only slightly and prepares the way for greater trouble. May God help us to be honest, for the stakes are high.

Next, *a peacemaker is willing to risk pain*. Anytime one attempts to bring peace societally or personally, he risks misunderstanding and failure. If we have been wrong, there is the pain of apologizing. Or we may have to endure the equally difficult pain of rebuking another. It is so much easier to let things slide, but that is not the way of the peacemaker.

These two qualities of the peacemaker (honesty about the true status of peace and willingness to risk pain in pursuing it) beautifully anticipate the next quality, which is a paradox: *the peacemaker is a fighter*. The peacemaker makes trouble to make peace. The Scriptures enjoin the aggressive pursuit of peace, telling us to "make every effort to do what leads to peace and to mutual edification" (Romans 14:19). "If it is possible, as far as it depends on you, live at peace with everyone" (Romans 12:18). St. Francis of Assisi understood this call to the active pursuit of peace, as his prayer so beautifully recalls:

> *Lord, make me an instrument of Thy peace.*
> *Where there is hate, may I bring love;*
> *Where offense, may I bring pardon;*
> *May I bring union in place of discord.*

Though the peacemaker is a fighter, he is not to be thoughtless or pugnacious. Rather, his character and personality are to be permeated with the *shalom* of God. He is gentle. James wrote, "But the wisdom that comes from heaven is first of all pure; then peace loving, considerate, submissive, full of mercy and good fruit, impartial and sincere. Peacemakers who sow in peace raise a harvest of righteousness" (James 3:17, 18). The peacemaker is tolerant in the best sense of the word. He realizes we are all of fallen stock and so does not demand perfection of others. He is humble. And most of all he is loving.

How beautiful true peacemakers are. Filled with peace themselves, they are honest about the state of the relationships around them. They are honest about what is in their own hearts and sensitive to where others are. They refuse to say "peace, peace" when there is none. They are willing to risk pain and misunderstanding to make things right. Peacemakers will even fight for peace. Are we like this?

There are lonely, alienated people all around us who long for a new humanity where there is peace and love and acceptance. And if they see the Church living out its indestructible unity with humility and gentleness and patience and forbearing love, they will be drawn to it. Jesus prayed, "May they also be in us so that the world may believe that you have sent me. I have given them the glory that you gave me, that they may be one as we are one: I in them and you in me. May they be brought to complete unity to let the world know that you sent me and have loved them even as you have loved me" (John 17:21-23). If the Church reaches out to the people of the world, those people will come and find the unity they need. "We proclaim to you what we have seen and heard, so that you also may have fellowship with us. And our fellowship is with the Father and with his Son, Jesus Christ" (1 John 1:3).

Are we walking in unity? If not, or if we wish to enhance it, we must do four things:

First, *we must reflect on our unity*, deeply rooted in the Holy Trinity, and its sevenfold basis. Our unity with fellow believers is indestructible.

Second, as an extension of this, *we ought to focus on Christ*. We should often read 1 John 1:3, 4 — or even better, memorize it. We must honestly confess our lack of focus and then spend several minutes each day focusing on him. In prayer, we can ask him to help us maintain his unity.

Third, *we need to consciously ask the Holy Spirit to help us* cultivate a character which builds unity — a character of humility, gentleness, patience, and loving forbearance.

Fourth, *we must be peacemakers*: "Make every effort to keep the unity of the Spirit through the bond of peace" (v. 3). We must admit the absence of peace when there is none. We need to confess our culpability if there is any. We must take the steps which make for peace.

But to each one of us grace has been given as Christ apportioned it. This is why it says: "When he ascended on high, he led captives in his train and gave gifts to men." (What does "he ascended" mean except that he also descended to the lower, earthly regions? He who descended is the very one who ascended higher than all the heavens, in order to fill the whole universe.) It was he who gave some to be apostles, some to be prophets, some to be evangelists, and some to be pastors and teachers, to prepare God's people for works of service, so that the body of Christ may be built up until we all reach unity in the faith and in the knowledge of the Son of God and become mature, attaining to the whole measure of the fullness of Christ. Then we will no longer be infants, tossed back and forth by the waves, and blown here and there by every wind of teaching and by the cunning and craftiness of men in their deceitful scheming. Instead, speaking the truth in love, we will in all things grow up into him who is the Head, that is, Christ. From him the whole body, joined and held together by every supporting ligament, grows and builds itself up in love, as each part does its work. (4:7-16)

15

Growing the Church

Ephesians 4:7-16

During the last twenty years much has been written on the subject of growing churches. But Paul's Ephesian treatise is still *the* book, for it is radically true in its principles and unfailing in its effectiveness.

In verses 7-16 Paul explains how God grows a church through its living out the theological fact of its spiritual unity. The passage gives us the keys to church growth, not in numbers, but in the pure sense of what develops the members of the Body of Christ. The first element introduced is that of spiritual endowments in general and gifted leadership in particular.

ESSENTIAL FOR GROWTH: GIFTED LEADERSHIP (vv. 7-11)

The apostle begins by announcing in verse 7, "But to each one of us grace has been given as Christ apportioned it." "Grace" here means the ability to perform the task God has called us to. In Romans 12:6 he similarly explains, "We have different gifts, according to the grace given us." And likewise in 3:7, 8 Paul says that his apostleship came with the gift of God's grace. The point for us is: *each of us has received this enabling grace in the exact proportion that Christ gave it.*

When I recently knelt with a longtime friend in his home and he asked Christ into his life, that very moment "grace [was] given as Christ apportioned it" (v. 7). My friend became a "graced" — a spiritually gifted — man. And as he matures in Christ, that grace will become more and more pervasive and evident in his life. The message of this verse is that all of us (no exceptions!) have a serving grace which has been given to us by Christ in perfect measure. We all have a special part to perform.

Paul goes on to say in verses 8-10 that not only do we each have a

131

special grace, but our individual graces have a spectacular origin: "This is why it says: 'When he ascended on high, he led captives in his train and gave gifts to men.' (What does 'he ascended' mean except that he also descended to the lower, earthly regions? He who descended is the very one who ascended higher than all the heavens, in order to fill the whole universe.)" (vv. 8-10).

Here Paul borrows a line from Psalm 68:18. In verse 7 of that psalm God is pictured as marching in triumph before all Israel after the Exodus. When he comes to Sinai, the earth shakes under his feet (v. 8). Then in verses 11-14 kings and armies are described as fleeing before him while his people sleep peacefully before their fires. Finally, in verses 16 and 17, from Mt. Sinai God sets his sight on Mt. Zion and moves with "tens of thousands and thousands of thousands" of chariots up the slopes of Jerusalem in victory, leading captives in his train and *receiving* gifts from men (v. 18).

Paul, in applying this line to Christ in Ephesians, changes the line from "receiving" to "*giving*" — the triumphant Christ "gave gifts to men." On what basis Paul made this change we do not know. Possibly he borrowed it from an Aramaic *targum*, for we know that there were *targums* which read exactly this way and it was a very acceptable rendering in the first century.[1] Whatever the case, the difference was only formal and not substantial, for ancient military victories precipitated the receiving of tribute and the distribution of the largess.[2]

Paul is simply borrowing the imagery of Psalm 68 and applying it to Christ's incarnation and ascension. The fact that he "ascended" implies that he descended in the Incarnation to the "lower, earthly regions," which is another way of indicating the humiliation of coming to earth (cf. John 3:13).[3] His descent to earth meant that he set aside the independent exercise of his attributes (such as his omnipresence), submitting the exercise of them to the Father's will, and went down, down, down in the Incarnation, and then went even further down in his death, actually becoming sin for us (2 Corinthians 5:21). But then he burst up in exaltation — so that now he fills the whole universe as a conquering King and joyously lavishes gifts upon his children. He bestows abundant gifts to his Church and gives his people power to fulfill their gifts.

The gifts and enabling grace which we have, have been given to us as Christ apportioned them. They came from the conquering King. They are given with great expectation on his part, for he expects us to use them to bring power and victory in the Church.

What are the graces he gives? The answer can be partially seen in the five lists of spiritual gifts in the Scriptures (4:11; 1 Corinthians 12:8-10; 12:28-30; Romans 12:6-8; 1 Peter 4:11). But here Paul focuses on four gifted persons who are gifts to the church: "It was he who gave some to be apostles, some to be prophets, some to be evangelists, and some to be pastors and teachers" (v. 11). From our study of Ephesians thus far we understand that the apostles and prophets are *foundational gifts* to the Church. The previous mentions of apostles and prophets in 2:20 and 3:5 indicate that "apostles" were the Twelve, and "prophets" were those who preached in association with the apostles (cf. Acts 11:27ff.; 13:1ff.; 21:4, 9; 1 Corinthians 14:1). The apostles and the prophets were given to the Church to get her established, but now their role is assumed by the canonical writings of the New Testament. The apostles and prophets with their unique endowments did not extend beyond the apostolic age.

But there is a group which God gives to every generation, and that is evangelists and pastor/teachers. F. F. Bruce says:

> The apostles as an order of the ministry of the church, were not perpetuated beyond the apostolic age, but the various functions they discharged did not lapse with their departure, but continued to be performed by others — notably the evangelists and pastors and teachers.[4]

Today "evangelists" are the *obstetricians* of the Church — those gifted in bringing new births. One of the sorrows of our day is that this name has become a term of derision because of the disgrace of *self-styled* and *so-called* evangelists. To me it is the highest of titles. Billy Graham, evangelist! Luis Palau, evangelist! All who are gifted in making the gospel plain and relevant to the lost or helping fearful people share their faith, evangelists! What marvelous gifts to the Church!

Then there are the *pediatricians*, the pastor/teachers. Notice I have combined the words into a single title. This is nothing new, for the Greek structure suggests it, and the ancients Chrysostom and Augustine translated it this way. "Pastor" literally means *shepherd*. Peter says, "Be shepherds of God's flock that is under your care" (1 Peter 5:2). Paul says, "Be shepherds of the church of God, which he bought with his own blood" (Acts 20:28). This tender, caring, nurturing title suggests a touch here, a kind word there, a gentle prod at the right time. Yet it also suggests resolute strength and protection of the flock. A pastor/teacher is to make feeding the sheep a top priority — as Christ three times charged Peter to do (John 21:15-17).

If there is one thing which characterizes all four of these gifts to the Church, it is teaching! John Stott, a man not given to overstatement, believes that this is *sine qua non* of the pastoral ministry, the greatest need of the Church universal,[5] and I agree. I once lunched with a seminary president as he mourned the lack of Biblical exposition from our pulpits, saying, "I would get on my knees and crawl across America to find someone who will teach my students to preach the text of the Bible."

Recently I heard of a pastor who often began preparation of his Sunday morning sermons on Saturday night as he watched television in his easy chair! Many pastors have a two- or three-year barrel of sermons which they recycle — usually in succeeding churches. No wonder so many churches are stagnant. Lame sermonettes produce Christianettes. Those who stand in the stead of the foundational apostles and prophets as evangelists and pastor/teachers must open wide the foundational teaching of the Old and New Testaments if there is to be true church growth. And those who receive the teaching must listen well, take notes, and put it to work.

MEANS OF GROWTH: DISCIPLESHIP (v. 12a)

Having spelled out that gifted leadership and people who cherish their gifts are essential to church growth, Paul goes on in verse 12 to state the means of growth — *discipleship*. He says quite simply that God has given gifted leadership to the church "to prepare God's people for works of service" (v. 12a) — or as it literally reads, *ministry*. This is a watershed text for the doctrine of the Church. It effectively eliminates the traditional model of the local church as a "pyramid, with the pastor perched precariously on its pinnacle, like a little pope in his own church, while the laity are arrayed beneath him in serried ranks of inferiority."[6] It also shoots down the model of a "bus, in which the pastor does all the driving while the congregation are the passengers slumbering in peaceful security behind him."[7]

The Biblical model is the Body of Christ in which those in pastoral roles prepare God's people for works of ministry. This is why I share the pulpit with my colleagues. While I am the senior pastor, I do not regard myself as *the* pastor and my associates as lesser ministers. We all have our part to do in building up the Body of Christ, and all our parts are equally important.

The bottom line for every Christian believer is that each one of us should be involved in some kind of ministry. Praise God — many have created their own areas of service: to refugees, unwed mothers, the homeless, the elderly, the handicapped, the pornography battle, pro-life witness — to name a few. But those who have no place of service are aberrations. Every believer is to minister! We all have a part to play!

When my wife and I were young parents, the school was presenting its annual Christmas program. Two of our children had parts in their class plays. Holly, our eighth-grader, had the lead of Della in O'Henry's *The Gift of the Magi,* and our fourth-grader, Kent, had four lines as a Wise Man in the Christmas pageant. Holly's play came first, and she articulated her lines perfectly, projecting them so the whole audience could hear. And she was dramatic — moving about the stage as a perfect nineteenth-century heroine — at times her hands extended imploringly, then her wrist to her head in a dither. She stole the show, and when it was over we proudly joined the chorus of applause.

Later came Kent's play. He had been working on his four lines since Thanksgiving and had found it difficult to remember them. Not only that, but he was terrified of the stage. Still, we will never forget the moment he stood in his shepherd's costume with his black tennies showing beneath the hem of his white robe, his eyes saucer-wide with stage fright and his hands repeatedly flexing at his sides. We held our breath as we heard him say,

> *Strange feelings come upon me*
> *Though I know not why.*
> *The night is still around me,*
> *The stars shine in the sky.*

There was no way we could applaud — it was the middle of the play. But our hearts applauded. How pleased we were — with both our children!

That evening we came to better understand that God is not so much interested in our being the star of the show as as he is in our doing our best with the part he has given us. As we all do our own part, we experience church growth.

THE GOAL OF GROWTH: MATURITY (vv. 12b-14)

What will result from the work of pastors who do their job and a people who are prepared for service? In a word — *maturity*. Verses 12-14 tell us:

> . . . to prepare God's people for works of service, so that the body of Christ may be built up until we all reach unity in the faith and in the knowledge of the Son of God and become mature, attaining to the whole measure of the fullness of Christ. Then we will no longer be infants, tossed back and forth by the waves, and blown here and there by every wind of teaching and by the cunning and craftiness of men in their deceitful scheming.

When my children were small, we paid many family visits to 31 Flavors ice cream stores. Thirty-one choices! Sometimes it took them *so long* to choose a flavor, and when we got in the car and they saw what the others had chosen they changed their minds. This is the way the immature believer is: fickle — unstable — gullible — easily influenced by the latest book or preacher or fad — vulnerable to the wolves, of which there are plenty.

But those who are mature are steady and focused. Paul describes here the *corporate maturity* possible for a church where "all reach unity in the faith and in the knowledge of the Son of God and become mature, attaining to the whole measure of the fullness of Christ." A mature church fosters a corporate elevation among its people, just as a fine educational institution promotes the mutual elevation of its students. But, of course, what happens in the church is far more substantial and dynamic, for the elevation is spiritual and eternal. What a vision this is! — Christians working together so that there is mutual growth.

MEDIUM OF GROWTH: TRUTHING (vv. 15, 16)

Lastly, there is the medium of growth, and this is exquisitely beautiful, for it is literally *"truthing in love."* Our text renders it in verse 15 as "speaking the truth in love," but it is the participle *aletheuontes*, which means *truthing*. This carries the idea of not only speaking the truth but doing it. This is the medium through which growth is maximized. When there is *"truthing in love,"* when true lives are married to love, the Spirit is free to do his work, and the result is wonderful. "Instead, speaking the truth in love, we will in all things grow up into him who is the Head, that is, Christ. From him the whole body, joined and held together by every supporting ligament, grows and builds itself up in love, as each part does its work" (vv. 15, 16).

How does Biblical church growth come? 1) Through *gifted leadership* which in dependence upon the Holy Spirit teaches and lives out God's Word. 2) Through *discipleship* in which God's people are prepared for works of service and are using their gifts to the fullest, whatever their parts may be. 3) Through a progressive *corporate maturity* of God's people, so all are riding high on the tide of one another's lives. 4) Through *truthing in love* — transparent, honest, loving speech and lives. This is church growth!

So I tell you this, and insist on it in the Lord, that you must no longer live as the Gentiles do, in the futility of their thinking. They are darkened in their understanding and separated from the life of God because of the ignorance that is in them due to the hardening of their hearts. Having lost all sensitivity, they have given themselves over to sensuality so as to indulge in every kind of impurity, with a continual lust for more. You, however, did not come to know Christ that way. Surely you heard of him and were taught in him in accordance with the truth that is in Jesus. You were taught, with regard to your former way of life, to put off your old self, which is being corrupted by its deceitful desires; to be made new in the attitude of your minds; to put on the new self, created to be like God in true righteousness and holiness. (4:17-24)

16

The Divine Wardrobe

EPHESIANS 4:17-24

If you have been abroad, you know there is a worldwide fascination with fashion. The *London Times* gives daily reports on what the royal family wears, especially the clothing of Princess Diana and the Duchess of York, even recording how many changes they make in one day. Prosperous Japan has become an obsessively clothes-conscious culture. The typical Japanese golfer dares not step on the golf course unless he or she is wearing thousands of dollars of designer clothing. (The average green fee of $450 has something to do with this, of course.) Whether you travel to Chicago or London or Geneva or Beijing or Nairobi, you find fashion-conscious people making fashion statements.

Much of this lure comes from fashion's enticing promise of a "new you." You have seen the ads — the *before* picture of a plain, unhappy-looking woman who lacks confidence, and then the photograph *after* she has come under the care of a salon and has a different hair color, cut, and eyebrows, a fresh paint job, and clothing to match. She is now a new person, brimming with confidence and appeal. Her husband and children love her now — and she is becoming rich! Men are subject to her enticement. "Clothes don't make the man (or woman), but they sure help," we hear. There are manuals on "power dressing." A dark pinstripe suit, a white button-down collar, and a muted red tie is power.

The promise from the fashion world to men and women is sartorial regeneration — new birth through clothing — and it sells and sells and sells! The problem is, not only does clothing not make the man or woman — it covers up the real you. Clothing can polish the image but not the soul.

Our text in Ephesians presents something far better — "a mantle for the soul divine" (to borrow William Blake's term) — a divine wardrobe which will really change one's life. Here we have the clothing for the third race — a heavenly, eternal style which will never go out of date — a wardrobe which wears increasingly better with time. Paul tells us what we need to shed and what we need to put on to be properly dressed. If we take his recommendation to heart, we'll be dressed for any occasion life may bring.

THE OLD WARDROBE (vv. 17-19)

Tragically, the old wardrobe is just as much in style today as it was in Paul's day. Paul describes the pagan lifestyle in verses 17-19 with severe disapproval as he exhorts the Ephesians to forsake it:

> So I tell you this, and insist on it in the Lord, that you must no longer live as the Gentiles do, in the futility of their thinking. They are darkened in their understanding and separated from the life of God because of the ignorance that is in them due to the hardening of their hearts. Having lost all sensitivity, they have given themselves over to sensuality so as to indulge in every kind of impurity, with a continual lust for more.

What a withering description! That kind of life, life apart from God, is a downward spiral which begins, as John Stott has outlined it, with 1) *hardness* of heart and then moves to 2) *darkness* of heart, and then 3) *deadness*, and finally 4) *recklessness* — unrestrained abandonment to sin.[1]

Some have questioned whether this chilling description is really true of the world apart from Christ. Others have called it an outright exaggeration. It is true that not all those who live apart from Christ and without grace go to the depths mentioned here. Yet, this is a valid portrait of pagan, Gentile life in general. In fact, all lives without Christ are dominated by sin. Moreover, the pagans of Paul's time would not disagree with these charges, as such documents as the letter of Aristides eloquently attest.[2] Today's tabloids and newspapers confirm the same terrible truths about our world: hardness — darkness — deadness — recklessness.

Hardness. Man's condition has at its root the hardening of the heart, as verse 18 describes: "They are darkened in their understanding and separated from the life of God because of the ignorance that is in them due to the hardening of their hearts." The Greek word for "hardening" is *porosis*, which comes from the word *poros*, which originally meant "a stone harder than marble." In our own terms we might call this "a heart of stone." This word is used elsewhere in Scripture to refer to the hearts of those in the synagogue who decided to kill Jesus as they witnessed his healing the man with the withered hand on the Sabbath (Mark 3:5, 6). In our text here "the hardening of their hearts" describes inability and unwillingness to respond to God's truth. The parallel text in Romans 1:18 describes "men who suppress the truth by their wickedness." They hold down the truth much like the little boy who smuggled his dog into his room to spend the night. When he heard his parents approaching, he put the dog in his toy box, sat on the lid, and talked with his parents, ignoring the repeated thumps of the poor pet. Paul is talking about aggressive suppression of the truth.

Darkness. From hardness comes darkness, as it says in verse 18a: "They are darkened in their understanding." This is, of course, an absence of spiritual understanding, because the intellects of the unsaved are active and capable. Paul says the same thing in Romans: "their thinking became futile and their foolish hearts were darkened" (1:21); "Although they claimed to be wise, they became fools" (1:22). The more they suppressed the truth, the less capable they became of discerning spiritual reality.

The full effect of such a darkening is seen, for example, in actress and occult leader Shirley MacLaine's standing on a Malibu beach with her arms flung open to the cosmos, shouting, "I am God! I am God! I am God!"[3] One day, if she continues in her darkness, she will stand before God as he judges her and will say, "Oh, God! Oh, God! Oh, God!" But it will be too late.

Deadness. From hardness and darkness comes deadness, as Paul says in verse 18: "separated from the life of God." This separation makes everything possible — John Gacy, Ted Bundy, the killing fields, perversion — sins hardly imaginable. This death-state makes it possible to call "evil good and good evil" and to "put darkness for light and light for darkness" (Isaiah 5:20).

Recklessness Finally, this death spawns recklessness: "Having lost all sensitivity, they have given themselves over to sensuality so as to indulge in every kind of impurity, with a continual lust for more" (v. 19). What a description! The opening phrase, "having lost all sensitivity," literally means they were beyond feeling — like callused skin. Bishop Moule renders this, "having got beyond the pain."[4] Nothing hurt, so they gave themselves over to "sensuality" (*aselgeia* — "vice that throws off all restraint and flaunts itself"[5]). They performed every impurity and lusted for more. Sensuality does not satisfy, but only creates a greater appetite.

The very nadir comes when such men and women flaunt their appetites and perversions. For example, when *Playboy* magazine publishes a parody on the conception of Christ in which an angel-like nymph tells Joseph that "the spirit of God" is on Mary's lover and then assures Joseph that the "offspring is going to be a tremendous genius whose ideas will make you a billionaire . . . The kid will be a Messiah." In such times our text is being lived out.[6] Our culture is hell-bent in its cavalier, reckless pursuit of sin, and it makes psychopaths its martyrs and drag queens its models.

Though many in our world-system never come close to approaching the debauchery so recklessly flaunted by some, still the culture provides a comfortable environment for their life's direction. Hearts which are hard and dark and dead to spirituality would rather keep their old clothing, musty and decaying as it is, than change. They may not like all that goes on, but as long as they are allowed to pursue life in their own way, everything and everyone is *simpatico* — "live and let live."

What is said here may seem harsh, but this is reality! Paul's opening line on the subject in verse 17, "So I tell you this, and insist on it in the Lord," means that these are not Paul's ideas, but Christ's. This is how the risen Lord sees the world. It is so important that we Christians embrace this assessment of the world without Christ because we then see that it is radically lost. We then comprehend why man cannot save himself and why Jesus came. A loss of the Biblical vision of the world is behind the erosion of orthodox Christianity in many places, because if you imagine the world is better than it is, the necessity of Christ and his cross is lessened and the potential of unregenerate man is elevated.

Is the picture Paul presents of the world gloomy pessimism? Far from it! Christianity presents an answer and vision for man far beyond any secular dreams. Now we turn from the world's wardrobe to the new apparel.

THE NEW WARDROBE (vv. 20-24)

As Paul warms to the subject of the new wardrobe, he uses the language of bold contrast: "You, however, did not come to know Christ that way. Surely you heard of him and were taught in him in accordance with the truth that is in Jesus" (vv. 20, 21). The Ephesian Christians were taught the exact opposite of the world's style by learning of Jesus Christ! Here Paul uses three remarkable pedagogical terms (teaching terms) which indicate respectively that Jesus was the *subject*, *teacher*, and *atmosphere* of their instruction.[7]

That Jesus was the *subject* of their instruction is indicated in the words "to know Christ" in verse 20 — which should be more accurately translated, "to learn Christ." The Ephesians learned of *the living Christ*.[8] They learned more than knowledge about him. They learned *him* — his life, his ethics, even his ambience.

Next we see that Jesus was their *teacher* (v. 21a): "Surely you heard of him . . ." The word "of" is not in the Greek, and the correct rendering is, "Surely you heard him." As Dr. Bruce says, "Christ himself is the Christian's teacher, even if the teaching is given through the lips of his followers; to receive the teaching is in the truest sense to hear him."[9] Jesus' sheep hear his voice (John 10:16). When true preaching takes place, Jesus is invisibly in the pulpit and walking the aisles personally teaching his own.

Last, we understand that Jesus is the *atmosphere* in which the instruction takes place, for the Ephesians "were taught in him in accordance with the truth that is in Jesus" (v. 21b). Everything was "in" Jesus." What dynamic instruction!

Jesus is the *subject, teacher,* and *atmosphere.* This is the Christian experience, as St. Patrick so beautifully put it in the fifth century:

> *Christ be with me, Christ within me,*
> *Christ behind me, Christ before me,*
> *Christ beside me, Christ to win me,*
> *Christ to comfort and restore me,*
> *Christ beneath me, Christ above me,*
> *Christ in quiet, Christ in danger,*
> *Christ in hearts of all that love me,*
> *Christ in mouth of friend and stranger.*

From Christ the Ephesian Christians were infused with the very antithesis to the downward spiral of the world plunging recklessly after its sin. Instead of hardness and darkness and deadness and recklessness, they had tenderness and light and life and an abandonment to the upward spiral!

What were the results of this dynamic instruction — in which Christ was the subject, teacher, and atmosphere — in their lives? The answer is in verses 22-24. First, verse 22: "You were taught, with regard to your former way of life, to put off your old self, which is being corrupted by its deceitful desires." Second, verse 23: "to be made new in the attitude of your minds." Third, verse 24: "and to put on the new self, created to be like God in true righteousness and holiness."

First, though the Ephesians had put off the old self (the life described in vv. 17-19) when they first came to Christ, in verse 22 Paul in effect challenges them to a repeated putting off of the old garments, the old style of life. Scripture and experience teach us that no one has ever succeeded in shedding the garments of the old life with a solitary, unrepeated action. Those who live holy lives do so by repeated putting offs. The problem is, the old garments are so comfortable and natural. Not only that, many of us have worn them so long that they naturally drape over us and we scarcely know we are wearing them until the Holy Spirit reproves us. If you are fighting lust, it must daily be shed. This is equally true of pride and bitterness and covetousness and all their relatives. Many Christians stumble because they don't realize this. But the truth is, our sins will have to be put off daily as long as we live.

Second, sandwiched between putting off and putting on is the necessity that we "be made new in the attitude of [our] minds" (v. 23). We cannot effectively put on our new clothing unless our thinking is altered and renewed. This is an echo of Romans 12:2 — ". . . be transformed by the renewing of your mind. Then you will be able to test and approve what

God's will is — his good, pleasing and perfect will." This is done by reading and studying God's Word, and by asking the Holy Spirit to continue his renewing work. The Word gives us God's very thoughts, and prayerful meditation upon it will infuse his mind into ours in constant renewal. This is why every Christian should be regularly — daily — reading God's Word. This is also why it is valuable to read the Bible through once a year. It is imperative that we read the Word expectantly, praying for God to speak to us by his Holy Spirit.

Finally, there is the putting on: ". . . and to put on the new self, created to be like God in true righteousness and holiness" (v. 24). The fact is, we have this new self if we are Christians. We received the old man at birth, and we were given the new man in our heavenly birth. The new man is not our work — it is God's creation and gift. Our task is not to weave it, but to wear it. Paul is commanding a daily appropriation of that which we already possess.

Here we must keep in mind that we do not put on the new man merely by putting off the old. We need to put on love, to put on peace, to put on joy, to put on patience, etc. (cf. Galatians 5:22). For example, I may have lost my temper with my children, and I have repented and put it off. But I have not completed my responsibility unless I have also put on love and patience.

All of this is through God's grace. Works have no place in obtaining salvation or in gaining merit in the Christian life. The Christian life is *sola gratia*, grace alone. Nevertheless, the Apostle Paul said, "continue to work out your salvation with fear and trembling, for it is God who works in you to will and to act according to his good purpose" (Philippians 2:12b, 13). God is at work in his people. But as children of grace we must work at our Christian lives. This divinely ordained synergism is required of all Christians. This same apostle, though he fought the legalists and Judaizers all across Asia and despised works-religion, said, "discipline yourself for the purpose of godliness" (1 Timothy 4:7, NASB).

We have our part to do in dressing ourselves with the divine wardrobe, for here clothes do make the man — and the woman! We must daily set aside the rotting garments of the old man. We must formally reject sensuality and selfish pride and materialism and bitterness. We must read the Word and ask God to to renew our minds through the Spirit. We must work out our salvation by doing those things that will develop a Biblical mind. We must put on our new, shining garments of light. We must put on what we are!

Therefore each of you must put off falsehood and speak truthfully to his neighbor, for we are all members of one body. "In your anger do not sin": Do not let the sun go down while you are still angry, and do not give the devil a foothold. He who has been stealing must steal no longer, but must work, doing something useful with his own hands, that he may have something to share with those in need. Do not let any unwholesome talk come out of your mouths, but only what is helpful for building others up according to their needs, that it may benefit those who listen. And do not grieve the Holy Spirit of God, with whom you were sealed for the day of redemption. Get rid of all bitterness, rage and anger, brawling and slander, along with every form of malice. Be kind and compassionate to one another, forgiving each other, just as in Christ God forgave you. (4:25-32)

17

Living Under the Smile

EPHESIANS 4:25-32

The average Christian has a theological "black hole" in his or her doctrine of God when it comes to the subject of the Holy Spirit. Many regard the Holy Spirit as a mysterious manifestation of God, or as a spiritual emanation or divine influence. The confusion was well expressed in a cartoon I once saw of two children, dressed in bedsheets, playing "ghost." The caption said, "Boo! I'm the Holy Ghost."

It is no exaggeration to say that many orthodox believers who affirm the doctrine of the Trinity when they recite the Apostles' Creed really view the divine nature as a duality of Father and Son instead of a Trinity. Those who have such a defective understanding will have a dark area not only in their theology, but in their life, for *the Holy Spirit is a divine being who is fully personal*. One of the clear proofs of this is verse 30 of our text: "And do not grieve the Holy Spirit of God, with whom you were sealed for the day of redemption." The root idea of the word "grieve" is "to cause pain," and the fact that the Holy Spirit can experience pain and sorrow and personal distress argues for his personal nature.

Understanding that the Holy Spirit is a Person who experiences joy and grief through the lives of those he indwells makes possible great spiritual advance, for two reasons. First, because we are able to better see how much we are loved. As we grieve over the failures of those we love, so does the Holy Spirit over us. Spurgeon said, "For it is an inexpressibly delightful thought, that He who rules heaven and earth, and is the creator of all things, and the infinite and ever blessed God, condescends to enter into such infinite relationships with his people that his divine mind may be affected by their actions."[1] His great love for us makes possible his grief.

Second, we are motivated to holiness. Innumerable sons and daughters have drawn back from sin at the thought of the pain it would bring their parents, and there is a similar effect on those who fully understand that their sin will hurt the Holy Spirit.

None of us who are truly Christian wants to grieve the Holy Spirit. His loving ministry draws our hearts to him, especially when we think of what he has done. He *baptized* us into the Body of Christ at the moment of our salvation (1 Corinthians 12:13). It was then that he also *sealed* us, declaring us to be his possession (1:13; 4:30). He has also *indwelt* us, just as God promised to Ezekiel: "And I will put my Spirit in you and move you to follow my decrees and be careful to keep my laws" (Ezekiel 36:27). Regarding this, Jesus similarly said in John 14:16, 17, "And I will ask the Father, and he will give you another Counselor to be with you forever — the Spirit of truth. The world cannot accept him, because it neither sees him nor knows him. But you know him, for he lives with you and will be in you." As a result the Apostle Paul could say, "Do you not know that your body is a temple of the Holy Spirit, who is in you, whom you have received from God?" (1 Corinthians 6:19). What a wondrous truth this is. He comes to us in the clay of our sinful humanity, and though the walls are covered over with spiritual leprosy, he indwells us.

Next, the Holy Spirit *teaches* us. Jesus said in John 16:12, 13, "I have much more to say to you, more than you can now bear. But when he, the Spirit of truth, comes, he will guide you into all truth." First John 2:20 makes a similar statement: "But you have an anointing from the Holy One, and all of you know the truth." Verse 27 continues, "As for you, the anointing you received from him remains in you, and you do not need anyone to teach you." As part of this, the Holy Spirit teaches us to *pray*. "We do not know what we ought to pray, but the Spirit himself intercedes for us with groans that words cannot express. And he who searches our hearts knows the mind of the Spirit, because the Spirit intercedes for the saints in accordance with God's will" (Romans 8:26, 27).

Seeing all of this (that he *baptized* us, *sealed* us, *teaches* us, and *prays* for us), it is inconceivable that any true believer would want to grieve the Holy Spirit. But it is probable that many Christians constantly grieve the Holy Spirit with their lives — given the powerlessness of the Church today and its accommodation to this age.

How can we lead lives which bring a smile to the Person of the Holy Spirit instead of the frown of grief? As we follow the discussion, we will see that Paul conveniently organizes this under four topics and so tells us what to discard and what to take up if we are to have the divine smile.

A LIFE FREE FROM FALSEHOOD (v. 25)

The first topic is *lying*: "Therefore each of you must put off falsehood and speak truthfully to his neighbor, for we are all members of one body."

Paul's words were pointedly relevant to his ancient culture, for lying was endemic to the Greeks as well as Israel's Semitic neighbors, and some who had recently become Christians had brought the practice right into the Church. The parallel exhortation is Colossians 3:9, 10 which says, "Do not lie to each other, since you have taken off your old self with its practices and have put on the new self." This shows that Paul regarded lying as a dominant characteristic of the old life. His message left no room for equivocation — there is no place for lying in the Church.

His message is no less needed today. We are immersed in a culture which oozes deception and falsehood. For instance, take the case of the baker who suspected that the farmer who was supplying his butter was giving him short weight. His suspicions were confirmed when he carefully checked the weight of the butter for several days. Incensed, he had the farmer arrested. But the judge threw the case out when the farmer explained that he had no scales, so he used a one-pound loaf of bread purchased from the baker as his counterbalance! Whether on Main Street or Wall Street, our culture is in an ethical crisis.

The public media blatantly traffic in deception. Use a certain toothpaste and your teeth will glisten with animal magnetism. In fact, your whole life will be changed. Drink a recommended brew and you will imbibe the machismo of an NFL athlete. Don a plaid flannel shirt and life will be a perpetual fishing trip with athletic has-beens.

None less than Mortimer Adler mourns the loss of truth as a criterion for literary excellence. He writes:

> Books win the plaudits of the critics and gain widespread popular attention almost to the extent that they flout the truth — the more outrageously they do so, the better. Many readers, and most particularly those who review current publications, employ other standards for judging, and praising or condemning, the books they read — their novelty, their sensationalism, their seductiveness, their force, and even their power to bemuse or befuddle the mind, but not their truth, their clarity, or their power to enlighten.[2]

Disregard for truth and a disposition for lying are everywhere, and the Church is no exception. We are so enculturated that many lie without even knowing they are doing so. It's an unconscious survival technique. There are, of course, also members of the Body of Christ who consciously lie — and find some subtle justification for it. None of this should exist among followers of him who is the Truth!

Why is lying forbidden? In his answer Paul ignores the greatest reason — that it is a sin against God — and answers rather that it is a sin against the Body of Christ. In Christ we have a mutual solidarity — "for we are all members of one body" (cf. Romans 12:4, 5; 1 Corinthians 12:14-26). Lies, false messages among the members, actually render the Body dysfunctional. For this reason Calvin called lying a monstrosity.[3] John Mackay put it this way:

> A lie is a stab into the very vitals of the Body of Christ. This is so because a lie is a sable shaft from the kingdom of darkness. . . . There is no place in the Christian ethic for the well-intentioned lie. In the moral behavior which Christ inspires, the end never justifies the means.[4]

Paul says here, "put off falsehood and speak truthfully." That is it, pure and simple. Have we told any lies lately? Any "white" lies? Are we presently lying? In words? By silence? These are great sins against Christ and his Body. If so, for this reason the Holy Spirit is not smiling on our life. If this is true of us, may we repent and ask the Holy Spirit to make us truthful persons.

A LIFE FREE FROM ANGER (vv. 26, 27)

The next concern of the Holy Spirit is *anger*: "'In your anger do not sin': Do not let the sun go down while you are still angry, and do not give the devil a foothold" (vv. 26, 27).

The opening phrase, "In your anger do not sin," drawn from Psalm 4:4, indicates there is a proper anger — a good anger. God himself is sometimes angered. Jesus was angry when, for instance, he cleansed the Temple (Mark 11:15). If we are imitators of God (5:1), we will sometimes be angry. We need the anger of a Wesley or a Wilberforce at personal or societal sins, or of a Luther at doctrinal aberration. Proper anger is a sign of spiritual life and health.

But in our anger we must be very, very careful because anger often leads to sin, which will "give the devil a foothold." How does this work? It typically begins with a healthy anger at sin and its effects on others or perhaps on ourselves. We properly hate the sin, and we mourn the wreckage it has brought. But if anger is held or nursed, it becomes highly personal. Our hatred for the perpetrator swells and, as Jesus warns in the Sermon on the Mount, we become guilty of some degree of murder (Matthew 5:21, 22). What began so properly becomes a matter of pride and then, as the Puritan Thomas Boston said, becomes "evil in itself, and dishonorable to God; being the vomit of a proud heart and unmeekened spirit."[5] You can then become worse than the offender, and an unwitting victim. As Frederick Buechner so perfectly expressed it:

Of the seven deadly sins, anger is possibly the most fun. To lick your wounds, to smack your lips over grievances long past, to roll over your tongue the prospect of bitter confrontation still to come, to savor to the last toothsome morsel both the pain you are given and the pain you are giving back; in many ways it is a feast fit for a king. The chief drawback is that what you are wolfing down is yourself. The skeleton at the feast is you.[6]

How many of us are gnawing on our own souls?

If this describes us, we must heed Paul's time-honored advice: "Do not let the sun go down while you are still angry." The day of our anger should be the day we deal with it.

A life filled with anger — a church full of angry people — is a pain to the Spirit. He will not work, indeed cannot, for he abides by his own laws. The great evangelist D. L. Moody related a story which demonstrates this truth:

I remember one town that Mr. Sankey and I visited. For a week it seemed as if we were beating the air; there was no power in the meetings. At last, one day, I said that perhaps there was someone cultivating the unforgiving spirit. The chairman of our committee, who was sitting next to me, got up and left the meeting right in view of the audience. The arrow had hit the mark, and gone home to the heart of the chairman of the committee. He had had trouble with someone for about six months. He at once hunted up this man and asked him to forgive him. He came to me with tears in his eyes, and said: "I thank God you ever came here." That night the inquiry room was thronged.

We must deal with our anger for the sake of our own souls and the life of the Church.

A LIFE FREE FROM THEFT (v. 28)

What else concerns the Spirit in the Church? Verse 28 gives the surprising answer: "He who has been stealing must steal no longer, but must work, doing something useful with his own hands, that he may have something to share with those in need."

The English preacher Rowland Hill astounded the mourners at his favorite employee's funeral when he told a story in his funeral oration which he had kept secret for thirty years: his first meeting with the man had been when the man attempted to hold Dr. Hill up. Hill had argued with him, offering the highwayman an honest job if he would visit him later. And this the robber did, becoming a devout Christian and devoted worker![7] This man lived out the standard Paul calls the Church to in verse 28.

Unfortunately, this has not always been the case. There were believers in the first-century Church who continued their pilfering — until they faced the challenge of God's Word. Does this have any relevance today? Theft is a major problem in our land. A paper given at an American Psychological Association symposium on employee theft presented a breakdown on the 8 billion dollars that inventory shortages cost department and chain stores every year. Of these losses, 10 percent were due to clerical error, 30 percent to shoplifting, and a shocking 60 percent (sixteen million dollars a day!) to theft by employees. The ethics of the land have penetrated the Church as well, just as in the first century. But in most cases it is far more subtle: padded expense accounts, inadequate income tax reporting, customs dodges, "borrowing" and forgetting to return, and using the employer's time for things other than work.

The Holy Spirit cannot smile on such lives, or on the churches they lead or minister in. The Scriptural call is to liberate ourselves from covetousness and grasping, and to work hard so we can generously share with others. The church which has the Spirit's smile is like the Macedonian church:

> And now, brothers, we want you to know about the grace that God has given the Macedonian churches. Out of the most severe trial, their overflowing joy and their extreme poverty welled up in rich generosity. For I testify that they gave as much as they were able, and even beyond their ability. Entirely on their own, they urgently pleaded with us for the privilege of sharing in this service to the saints. And they did not do as we expected, but they gave themselves first to the Lord and then to us in keeping with God's will. (2 Corinthians 8:1-5)

A LIFE FREE FROM ROT (v. 29)

Finally, our text reveals the Holy Spirit's concern that our speech be constructive: "Do not let any unwholesome talk come out of your mouths, but only what is helpful for building others up according to their needs, that it may benefit those who listen" (v. 29).

The language Paul uses is very descriptive. "[U]nwholesome talk" literally means "rotten, putrid or filthy."[8] This includes obscene language, but the emphasis is on decay-spreading conversation which runs others down and delights in their weaknesses. A person who engages in this is like the fabled slave who took poison into her system a little at a time, and then more and more, until at last her whole being was so full of poison that her very breath would wither the flowers. There are Christians who unwittingly become like this. To them wicked witticisms come as naturally as breathing.

Such talk must not be part of the believer's life. St. Augustine, in recognition of this principle, hung this motto on his dining room wall: "He who speaks evil of an absent man or woman is not welcome at this table."

Our text concludes that we are to speak "only what is helpful for building others up according to their needs, that it may benefit [literally grace] those who listen." We are to converse in such a way that our words become a vehicle and demonstration of the grace of God. We are to be like Alexander Whyte, of whom it was said, "All of his geese became swans." We should speak constructive talk, talk that builds others up. As Eliphaz said of Job, "Your words have supported those who stumbled; you have strengthened faltering knees" (Job 4:4). Instead of being rot, our speech should be "always full of grace, seasoned with salt" (Colossians 4:6). Salt preserves that to which it is supplied. It retards decay. Our talk must maintain and elevate others. "[T]he tongue of the wise brings healing" (Proverbs 12:18b). It also brings the smile of the Holy Spirit.

The Holy Spirit is not a phantom — he is a Person. In infinite love he has condescended to indwell us and to suffer pain and joy through us. Is he grieved with us, or is he singing over us?

Our text calls to us in summary, "Do not grieve the Holy Spirit of God, with whom you were sealed for the day of redemption. Get rid of all bitterness, rage and anger, brawling and slander, along with every form of malice. Be kind and compassionate to one another, forgiving each other, just as in Christ God forgave you" (vv. 30-32).

Do we have the frown or smile of the Holy Spirit upon us? To gain his smile, I would like to suggest a spiritual exercise which can be done alone, but may be enhanced in tandem. If you are married, ask your spouse to participate. If you are single, invite a Christian friend to go through this exercise with you. Take each of the four categories in succession — *truth* (v. 25), *anger* (vv. 26, 27), *theft* (v. 28), and *speech* (v. 29) — and reflect out loud to your partner as to whether this area of your life has the smile or frown of the Holy Spirit. If you fall short, confess your sins to God and each other, and invite your partner to pray for you. Be assured that the Holy Spirit will attend your conversation with great joy.

Be imitators of God, therefore, as dearly loved children and live a life of love, just as Christ loved us and gave himself up for us as a fragrant offering and sacrifice to God. But among you there must not be even a hint of sexual immorality, or of any kind of impurity, or of greed, because these are improper for God's holy people. Nor should there be obscenity, foolish talk or coarse joking, which are out of place, but rather thanksgiving. For of this you can be sure: No immoral, impure or greedy person — such a man is an idolater — has any inheritance in the kingdom of Christ and of God. Let no one deceive you with empty words, for because of such things God's wrath comes on those who are disobedient. Therefore do not be partners with them. (5:1-7)

18

The Cookie Jar Syndrome

EPHESIANS 5:1-7

For many years he had been an honored Bible professor at a fine Christian college in the West. He was a vigilant guardian of Biblical orthodoxy. He was an author. His encyclopedic knowledge of the Bible made him a man people looked to for wisdom. He was the confidant and advisor of college presidents, prominent pastors, and Christian executives. Yet, his long association with the college came to be irreparably severed because of adultery. He was unrepentant then and to my knowledge remains so today.

Tragically, this was neither the first nor last such incident. I have known Christian executives, celebrated speakers, and well-known pastors of churches large and small who have succumbed to sensuality. Best friends have left their families and ministries.

What immense human suffering has come to God's people because of sensuality. And what tragic irony, for Christianity has by far the most exalted sexual ethics of any religion. The New Testament not only enjoins absolute chastity outside marriage, but a chaste mind, as Jesus so forcefully demands in the Sermon on the Mount (Matthew 5:27-30). None of the other great world religions — whether Buddhism, Hinduism, Islam, or any other — has such profound sexual ethics. Yet the Church of Christ is too often rocked with repeated scandal. Why is this so?

Part of the answer, I believe, is the "cookie jar syndrome." A little boy's mother had just baked a fresh batch of cookies and placed them in the cookie jar, giving instructions that no one touch them until after dinner. But it was not long until she heard the lid of the jar move, and she called out, "My son, what are you doing?" To which a meek voice called back, "My hand is in the cookie jar resisting temptation!" The fact is, no one can resist temptation with his or her hand in the cookie jar.

There are open cookie jars all around us. The ubiquitous cookie jar of our culture is the television, dwelling in the heart of nearly every home in America. Turn it off, and the goodies are present in an open magazine or a billboard. There are living cookie jars everywhere, inviting passersby to taste their wares. It would be so easy . . . But when these wares are removed from the jar, their sweetness soon turns to rot, and the decay is shared by the hand that plucked them, resulting in gangrene of the soul.

Keeping one's hand out of the cookie jar is a challenge for all of God's children, and Paul addresses this problem in verses 3 through 7 of our text.

Bear in mind that these verses were addressed to Christians who had come to Christ while living in the notoriously sinful port city of Ephesus. In that wicked metropolis the dominant religion was the worship of the multibreasted goddess Diana, and ritual prostitution was a way of life. Moreover, there was cultural acceptance of sexual perversion as a valid, and even exalted, way of life. Ephesus is a paradigm of any of the great cities of today's world — San Francisco, Berlin, Hong Kong, Moscow, Chicago . . .

THE PROHIBITIONS OF CHRISTIANITY'S EXALTED SEXUAL ETHICS (vv. 3, 4)

Paul abruptly tackles the issue in no uncertain terms in verse 3: "But among you there must not be even a hint of sexual immorality, or of any kind of impurity, or of greed, because these are improper for God's holy people." To catch the force of Paul's words, we need to understand that the word "greed" is sexually freighted in this context. It means greed for someone else's body. Marcus Barth renders it as "Insatiability."[1]

The television ad for Calvin Klein's Obsession perfectly portrays this idea. The camera focuses close up, in black and white, on an intense, lustful male face, which then has superimposed on it an amber flame which becomes the amber bottle of Obsession as he intones his desire.

Paul says there must be none of this — no "sexual immorality, or . . . any kind of impurity, or . . . greed" for others. There must "not be even a hint" of it! Literally, it is not to be named (or discussed) among them. They should also refrain from discussing and rehashing the sins and immoralities of others. While Paul always demanded that Christians call sins by their names, however loathsome they were, he regarded extended conversation about such sins as dangerous to spiritual health.[2] Too much discussion of evil often functions like an incantation, bringing the very thing we say we despise into our lives. The old English poet Alexander Pope gave this warning:

Vice is a monster of such
frightful mien
That to be hated needs
but to be seen.

But seen too often
familiar with his face
We first endure, then pity,
then embrace.[3]

Paul warned the Ephesians in their debauched culture, and now warns us in ours, to refrain from the delectable temptation to dine together on the juicy morsels of sensual gossip which come our way. Had he been writing today amidst the piles of tabloids and slick magazines which grovel in the dirt of the "lives of the stars," he would include such foolishness in his prohibitions. If you are watching the soap operas or the debased evening detective thrillers, or are reading the tabloids, the star mags, or even the drivel in more respected publications, you are ignoring Scriptural warnings and are sinning. This is wisdom for the soul who wants to avoid the cookie jar.

Paul continues his challenge in verse 4 with advice regarding the purity of the Christian's speech: "Nor should there be obscenity, foolish talk or coarse joking, which are out of place, but rather thanksgiving." "Obscenity" is oral filth, dirty language. Most Christians would agree with Paul that this is wrong. But when it comes to "foolish talk" and "coarse joking," there is divided opinion, as the conversation habits of many Christians attest. Paul's word for "foolish talk" is *morologia* — moronic talk. Proverbs 15:2 says, "The tongue of the wise commends knowledge, but the mouth of the fool gushes folly." Empty, wasteful, idiotic talk is sub-Christian. The implication here is that such empty talking goes hand-in-hand with "coarse joking."

Do not misunderstand — humor and merriment are recommended by both Scripture and life. Proverbs 17:22 says, "A cheerful heart is good medicine." The Preacher of Ecclesiastes says there is a "time to laugh" (Ecclesiastes 3:4). Laughter can exhilarate the human spirit for God's service. Medically a good laugh is like "inner jogging," according to *American Health* magazine, which suggests a "Laugh Diet." We ought to "laughercize."[4]

Admittedly, "coarse joking" may produce a similar effect, but it is poison to the soul. Such joking is quick wit that revels in *double entendre* and urbane vulgarity. It is the kind of talk some talk-show hosts major in while they roll their eyes and mug for the camera. This is witty talk but dirty — sleazy repartee. People who use this type of humor are in hog-heaven with the naive, whom they use as props to showcase their brilliance. It is a matter of historical record that the Ephesians were masters at this,[5] and thus it was easy to them to carry such coarse wit right into the Church. But Paul forbids such arsenic to the soul. What makes it so bad?

First, humor that flirts with the boundaries of what is proper can easily degenerate. I remember this happening, especially in the company of other men, on several occasions over the years. Someone says something that is off-color and humorously clever, and everyone has a knee-slapping laugh. Then someone else shares another witticism which is a little coarser, the conversation begins a shameful spiral, and sacred relationships are verbally profaned by God's own children.

Second, humor can make us vulnerable to degrading moral change. Have you ever been made to laugh at something which is no laughing matter at all through clever humor — say, a crime or a seduction? This is very dangerous, because if you laugh often enough at evil your moral perception may begin to blur, and ultimately your moral conduct may be subverted. In a nutshell, filthy laughter naturally promotes sensual, degenerating voyeurism.

Third, there is a dynamic exchange between our speech and our inner morality. The sixteenth-century Puritan preacher Thomas Manton quaintly told it like it is: "Men usually discourse as their hearts are . . . for the tap runneth according to the liquor wherewith the vessel is filled."[6] Or as Jesus said, "For from within, out of men's hearts, come evil thoughts, sexual immorality . . ." (Mark 7:21). One thing is sure — filthy speech means a filthy heart. We must never rationalize this truth.

Lastly, we will give account of every word, as Jesus ominously warned: "But I tell you that men will have to give account on the day of judgment for every careless word they have spoken. For by your words you will be acquitted, and by your words you will be condemned" (Matthew 12:36, 37).

Paul is crystal-clear: we are not to read, watch, or talk about the immoral escapades of others, and even more, there is to be no obscenity, moronic talk, or coarse joking, no matter how urbane it is. If this is any part of our life, our hand is in the cookie jar. And if that is so, Paul says we must pull it out and replace our degrading speech with "thanksgiving" (v. 4b). That is, we are not to joke about our sexuality, but to give God thanks for it. Christians are not repressive about sexuality. Rather, they hold it in highest respect. Joking degrades it. Thanksgiving preserves it.

THE REASONS FOR THE PROHIBITIONS OF CHRISTIAN SEXUAL ETHICS (vv. 5, 6)

Here Paul gives his reasons for his strong teaching about guarding oneself against sensuality. Foremost among these is that no sensualist will go to

Heaven: "For of this you can be sure: No immoral, impure or greedy person — such a man is an idolater — has any inheritance in the kingdom of Christ and of God. Let no one deceive you with empty words, for because of such things God's wrath comes on those who are disobedient." It does not matter what theological construct you are under — whether you are a Calvinist or an Arminian. The passage in its context says that people whose "lust has become an idolatrous obsession" will not be any part of the Kingdom.[7] The Scripture repeats this truth elsewhere — for example, 1 Corinthians 6:9, 10:

> Do you not know that the wicked will not inherit the kingdom of God? Do not be deceived: Neither the sexually immoral nor idolaters nor adulterers nor male prostitutes nor homosexual offenders nor thieves nor the greedy nor drunkards nor slanderers nor swindlers will inherit the kingdom of God.

Note that the three vices in our Ephesians passage are repeated here among the ten vices which keep people from eternal life. Consider also Galatians 5:19-21:

> The acts of the sinful nature are obvious: sexual immorality, impurity and debauchery; idolatry and witchcraft; hatred, discord, jealousy, fits of rage, selfish ambition, dissensions, factions and envy; drunkenness, orgies, and the like. I warn you, as I did before, that those who live like this will not inherit the kingdom of God.

And the Apostle John says essentially the same thing in different words:

> Dear children, do not let anyone lead you astray. He who does what is right is righteous, just as he is righteous. He who does what is sinful is of the devil, because the devil has been sinning from the beginning. The reason the Son of God appeared was to destroy the devil's work. No one who is born of God will continue to sin, because God's seed remains in him; he cannot go on sinning, because he has been born of God. This is how we know who the children of God are and who the children of the devil are: Anyone who does not do what is right is not a child of God. . . . (1 John 3:7–10)

So the Scriptures are in concert: No practicing sinner, no unrepentant sensualist, has eternal life.

Do Christians fall into these sins? Of course! But true Christians will not persist in them, for persistence in sensuality is evidence of a graceless state.

We conclude on the authority of God's Word that anyone who is living a lustful life of sensuality and is unwilling to turn from it is lost and has no inheritance in the Kingdom of God and Christ. Such a person is an "idolater" because he has put his sensual desire in the central place only God should occupy.

Paul says, "Let no one deceive you with empty words, for because of such things God's wrath comes on those who are disobedient" (v. 6). The "empty words" we hear today go like this: "God is too kind to condemn to Hell those whose behavior doesn't measure up. Love will prevail. God is sympathetic with our frail human nature." These are clever reasonings, but they will not convince God to turn aside his wrath. Yet there is hope, for the damning list in 1 Corinthians ends with, "And that is what some of you were. But you were washed, you were sanctified, you were justified in the name of the Lord Jesus Christ and by the Spirit of our God" (1 Corinthians 6:11).

There are open cookie jars everywhere the believer goes. All around us we see the misery of those who have helped themselves. What are we to do? Negatively, "Therefore do not be partners with them" (v. 7). We must not join them in their sin. We must reprove those who claim to be believers but are obsessed with lust. We must risk their ostracism. We do not need friends like that.

Positively, take to heart the words which sum up the preceding passage and provide the introduction to this one: "Be imitators of God, therefore, as dearly loved children and live a life of love, just as Christ loved us and gave himself up for us as a fragrant offering and sacrifice to God" (vv. 1, 2). Imitation of Christ will beautifully change us from the old way of life to the new. Jesus never came close to having his hand in the cookie jar. He was never obsessed with lust. He never uttered an obscenity. There was no foolish talk, no coarse joking, no sly off-color humor, no vulgarities, no laughter over what ought not to be laughed at.

Does that sound like a bit much? That is because we are children of this age. But a godly life is possible, for we have his Spirit, who is just like him (John 14:16).

For you were once darkness, but now you are light in the Lord. Live as children of light (for the fruit of the light consists in all goodness, righteousness and truth) and find out what pleases the Lord. Have nothing to do with the fruitless deeds of darkness, but rather expose them. For it is shameful even to mention what the disobedient do in secret. But everything exposed by the light becomes visible, for it is light that makes everything visible. This is why it is said, "Wake up, O sleeper, rise from the dead, and Christ will shine on you." (5:8-14)

19

Shades of Life

EPHESIANS 5:8-14

The story of Jesus identifying himself as the "light of the world" captured my heart the very first time I came to understand it. Jesus did that at the end of the Feast of Tabernacles on the day after the spectacular nighttime ceremony known as the Illumination of the Temple. That event took place in the Temple treasury before four massive golden candelabra topped with huge torches. It is said that the candelabra were as tall as the highest walls of the Temple, and that at the top of three candelabra were mounted great bowls holding sixty-five liters of oil. There was a ladder for each candelabrum, and when that evening came, healthy young priests would carry oil up to the great bowls and light the protruding wicks. Eyewitnesses said the huge flames which leapt from these torches illuminated not only the Temple but all of Jerusalem. *The Mishnah* tells us that "Men of piety and good works used to dance before them [the candelabra] with burning torches in their hands singing songs and praise and countless Levites played on harps, lyres, cymbals and trumpets and instruments of music."[1] Imagine the smell of the oil, the heat of the smoking torches, and the shadows of perspiring, bearded priests as they whirled and danced before the fire-dazzled throng. This exotic rite celebrated the great pillar of fire (the glorious cloud of God's presence) which led the Israelites during their sojourn in the wilderness and spread its fiery billows over the Tabernacle.

It was after this ceremony, and in the same Temple treasury the following morning, with the great charred torches still in place, that Jesus lifted his voice above the crowd and proclaimed, "I am the light of the world" (John 8:12). There could scarcely be a more emphatic way to announce one of the supreme truths of Jesus Christ! Christ was saying in effect, "The pillar of fire that came between you and the Egyptians, the cloud that guided you by day in the wilderness and illumined the night and enveloped the Tabernacle, the glorious cloud that filled Solomon's Temple, is me!" — "I am the light of the world. Whoever follows me will never walk in darkness, but will have the light of life" (John 8:12). He is everything suggested by the sublime metaphor of light — and much more.

The immense truth that Christ is the light of the world must be foundational to our thinking as we study our next Ephesians text, the opening words of which amazingly apply the metaphor to us: "For you were once darkness, but now you are light in the Lord" (v. 8a). We are light!

Dr. Donald Grey Barnhouse, a master of illustration, explained it this way: When Christ was in the world, he was like the shining sun. When the sun sets, the moon comes up. The moon is a picture of believers, the Church. The Church shines, but not with its own light. It shines with reflected light. At times the Church has been a full moon dazzling the world with an almost daytime light. Those were times of great enlightenment — for example, in the days of Paul and Luther and Wesley. At other times the Church has been only a thumbnail moon, and in those days very little light shone on the earth. But whether the Church is a full or thumbnail moon, whether waxing or waning, it reflects the light of Christ. Our light does not originate with us.[2]

But our text suggests even more than reflection — we actually *become light ourselves*: "For you were once darkness, but now you are light in the Lord" (v. 8a). Our light is derived from him — not a ray of it comes from ourselves. But somehow our incorporation in Christ allows us to actually be light, however imperfect. We "participate in the divine nature," says Peter (2 Peter 1:4). So authentic is our participation, so real is our light, that in eternity we will actually be part of the light ourselves. Jesus said in his Mystery Parables, "Then the righteous will shine like the sun in the kingdom of their Father" (Matthew 13:43).

As C. S. Lewis noted, the heavens reflect the glory of God. But we share the glory of the Father in Christ — and we shall be more glorious than the heavens. Lewis said:

> Nature is mortal. We shall outlive her. When all the suns and nebulae have passed away, each one of you will still be alive. Nature is only the image, the symbol. . . . We are summoned to pass in through nature beyond her to the splendor which she fitfully reflects.[3]

As Christians there is a glory awaiting us that involves, in some mysterious way, *shining*. Somehow we are going to enter into the fame and approval of God, and we will be glorious beings far beyond description.

Because we are light, we have a huge responsibility in the world.

How are we who have been transferred from darkness to light to live? Our text speaks to this first positively and then negatively and then with a stirring charge.

POSITIVE INSTRUCTION FOR THE "LIGHT" (vv. 8b-10)

Paul scrambles his metaphorical thought to drive home his positive instruction on how we are to live: "Live as children of light (for the fruit of the light consists in all goodness, righteousness and truth) and find out what pleases the Lord" (vv. 8b-10).

Light, strictly speaking, does not bear fruit. But here Paul views Christ's light as reflected through the prisms of our lives and thus producing the threefold qualities of "goodness," "righteousness," and "truth" — in a word, the fruit of sterling character.

Corrie ten Boom tells how during hard times in the watchmaking business, when the family was in extreme financial need, she observed her father and a wealthy customer. The wealthy man had decided to purchase a costly timepiece with cash which would have met all their needs. But as her father was handling the cash, the customer related that he was buying the watch because Mr. ten Boom's young competitor could not fix the fine old watch. Corrie's father asked to see it, opened it, made a slight adjustment, and handed it back saying, "There, that was a very little mistake. It will be fine now. Sir, I trust the young watchmaker. Someday he will be just as good as his father. So if you ever have a problem with one of his watches, come to me. I'll help you out. Now I shall give you back your money and you return my watch."

Corrie watched horrified as she saw the exchange, and then observed her father open the door for the man and bow deeply in his old-fashioned way. She flew at her father in reproof, only to be herself reproved by his patient regard through his steel-rimmed glasses and his gentle question, "Corrie, what do you think that young man would have said when he heard that one of his good customers had gone to Mr. ten Boom? Do you think that the name of the Lord would be honored? As for the money, trust the Lord, Corrie. He owns the cattle on a thousand hills and He will take care of us."[4]

How beautiful impeccable character is! First, "goodness," which here means something like "generosity."[5] Then, "righteousness," which means integrity in all dealings with God and man. And finally, "truth," the absence of falsehood and deception. These are the ethics of light. When the light of Jesus is refracted through the prisms of our lives, there will be sanctifying shades of life for others to see. We then "find out what pleases the Lord," and so do others.

As Christians, we are "light in the Lord." Jesus said in the Sermon on the Mount, "You are the light of the world" (Matthew. 5:14). The more luminous our integrity — our goodness, righteousness, and truth — the brighter the light. How can we shine more brightly? A man returning from a journey brought his wife a matchbox that would glow in the dark. After giving it to her she turned out the light, but the matchbox could not be seen. Both thought they had been cheated. Then the wife noticed some French words on the box and asked a friend to translate them. The inscription said: "If you want me to shine in the night, keep me in the light." We need to spend time alone with Jesus — the Light — in prayer, exposing our lives like photographic plates to his presence so that his image, his character, is burnt into ours. If we do this, we will spiritually be like Moses when he descended Sinai after being alone with God — his face shone with the light of God. We need to open our Bibles and allow God's truth to illumine our eager faces with goodness and righteousness and truth. *If you want to shine in the night, keep in the light of Christ.*

NEGATIVE INSTRUCTION FOR THE "LIGHT" (vv. 11-14a)

Paul moves from the positive to the negative with some equally wise instruction: "Have nothing to do with the fruitless deeds of darkness, but rather expose them. For it is shameful even to mention what the disobedient do in secret. But everything exposed by the light becomes visible, for it is light that makes everything visible" (vv. 11-14a).

The effects of darkness and light are antithetical. From the perspective of the sciences, disease flourishes in the dark, and total darkness brings death to earth's fauna and flora. Similarly, spiritual darkness brings sterility — "fruitless deeds," as Paul calls them in verse 11. The siren songs of darkness promise great things but give only desolation — the "apples of Sodom" as some have called it. Darkness shelters evil and helps it fester, so that "it is shameful even to mention what the disobedient do in secret" (v. 12). "Night has no shame."[6] The leaven of sin silently swells in the darkness until the whole life is infected.

Light, on the other hand, promotes life. Patio plants flourish in a basement during winter if we provide them with enough light — even artificial light. Broken bodies heal faster if we can soak up some sunlight. Light awakens too. We have probably all "heard" the sun rise as it awakens nature. Light is also persistent, constantly assaulting the earth and penetrating the smallest opening. The darkest place is not safe from it, as verses 13 and 14 make so clear: "But everything exposed by the light becomes visible, for it is light that makes everything visible" (vv. 13, 14a).

In view of all this, what are we to do? Paul is most explicit: "Have nothing to do with the fruitless deeds of darkness, but rather expose them" (v. 11). This is where the going has always been rough, and it is especially so today because our culture has come to put such emphasis on what it perceives as "tolerance." Christians who would make moral judgments are defined as "sub-Christian" or "subhuman." The motto of modern man is, "The one thing I will not tolerate is intolerance." According to the world, Christianity ought to be as broad and accepting as possible. And the fact is that clergy who think in this way, who baptize every form of sin as OK, become the darlings of the media. A cultured accent, a fuchsia-colored bishop's shirt, and the urging to place condoms in Gideon Bibles will get you a spot on *Good Morning, America*. Our culture loves the "open-minded," nonjudgmental, "live and let live" personality.

The problem is, God's Word allows us no such luxury. If the Scripture calls something wrong, we dare not call it otherwise. This is not to suggest that believers have a license to go around looking as grim as death, maliciously mouthing our "Don'ts." What it does mean is that we must call sin what it is and expose it. This is one of the things I so much appreciated about Joe Bayly (popular author and columnist) in his writings and in person. He told the truth about sin, whether it was the obvious pornography and abortion industries, or materialistic, self-seeking evangelicals, or Bible theme parks, or errant public officials. Moreover, his prophetic vane was not doctrinaire Left or Right but radically Biblical. Our call is to expose sin wherever it is — within our camp and outside it. Adultery is sin. Lying is sin. Materialism is sin. Neglect of the poor is sin. Child neglect is sin, even in expensive suburban wrappers.

We need to be ethical light when we are in the office, in the classroom, in the shop, and in the Church. We must be willing to risk being called "negative," "narrow," "judgmental," "puritanical," or "bigoted." If God's Spirit is calling us to stand up against wrong, it is up to us to be faithful.

Considering that Jesus Christ is "the light of the world," and that we are "light in the Lord" by virtue of our incorporation in him, and, further, that we have a *positive* charge to "Live as children of light," as well as a *negative* responsibility to "Have nothing to do with the fruitless deeds of darkness, but rather expose them" — *the Church needs to wake up!* So Paul concludes this section with verse 14:

> "Wake up, O sleeper,
>   rise from the dead,
>   and Christ will shine on you."

We do not know whom Paul is quoting here. Many think it was a line from an apostolic baptismal hymn sung as the convert emerged "sacramentally from the sleep of spiritual death into the light of life."[7]

Whatever its origin, Paul's application is clear. Some people who are "light in the Lord" are slumbering and need to wake up. It is an obvious fact that Christians who are asleep do not know it.

It is possible to be slumbering light and even to be well-regarded by others in the Church (especially by others who are in the same state). It is possible to be asleep and appear awake. It is possible to *pray* while asleep, mouthing phrases others have used before. It is possible to *sing* a hymn without being awake to the words. It is possible to *walk* while asleep and end up in harm's way. It is possible to live a *dreamy* life of unreality in the netherland of inaction.[8]

That is why Paul says,

> "Wake up, O sleeper,
>   rise from the dead . . ."

If we are light we must act as light, manifesting its brilliant functions, both positive and negative. We must live out the ethics of light in "goodness" and "righteousness" and "truth," and we must at times "expose . . . the fruitless deeds of darkness."

Then comes the reward: "and Christ will shine on you" (v. 14). Slumbering light awakened resounds with more light! I cannot get over the picture of Jesus standing before the huge blackened torches which symbolized, as they had flared the night before, the Shekinah glory and calling out, "I am the light of the world" — "I am the glory returned, the Eternal Light." Neither can I get over his amazing identification of us as "the light of the world" (Matthew 5:14), "light in the Lord" (v. 8).

We must allow the full light of Jesus to shine upon and through the prisms of our lives, so that we will radiate the ethics of light in glowing character. Jesus said, "You are the light of the world." May we be the light indeed!

Be very careful, then, how you live — not as unwise but as wise, making the most of every opportunity, because the days are evil. Therefore do not be foolish, but understand what the Lord's will is. Do not get drunk on wine, which leads to debauchery. Instead, be filled with the Spirit. Speak to one another with psalms, hymns and spiritual songs. Sing and make music in your heart to the Lord, always giving thanks to God the Father for everything, in the name of our Lord Jesus Christ. Submit to one another out of reverence for Christ. (5:15-21)

20

The Fullness of the Spirit

EPHESIANS 5:15-21

A recent issue of *Time* Magazine carried the cover story "How America Has Run Out of Time." It began:

> If you have a moment to read this story with your feet up, free of interruption, at your leisure . . . put it down. It's not for you.
>
> If, like almost everyone else, you're trying to do something else at the same time — if you are stuck in traffic, waiting in the airport lounge, watching the news, if you're stirring the soup, shining your shoes, drying your hair . . . read on. Or hire someone to read it for you and give you a report.[1]

It is a great article which I think everyone should read. As of this writing I am about halfway through it and hope to finish it . . . if I can find the time.

Our lives are so busy! If you do not think so, hesitate for a moment the next time the light turns green and listen to the whole world honking! We are so harried that we think our timing is off if we miss one panel of a revolving door. We have become like the Queen who, informed that the inhabitants of Wonderland had to run very fast to get anywhere, replied to Alice, "It takes all the running you can do, to keep in the same place. If you want to get somewhere else you must run at least twice as fast as that."[2] *We* could have written that. We are busy, busy, busy, busy!

And in our busy lives we have the added pressure of knowing that things tend toward degeneration and evil if we do not attend to them. Ignore your garden and it will be overrun with weeds and the fruit will fail. Forget your body and it will vegetate and degenerate. And, far more important, lack of attention to the interior life and one's important relationships will

171

mean personal decline. In this world there is a natural tendency toward corruption.

I have emphasized our busyness and the attendant dangers of inattention because Paul's words in verses 15 and 16 radiate with relevance: "Be very careful, then, how you live — not as unwise but as wise, making the most of every opportunity [literally, buying up the time], because the days are evil." Paul knew, as we well know, that the days are evil and time is fleeting, and that as Christians we must purposely engage in buying them back from the mere use of self if our life is going to amount to anything.

The natural question is, how are we to do this? Paul answers with a statement which, although it does not give detailed instructions, provides the inner principle which will redeem our time and, indeed, our days. This is a famous dual command: "Therefore do not be foolish, but understand what the Lord's will is. Do not get drunk on wine, which leads to debauchery. Instead, be filled with the Spirit" (vv. 17, 18). It is never the Lord's will for a Christian to be drunk. This especially needed to be said in Ephesus, the heart of Greek culture and a wine country where overindulgence was common. The wine-god Bacchus dominated many lives and even enslaved some in the Church — just as it does today.

Here Paul forbids drunkenness because it "leads to debauchery." It degrades the drinker and others. People get drunk for various reasons. Some do so to interrupt the monotony of life, others to escape themselves. Typically drunkenness brings a temporary personality change. Some become morose, others giddy; some are belligerent, others weepy; some sing, and some shout; some become generous, and others steal. With many there is a temporary ego elevation. The coward becomes a hero, the boor a philosopher, the least great, the wimp a "terminator." They become legends in their own minds. The heavy drinker thinks he has a "good time" by losing control of his life. But in reality drunkenness degrades.

> Who has woe? Who has sorrow?
>   Who has strife? Who has complaints?
> Who has needless bruises?
>   Who has bloodshot eyes?
> Those who linger over wine,
>   who go to sample bowls of mixed wine.
> Do not gaze at wine when it is red,
>   when it sparkles in the cup,
>   when it goes down smoothly!
> In the end it bites like a snake
>   and poisons like a viper.
> Your eyes will see strange sights
>   and your mind imagine confusing things.

You will be like one sleeping on the high seas,
    lying on top of the rigging.
"They hit me," you will say, "but I'm not hurt!
    They beat me, but I don't feel it!
When will I wake up
    so I can find another drink?"
                         (Proverbs 23:29-35)

In reference to the concern of our text in Ephesians, drunkenness immerses one in the flow of the evil days and makes life a series of missed opportunities. This is a tragic waste! "Instead," says Paul, we are to "be filled with the Spirit" (v. 18).

The mention of drunkenness and being filled with the Spirit may suggest an exact parallel. But this is not so, for the parallels between drunkenness and the filling of the Spirit are merely superficial. It is true that when someone is drunk he is "under the influence," and when one is filled with the Spirit he is under the Spirit's influence. But the comparison ends here, and the rest is contrast. Being filled with the Spirit is not a kind of spiritual intoxication in which we lose self-control, for "self-control" is a fruit of the Spirit (Galatians 5:22, 23; 2 Timothy 1:7). To be sure, at Pentecost the disciples were accused of having "had too much wine" (Acts 2:13), but only by their detractors, who were making fun of them. The rest of the people were awed by the Spirit's power manifested in the disciples.[3] Those filled with the Spirit are not drunk with the Spirit! In addition to this, we must understand that alcohol is a *depressant*, while the Spirit is a *stimulant*.

Dr. Martyn Lloyd-Jones, a brilliant physician who became a pastor and ministered for nearly forty years at Westminster Chapel, London, wrote:

> Drink is not a stimulus, it is a depressant. It depresses first and foremost the highest centers of all in the brain. They are the very first to be influenced and affected by drink. They control everything that gives a man self-control, wisdom, understanding, discrimination, judgment, balance, the power to assess everything; in other words everything that makes a man behave at his very best and highest. The better a man's control, the better man he is. . . . But drink is something which immediately gets rid of control; that indeed is the first thing it does.[4]

Today the church needs the Holy Spirit in this way more than anything else! Those in the Church have received many blessings of the Spirit. They have been *baptized* into Christ's Body (1 Corinthians 12:13), *sealed* by the Holy Spirit (1:13), *reconciled* (2:16), and given the Holy Spirit as a *deposit* (1:14). Yet the Church is often so spiritually empty! Some, like ancient Israel, "have forsaken . . . the spring of living water, and have dug their own cisterns, broken cisterns that cannot hold water" (Jeremiah 2:13b). Others have made no conscious departure and are present at the Lord's Table, read their Bibles, and lead steady lives, but have no joy or delight in God.

What is needed is the flood of the Spirit. Jesus told the Samaritan woman, ". . . whoever drinks the water I give him will never thirst. Indeed, the water I give him will become in him a spring of water welling up to eternal life" (John 4:14). That woman got it and still has it! Then, at the Feast of Tabernacles, "On the last and greatest day of the Feast, Jesus stood and said in a loud voice, 'If a man is thirsty, let him come to me and drink. Whoever believes in me, as the Scripture has said, streams of living water will flow from within him'" (John 7:37, 38). That promise has been fulfilled again and again and again. We need to long for this like a thirsty deer. "The Spirit and the bride say, 'Come!' And let him who hears say, 'Come!' Whoever is thirsty, let him come; and whoever wishes, let him take the free gift of the water of life" (Revelation 22:17). What is the fullness of the Spirit like? And how do we become filled? Paul now answers these questions.

FIRST, THERE IS A FULLNESS OF SPIRITUAL COMMUNICATIONS (v. 19)

The apostle says that those who are full of the Spirit should "Speak to one another with psalms, hymns and spiritual songs" and "Sing and make music in your heart to the Lord" (v. 19). This does not mean that we abandon normal speech and confine our communication to song so that church life becomes an opera: ♩ ♩ ♪ ♩ "How are you, Brother Jones? Good! I'm glad. God bless you!" ♩ ♪ ♩ ♪ But there develops in Spirit-filled believers a vertical music of the heart, so that those full of the Spirit "Sing and make music" in their hearts to the Lord. This outflow is artesian, silently coming from one's depths. It is informed and motivated by God's words richly dwelling within (Colossians 3:16). And it is passionately joyful. Inevitably this heart-music becomes verbal.

> *My life flows on in endless song*
> *above earth's lamentation.*
> *I hear the real, though far-off hymn*
> *that hails a new creation.*
> *No storm can shake my inmost calm*
> *while to that rock I'm clinging.*

It sounds an echo in my soul,
How can I keep from singing?
(Source unknown)

The public result of this inner music is that when the church comes together there is verbal, musical communication — both horizontal and vertical. They "speak to one another with psalms, hymns and spiritual songs." The Roman governor Pliny, in his famous letter to the Emperor Trajan in A.D. 112, tells how the Christians in his province had the custom of meeting on a fixed day before dawn and "reciting a hymn antiphonally to Christ as God."[5] Tertullian, writing from North Africa toward the end of the same century, describes a Christian feast at which "Each is invited to sing to God in the presence of others from what he knows of the holy scripture or from his own heart."[6] Putting all this together we get the idea: some sang "psalms" from the Old Testament Psalter, some sang new Christian "hymns," perhaps like those in Revelation 4 and 5, and some sang "spiritual songs" — unpremeditated praise from the heart. Imagine how beautiful and soul-satisfying these meetings must have been under the orchestration of the Holy Spirit.

Spirit-filled people overflow in song! This has been attested again and again in times of great spiritual blessing. That is the way it was in the awakening under St. Francis, the Troubadour of God. In the Reformation, Martin Luther brought hymn singing to the Church. During the Wesleyan Revival, Charles Wesley wrote 6,000 hymns. When Charles Simeon preached in Holy Trinity in Cambridge and there was that great outpouring of blessing among his enthusiastic people at the beginning of the evangelical movement, another disapproving church in Cambridge hung a new bell in its tower with the inscription, "Glory to the Church and damnation to the enthusiasts."[7] One wonders whose damnation it rang. Think of the music which came with Moody and Sankey, and more recently during the spiritual harvest of the late 1960s. There is a sense in which when people are born again, music is "born again" in their souls. And if they remain full of the Spirit, life brings an ongoing symphony of soul.

SECOND, THERE IS FULLNESS IN THANKSGIVING (v. 20)

Verse 20 says that those full of the Spirit are "always giving thanks to God the Father for everything, in the name of our Lord Jesus Christ." These words have sometimes been misappropriated through a literalness which has done great harm to many sincere believers. The words "for everything" have been interpreted without reference to God's character or to the absurdity of thanking God for something he loathes. The false reasoning is that "for everything" means literally for everything regardless of how evil it is. Some have taken what they call "unconditional praise" to be the key to spiritual victory. Thus they praise God for a spouse's adultery, a daughter's rape, a child's death, a church split, a fellow Christian's fall. True, we praise God for being God in the midst of these miseries and for being able to bring good out of evil. "But," as John Stott says, "that is praising God for being God; it is not praising him for evil. . . . God abominates evil, and we cannot praise or thank him for what he abominates."[8]

Nevertheless, the fullness of the Spirit does call us to a radical spirit of gratitude. We are to thank God in the midst of difficulties for everything which is consistent with his Fatherhood and his loving Son.

One day Tauler, the fourteenth-century mystic and preacher, met a beggar. "God give you a good day, my friend," he said. The beggar answered, "I thank God I never had a bad one." Tauler said, "God give you a happy life, my friend." "I thank God," said the beggar, "I am never unhappy." Tauler, in amazement, responded, "What do you mean?" "Well," said the beggar, "when it is fine, I thank God; when it rains, I thank God; when I have plenty, I thank God; when I am hungry I thank God . . . why should I say I am unhappy when I am not?"

The fullness of the Spirit rules out a grumbling, complaining, negative, sour spirit. No one can be Spirit-filled and traffic in these things. In America we, as a people, have so much. Yet we characteristically mourn what we do not have: another's house, car, job, vacation, even family! Such thanklessness indicates a life missing the fullness of the Holy Spirit.

On the other hand, a positive, thankful attitude announces the presence of the Spirit. I once met a pastor in a remote little western town. His church met in rented facilities, and his car had seen better days, as had his house-trailer. But as we walked down Main Street, stepping around the tumbleweeds, he remarked, "I can't believe how good God is to me. I have a wonderful wife, a church to serve, and sunshine 365 days a year!" And then he spent the day helping me set up a week-long outreach. What an argument for the reality of Christ and the life-changing power of the gospel in a world which has forgotten to be thankful (cf. Romans 1:21).

THIRD, THERE IS FULLNESS IN SUBMISSION (v. 21)

Those full of the Spirit obey the Scriptural admonition to "Submit to one another out of reverence for Christ" (v. 21). In the Greek text verses 18 to 21 form one long sentence, with mutual submission being the final result of the Spirit's filling. The supreme model for our submission is Jesus Christ. He, the Incarnate Son, God himself, in an electrifying moment stripped himself naked and washed the feet of his prideful, arrogant disciples. He then said, "Now that I, your Lord and Teacher, have washed your feet, you also should wash one another's feet. I have set you an example that you should do as I have done for you. I tell you the truth, no servant is greater than his master, nor is a messenger greater than the one who sent him" (John 13:14-16). Jesus used the ancient logic, If it is true for the greater (me), then it must be true for the lesser (you). This is always a powerful argument. But coming from the majesty of his greatness, it is infinitely compelling.

The Scriptures are clear. "[I]n humility" we are to "consider others better than [ourselves]" (Philippians 2:3). "For we do not preach ourselves, but Jesus Christ as Lord, and ourselves as your servants for Jesus' sake" (2 Corinthians 4:5). Sometimes we meet Christians who claim to be Spirit-filled but are brash, assertive, and self-promoting — and thus they give their claim the lie, for neither Christ nor the Holy Spirit is like this.

The key to submission is profound, reverent submission to Christ. What a beautiful grace this is in today's assertive, rung-dropping world! What a magnet for Christ!

The fullness of the Holy Spirit produces a life of profound beauty. Each of the resulting characteristics is exquisite in itself, but in bouquet they are sublime. When a heart is full of *spiritual music* which flows back up to God and then out to brothers and sisters in psalms, hymns, and spiritual songs — a spiritual symphony — when this heart is radically *giving thanks* for all things with radical constancy — when this heart is *joyfully submitting* to its brothers and sisters — this is absolutely, ineluctably compelling.

Even more, in a busy, decaying world such a bouquet brings the cadence and perspective of ultimate sanity. Though honked at and jostled and squeezed, such a life buys up the time, "making the most of every opportunity." It knows what is important. It orders its priorities. It gives its time to the eternal.

Are we filled with the Spirit? Is there music in our souls? Is there thankfulness and praise? Is there submission in our lives?

Do we want to be so filled? If so, there are several points we need to understand about the call to "be filled with the Holy Spirit."

1) It is a *command*, not a suggestion. We are not free to ignore it.

2) It is a *plural command* to the whole Church. *None* of us is to get drunk. *All* of us are to be filled with the Spirit. It is not for the few or for some elite.

3) It is a *passive command*. It means, "Let the Holy Spirit fill you" (NEB). There is no ritual, no formula. We must turn from any known sin. We must open ourselves to God's Word so it dwells richly in us (Colossians 3:16). We must yield to the Spirit.

4) Last, it is a *present tense command*. It is not once for all but contin-
uous. We are to go on being filled. We are to keep drinking and drinking
and drinking.

We have capacities for spiritual life and power which we scarcely can
imagine. "The Spirit and the bride say, 'Come!' . . . Whoever is thirsty, let
him come; and whoever wishes, let him take the free gift of the water of
life" (Revelation 22:17).

Submit to one another out of reverence for Christ. Wives, submit to your husbands as to the Lord. For the husband is the head of the wife as Christ is the head of the church, his body, of which he is the Savior. Now as the church submits to Christ, so also wives should submit to their husbands in everything. (5:21-24)

21

The Mystery of
Marriage (I)

EPHESIANS 5:21-24

As we have noted in our preceding studies, the Letter to the Ephesians takes a dramatic change at chapter 4. Chapters 1 through 3 are given to Christian *doctrine*, whereas 4 through 6 are Christian *duty*. Now, as we take up the last half of chapter 5, the instruction becomes intensely practical as we are given explicit instruction for the Christian home in the section beginning at 5:21 and ending with 6:9. Traditionally this has been called the Ephesian *Haustafel* ("house table," in deference to the fitting name Martin Luther gave it 500 years ago). Here the household table of duties covers three areas: wives and husbands (5:22-33), children and parents (6:1-4), and slaves and masters (6:5-9). This study will consider the *Haustafel* for wives (5:22-24). The following exposition will cover the Haustafel for husbands (5:25-33).

The exposition of this brief text must be done with measured care and, frankly, with some trepidation, for several reasons. First, the text teaches that there is a divinely given order in the marriage relationship and uses the word "submit," which is an incendiary word in today's western culture. This is the age of liberation. Talk about "submission" is today seen as countercultural and connotes for many putative synonyms like "oppression," "subjugation," or "dominance." In discussing the subject, one runs the risk of being misunderstood and possibly vilified.

Second, the truths of this text have been perverted and abused by disordered and sinful men. God's holy Word in the hands of a religious fool can do immense harm. I have seen "couch potatoes" who order their wives and children around like the grand sultan of Morocco — adulterous misogynists with the domestic ethics of "Jabba the Hut" who cow their wives around with Bible verses about submission — insecure men whose wives do not dare go to the grocery without permission, who even tell their wives how to dress. But the fact that evil, disordered men have perverted God's Word is no reason to throw it out.

Many of the problems in Christian marriages come from either an ignorance of or a cavalier disregard for the Scriptural teaching on the roles of men and women in marriage. Many Christians have adopted the ego-centered canon of "self-fulfillment" as the ground for their union. Marriage is seen more as an alliance to promote personal growth than a lifelong commitment to mutual love and service. Thus, when difficulties arise, Christian men and women simply step out of the situation, much as one does from a change of clothes. What is needed today is a clear understanding of and a return to the *Haustafel* of Scripture. There is nothing degrading or dehumanizing about the *ordered equality*[1] of these domestic instructions. Rather, they are the key to marital elevation.

We must keep in mind that this text is preceded by one long sentence in the Greek (vv. 18-21) which commands that we be filled with the Holy Spirit, describing it with four coordinated participles, the last of which calls for mutual submission by all believers to one another. "Submit to one another out of reverence for Christ" (v. 21). When we are full of the Holy Spirit, we all (husbands and wives, parents and children, slaves and masters) will defer to and serve each other in the spirit of Christ (cf. Philippians 2:5-8). The entire household teaching (5:21–6:9) rides on the joyous, surging tide of mutuality.

This emphasis on submission falls on three groups: wives, children, and slaves. Wives are told to submit to their husbands, children to obey their parents, and slaves to obey their masters. On the other hand, instead of being told to submit, husbands are told to love their wives, parents not to exasperate their children, and masters to treat their slaves fairly. So we see a call to Spirit-filled mutual submission, beginning with wifely submission.

The initial statement of this is in verse 22: "Wives, submit to your husbands as to the Lord." This does not mean, as some chauvinists have interpreted it, that wives are to treat their husbands like the Lord, but rather that their submission to their spouses is a duty which they owe to the Lord. This raises some important questions. Why this emphasis on wifely submission? And what does such submission entail?

THE RATIONALE FOR SUBMISSION (v. 23)

The answer to the first question regarding the reason for submission is in verse 23: "For the husband is the head of the wife as Christ is the head of the church, his body, of which he is the Savior." Some have attempted to reinterpret the obvious meaning of this verse by insisting that "head" (*kephale*) carries the idea of "source" rather than "authority over."[2] But this simply is not true, especially in this context.

Dr. Wayne Grudem, in a careful study of 2,336 instances of *kephale* from classical Greek literature — all the non-classical references from Philo, Josephus, the Apostolic Fathers, the Epistle of Aristias, the Testaments of the Twelve Patriarchs and Aquila, Symmachus, and Theodocian, says, "No instances were discovered in which *kephale* had the meaning 'source, origin.'"[3]

Moreover, during Paul's time, Philo of Alexandria made a statement which clearly explains that *head* means authority:

> Just as nature conferred the sovereignty of the body on the head when she granted it also possession of the citadel as the most suitable for its kingly rank, conducted it thither to take command and established it on high with the whole framework from neck to foot set below it, like the pedestal under the statue, so too she has given the lordship of the senses to the eyes.[4]

Finally, "head" has to mean authority here in its context. F. F. Bruce says, "But in this context the word 'head' has the idea of authority attached to it after the analogy of Christ's headship over the church."[5] *Head* has a clear enough connotation in English as in head of a corporation or head of a university — the authority over, the leader.

What does the headship in marriage call a husband to do or be? *Servant-leadership.* Verse 23 says Christ is the Savior of the Church, of which he is Head, and thus follows by analogy the conclusion that the husband is to exercise his headship with a Savior-style servant-leadership. He must lead with the kind of love that is willing to die. Jesus said, "For even the Son of Man did not come to be served, but to serve, and to give His life a ransom for many" (Mark 10:45, NASB). And again he said, "Let him who is the greatest among you become as the youngest, and the leader as the servant" (Luke 22:26, NASB).

God help the man who thinks his headship is a license for dominance or lordship. Headship has definite limits. It can never command what God forbids or forbid what God commands.[6] It can never be used selfishly. The *Haustafel* enjoins reciprocal duties. Husbands are to love their wives, parents are to care for their children, masters are to treat their slaves well. There is no room for tyranny — "Me Tarzan! You Jane!" — no bullying.

A husband's headship carries immense responsibility. In May 1943 Dietrich Bonhoeffer wrote his famous *Wedding Sermon from a Prison Cell* to his close friend Eberhard Bethge and his fiancée Renate Schleicher. As he came toward the end, he said,

Now when the husband is called "the head of the wife," and it goes on to say "as Christ is the head of the church" (Ephesians 5:23), something of the divine splendour is reflected in our earthly relationships, and this reflection we should recognize and honour. The dignity that is here ascribed to the man lies, not in any capacities or qualities of his own, but in the office conferred on him by his marriage. The wife should see her husband clothed in this dignity. But for him it is he who is responsible for his wife, for their marriage, and for their home. On him falls the care and protection of the family; he represents it to the outside world; he is its mainstay and comfort; he is the master of the house, who exhorts, punishes, helps, and comforts, and stands for it before God.[7]

Indeed, both husband and wife bear mutual responsibility, but he, by his position, stands in the way of greater judgment. Headship is a fearful thing! When a husband makes difficult decisions, he should do so with the full counsel of his wife. And he should do so with great humility and dependence on the Lord, realizing his fallibility and responsibility.

Headship modeled on the headship of Christ demands a profound life of devotion and intercessory prayer. It demands a warm heart which is constantly exposed to the light of Christ in prayer and Bible-reading. Husbands, if this does not characterize our lives, we are sinning. It demands the practice of detailed intercession for one's spouse and children like that of righteous Job (Job 1:5). Men, if we are not praying in detail for our wives and children, we are sinning. This is a leadership which will convict and draw the world. This is what our homes and world need more than anything else!

THE NATURE OF SUBMISSION (v. 24)

The reason for wifely submission is that the husband is the head of the wife, and the character of that submission is given in verse 24: "Now as the church submits to Christ, so also wives should submit to their husbands in everything." How are we to understand this?

First by noting what it does not mean. *It does not suggest spiritual inequality.* Both sexes are equal. Both bear the image of God and are equal in their standing and in their spiritual gifts for service. The New Testament Scripture supports this. "There is neither Jew nor Greek, slave nor free, male nor female, for you are all one in Christ Jesus" (Galatians 3:28). The *Haustafel* here in Ephesians presents men and women in an *ordered equality* in which there is no superiority or inferiority — simply differing roles. As John Howard Yoder has said, "Equality of *worth* is not equality of *role*."[8]

Next, *wifely submission does not mean slavish obedience.* Some women have taken "in everything" and uncritically absolutized it, not taking into account the fact that the example of Christ flavors "in everything" so that it means in everything consonant with his character. A woman must never follow her husband into sin. Christ alone is her supreme authority, and the Holy Spirit enlightens her conscience as to what is right and wrong.

What the Scripture is enjoining here is the disposition to yield in happy submission, the disposition to recognize and honor the husband's great responsibility to lead the home. When the husband is giving godly leadership — strong moral, loving headship to his family — the woman "will be no more squelched by the leadership of Jesus."[9] She will be elevated and enriched by her submission.

But then there is the matter of ungodly headship. What then? The fact that a wife wants to honor her husband's leadership if possible does not mean she will sit in mute silence. Questioning his reasoning or acquainting him with his error is not evidence of a rebellious spirit, but rather of love. Refusing to support his moral folly is not sin. A Christian wife can stand with Christ against her husband with a humble, loving spirit which indicates her longing to honor his headship. The attitude is, of course, key.

Concerning those who are married to a difficult man, my heart goes out to them, the Church's concern goes out to them, indeed the very heart of Christ goes out to them. Every day is filled with huge tensions and decisions which must be made on principle. Living a godly life in a fallen world can only be done through a profound dependence upon the grace of God.

The Fall has introduced distortions into the relationships between men and women. "In the home, the husband's loving humble headship tends to be replaced by domination or passivity; the wife's intelligent, willing submission tends to be replaced by usurpation or servility."[10] Husbands' domination on the one hand and passivity on the other are terrible sins against their wives, families, and the Church, "For the husband is the head of the wife as Christ is the head of the church" (v. 23). Wives' usurpation of their husbands' headship — or the opposite, servility to his sinfulness — is sin. A wife's submission should be informed by and in accord with the call of Christ.

The marital relationship is an exalted state, for it is a picture of Christ and his Church. I regularly have the best view in the house at Christian weddings as I stand about three feet from the joyous couple. Their skins glow with amber luminosity from the candles behind me. I see everything: the bride's blush which often extends to her shoulders — the moist eyes — the trembling hands — the surreptitious wink — their mutual earnestness of soul.

Sometimes in my enjoyment I let it all blur for a moment and imagine the ultimate wedding where Christ will officially take us to himself. I then blink back to the living parable before me. How will the couple fare? Will he love his beautiful bride as Christ loved the Church and gave himself for it? Will he be a loving, caring head who will provide moral leadership to his wife? I pray it will be so. Will she follow her present inclination to reverence her husband and submit to him as the Church submits to Christ? I pray it will be so.

When it is time for the vows, I call them to the seriousness of their commitment. They are not merely marrying one another. They are, in part, submitting themselves to the larger realities of life, to the survival of the Christian community. Their lives, their souls, their egos, bent and shaped by the pattern of Christ and his Church, will mean Christ to their children, to their parents, and to "the church, his body, of which he is the Savior."

They must be full of the Spirit to accomplish their vows — speaking to one another in psalms and hymns and spiritual songs, singing and making music in their hearts to the Lord, continually giving thanks to God their Father for all things, submitting to one another out of reverence for Christ (vv. 18-21).

The loving husband is like Christ. The submissive wife is like his glorious Church. What a mystery! What a marvel!

Husbands, love your wives, just as Christ loved the church and gave himself up for her to make her holy, cleansing her by the washing with water through the word, and to present her to himself as a radiant church, without stain or wrinkle or any other blemish, but holy and blameless. In this same way, husbands ought to love their wives as their own bodies. He who loves his wife loves himself. After all, no one ever hated his own body, but he feeds and cares for it, just as Christ does the church — for we are members of his body. "For this reason a man will leave his father and mother and be united to his wife, and the two will become one flesh." This is a profound mystery — but I am talking about Christ and the church. However, each one of you also must love his wife as he loves himself, and the wife must respect her husband. (5:25-33)

22

The Mystery of Marriage (II)

EPHESIANS 5:25-33

Winston Churchill once attended a formal banquet in London at which the attending dignitaries were asked the question, "If you could not be who you are, who would you like to be?" Naturally everyone was curious as to what Churchill, seated next to his beloved Clemmie, would say. When it finally came Churchill's turn, the old man, who was the dinner's last respondent to the question, rose and gave his answer. "If I could not be who I am, I would most like to be" — here he paused to take his wife's hand — "Lady Churchill's second husband."[1] The old boy made some points that night. But his comments also apply to everyone who has a good marriage.

As we begin to examine the husband's loving responsibility, we must fix in our minds the grand truth toward the end of our text (v. 31), where Paul refers to Genesis 2:24 — which says that when a man leaves his father and mother and is united to his wife "they will become one flesh" — and then adds in verse 32, "This is a profound mystery — but I am talking about Christ and the church." The truth here has two parts.

First, there is an amazing unity in marriage. The sexual union entails mysterious and sacred depths. That men and women become "one flesh" suggests an exchange of soul and indicates something of the psychological depth of the marital union. Marriage ideally produces two people who are as much the same person as two people can be. Christians in marriage have the same Lord, the same family, the same children, the same future, and the same destiny. This, in my opinion, is why old couples with extraordinarily different physical appearances yet often look so much alike — they are "one flesh." There has been an exchange of soul.

Second, the marriage union is illustrative of the union between Christ and his Church. Christ loved the Church from eternity, and the spiritual mystery which was hidden in the creation of Eve as the first Adam's wife, and in their becoming one flesh, is revealed in the creation of the Church to be the bride of Christ, the second Adam. Thus the union of Christ and his Church is partially illustrated by the marriage union. This is why he publicly identified himself as the Bridegroom. It is also why he did his first miracle at a wedding.

This also explains why in this *Haustafel* to husbands, Paul often uses language which is descriptive both of Christ and husbands and of the Church and wives. What the *Haustafel* enjoins first is *sacrificial love* (v. 25), then *sanctifying love* (vv. 26, 27), and then *self-love* (vv. 28-30).

SACRIFICIAL LOVE (v. 25)

The opening line is a clear call to sacrificial love: "Husbands, love your wives, just as Christ loved the church and gave himself up for her." The radicalness of this injunction is especially clear when we see that marriage in the ancient world had fallen on hard times. Pagan marriage was in shambles.

Demosthenes said, "We have courtesans for the sake of pleasure; we have concubines for the sake of daily cohabitation; we have wives for the purpose of having children legitimately, and of having a faithful guardian for all our household affairs." Xenophon said it was the husband's aim that a wife "might see as little as possible, hear as little as possible and ask as little as possible." Similarly Socrates said, "Is there anyone to whom you entrust more serious matters than to your wife — and is there anyone to whom you talk less?" The ancient pagan man breathed adultery. The marriage bond was virtually meaningless.[2] It was better with the Jews, of course, except that the ultra-liberal and very popular school of Hillel allowed a man to divorce his wife for virtually anything — like putting too much salt in his food or becoming less attractive in his eyes.[3]

Thus Paul's radical call to marital love was a bare-knuckled swing at the domestic ethics of his time — much as it is today. Taken seriously, the naked force of these words, "love your wives, just as Christ loved the church and gave himself up for her" is staggering! There is no honest Christian husband who can hear or read these words and not feel the punch.

What does such Christ-inspired love demand? First and foremost, the example of Christ involves death to self. I do not think it is a figment of Christian men's heroic Walter Mitty imaginations that even if we were presented with death in a dark alley or a tyrant's scaffold we would die for our wives. Hopefully we will never face such a situation. But we do repeatedly face the call to die to self for the sake of our wives.

For some men golf is synonymous to Dante's *Paridiso*, whereas the entrance to a department store, like the gates of Hell, bears the inscription, "Abandon all hope ye who enter here."[4] But if we love our wives we will forsake the platonic greens for the fiery gates because we value their interests and love to be with them.

A leaky kitchen faucet may not seem to be much to us, especially if we are exhausted at the end of the day. But if we were in the kitchen as much as our wives are, it would seem like oriental water torture. Sacrificial love dies to self and serves the one it loves in unsung domestic heroism.

Secondly, sacrificial love prays for its bride as Christ does for the Church. Again, if we are not praying for our wives in detail, we are not loving them as Christ loved the Church and are, in fact, sinning. We should be praying for their spiritual life, obligations, pressures, friendships, and dreams daily and passionately, for that is how Christ prays for us!

Thirdly, as Christ is attentive to the Church, so we must be with our wives. Years ago in the Midwest the story was told of a farmer and his wife who were lying in bed during a storm when suddenly the funnel of a tornado lifted the roof right off their house and sucked their bed away with them still in it. The wife began to cry. The farmer called to her that it was no time to cry. But she called back that she couldn't help it, as she was so happy. It was the first time they had been out together in twenty years!

In contrast, Christ loves his Church and rejoices in its presence — and in meeting its needs. A godly husband will follow this example.

Lastly, a husband who loves his wife "as Christ loved the church and gave himself up for her" will be ever faithful to her. One thing the Church can count on is the fidelity of the Bridegroom. And this is the one thing a wife whose husband loves like Christ can rest on. Jeremy Taylor, the great seventeenth-century preacher, in his sermon *The Marriage Ring or the Mysteriousness and Duties of Marriage*, gave this charge regarding fidelity:

> Above all . . . let him [the groom] preserve towards her an inviolable faith, and an unspotted chastity, for this is the marriage ring, it ties two hearts by an eternal band; it is like the cherubim's flaming sword set for the guard of paradise. . . . Chastity is the security of love, and preserves all the mysteriousness like the secrets of a temple. Under this lock is deposited security of families, the union of affections, the repairer of accidental breaches.[5]

What a slap Christ's sacrificial love is to many men's provisional commitments today. May it awaken us to our call to a *dying-to-self* love — a *praying* love which lives in continual intercession — an *attentive* love which lavishes time and care — a *faithful* love which extends to death. This is what our brides, the mothers of our children, our soul-partners, must have

— and nothing less! "Husbands, love your wives, just as Christ loved the church and gave himself up for her" (v. 25).

SANCTIFYING LOVE (vv. 26, 27)

The sanctifying effect of such love is beautifully set forth in verses 26 and 27: "to make her holy, cleansing her by the washing with water through the word, and to present her to himself as a radiant church, without stain or wrinkle or any other blemish, but holy and blameless." In order for us to understand this sanctifying love, I want us to think of three brief pictures: a very *Hebrew* picture, a *prophetic* picture, and a *marital* picture.

The Hebrew picture is this: It is the bride's wedding day, the day of her dreams. She rises with the dawn in anticipation. The hours speed by. Her women friends join her for her ritual, nuptial bathing.[6] The cleansing bath completed, she is clothed in her embroidered linen wedding dress and wedding sandals. She waits breathlessly, without spot or wrinkle, for her bridegroom.

That is a lovely picture, but the prophetic picture is even more so. It is of the individual members of the Church here on earth who, under the preaching of the Word, are joyously baptized, symbolizing full washing from sin and their regeneration as the bride of Christ. Then the picture switches to the return of Christ, when this washed and regenerated Church is presented by Christ to himself in absolute perfection. She radiates her perfection, completely free from any ethical or spiritual stain. The official wedding is ready to begin. This is a picture of the sealing of the romance of the ages.

Then there is the earthly marital picture. It is of a woman who throughout her life has grown to be ever more like Christ. Her salvation and sanctification are solely due to the work of Christ. Nevertheless, a prominent instrument in her progressive sanctification has been her loving husband. He has been a humble partner in developing her beauty. How did this come about? He was a man in whom the Word of God richly dwelled (Colossians 3:16). As God's Word and Spirit filled him, he lived out the ethics of the Kingdom. As her loving head, he served her and prayed for her and adored her with unconditional love. The tide of his authenticity encouraged her onward and upward in her beauty of soul. All was and is of Christ the Bridegroom — but the sanctifying love of the husband was an effective instrument in Christ's hands.

When we men read verses 25 through 27 together, we cannot escape our huge responsibility. Is our wife more like Christ because she is married to us? Or is she like Christ in spite of us? Whatever our effect, our call is clear: *sanctifying love*.

SELF-LOVE (vv. 28-30)

Greek mythology tells of a beautiful youth who loved no one until one day he saw his own reflection in the water and fell in love with that reflection. He was so lovesick that he finally wasted away and died and was turned into the flower that bears his name — *Narcissus*.[7] We are revulsed by narcissism and carefully seek to avoid it. But here the Scriptures actually call us to a self-love: "In this same way, husbands ought to love their wives as their own bodies. He who loves his wife loves himself. After all, no one ever hated his own body, but he feeds and cares for it, just as Christ does the church — for we are members of his body" (vv. 28-30).

The Golden Rule of Matrimony is, *You shall love your wife as yourself* (cf. Leviticus 19:18), and when you love her as yourself, you will be loving yourself because the two of you are one flesh.

This works out in marriage in a number of ways. It is evidenced in the husband's sensitivity to his wife's feelings and environment. I know how I feel physically, and I am aware of my emotions. Of course I can never have such intimate knowledge of my wife. But the call to love her as I love myself demands that I work at it. It demands that I be sensitive to her moods, her needs, her nonverbal communication. I'm not suggesting a nervous, self-conscious sensitivity: "How are you feeling, my dear? Are you sure? Now really tell me!" Rather, I am to practice patient love, to set myself to understand the pressures she faces.

I had a profitable experience in this regard some years ago when my wife visited her sister in Connecticut for a week. I had all four children with me, and I bathed them, dressed them, dropped them off at school, took them to lessons, cleaned house (sort of!), fixed the meals, and washed dishes. The whole experience so affected me that I invented a new kitchen. It has tiled walls, stainless-steel furniture, a tiled floor which slopes down to a large grate in the middle of the floor, and a high-pressure hose hanging on the wall!

This love is not only sensitive, it is courteous. One of the things I mourn in today's world is the passing of courtesy. I think husbands ought to open doors for their wives, not because their wives are weaker, but because courtesy displays the gospel. Putting the other first, finding her a seat, waiting for her to speak says, "My life for your life." It says, "I love you as I do my own body." This is legitimate self-love.

This valid self-love also demands communication. I communicate with myself all the time. I even talk to myself when I'm preaching! If we love our wives as we do ourselves, we will work at communication. We will be "speaking the truth in love" (literally, we will be "truthing in love," 4:15). Proverbs 24:26 says, "An honest answer is like a kiss on the lips." An honest answer is an act of love. When you lovingly communicate in truth, you join an elite group of people in the Western world, for only a small percentage ever experience this — and the resulting soul sanctification.

Legal self-love — what a way to go! It obliterates the tragic distinction between *mine* and *thine*. It facilitates a satisfying exchange of soul. It helps you find life, for whoever loses his life finds it.

The *Haustafel* for wives is, "Wives, submit to your husbands as to the Lord" (v. 22). The *Haustafel* for husbands is, "Husbands, love your wives, just as Christ loved the church and gave himself up for her" (v. 25). Together they form the divine order for Christian marriages.

Husbands, let us commit ourselves to *sacrificial* love, to the death of self for our wives — to *sanctifying* love, that they might grow to be more like Christ — to the liberating *self-love* of loving our wives as we love our own bodies. This is our holy call.

Children, obey your parents in the Lord, for this is right. "Honor your father and mother" — which is the first commandment with a promise — "that it may go well with you and that you may enjoy long life on the earth." Fathers, do not exasperate your children; instead, bring them up in the training and instruction of the Lord. (6:1-4)

23

Instructions to Children and Parents

EPHESIANS 6:1-4

I remember with technicolor clarity when our first child was born — August 10, 1963 — a blazing-hot Southern California night. It had been so hot that I had taken my round little wife to the ocean — Huntington Beach to be exact — to cool off. There I hollowed out a place in the sand for her tummy, and we stretched out under the sun while the cool breezes of the *Mar Pacifica* refreshed us (as we both unwittingly began to sunburn).

It was midafternoon when we headed back to the heat and smog of LA, so we rolled back the sunroof of our VW and foolishly baked some more. Soon we looked like Maine lobsters.

After dinner, when we lay smarting on the hot sheets of our bed, labor began, and that is about all we remember of our sunburns. My wife had another kind of pain to occupy her, and I was so excited that I forgot about mine — until the next day! That night brought one of the greatest events of our lives, for God gave us our firstborn, a beautiful little girl we named Holly. I remember everything, even the color of the hospital walls. It seems like only yesterday.

Another event has lodged in my mind with similar vividness. July 23, 1986, twenty-two years later, in another hospital in far-off Illinois, my baby Holly gave birth to *her* firstborn, a beautiful little boy, Brian Emory, and his father held him with the same rapture. The baby lifted his arms outward and upward as if to embrace life.

Where did the time go between these two indelible memories? To be honest, some of the years were long and hard. I thought we would never get through some of the stresses. But when these great events are recalled in all their color, there seems to be no time between them.

That is why whenever I have occasion to hold a baby in my arms, I often encourage his or her parents to savor every moment and not to rush through the experience — the child will be grown-up and gone in no time.

The realization that we have only a brief time to raise our children gives us huge motivation to make the most of it and makes Scriptural advice about raising children pulse with importance. The *Haustafel* for children and parents here in Ephesians brings the wisdom of eternity to bear on our domestic moments and is essential to make them count.

GOD'S WISDOM TO CHILDREN (vv. 1-3)

What is the divine wisdom for children? In a word, it is to honor and obey parents, as verses 1 through 3 so clearly say: "Children, obey your parents in the Lord, for this is right. 'Honor your father and mother' — which is the first commandment with a promise — 'that it may go well with you and that you may enjoy long life on the earth.'" There are two reasons for this call to honor and obedience.

First, because such a call accords with *natural law* — as Paul says, "for this is right." Virtually every culture and every society recognizes and is indeed built on the premise that children are to respect and obey their parents. When this is absent, it is a sign of decadence and degeneration. In Romans 1:30 Paul places disobedience to parents at the very nadir of the decadence to which people go as God gives them over to a "depraved mind" (Romans 1:28). To disobey and dishonor parents, however naturally such behavior may come to a child, is to live against the natural order of every civilization. It is "right" to honor and obey one's parents.

Second, we are to give honor and obedience to our parents because it not only is in accord with natural law, but with *divine law*. Here Paul refers to the fifth of the Ten Commandments: "'Honor your father and mother'" — which, he says, "is the first commandment with a promise" — the promise being, "'that it may go well with you and that you may enjoy long life on the earth'" (vv. 2, 3). Simply put: children must obey and honor their parents because it is commanded by God, period! If that is not enough, Paul adds a very practical reason, which is that it will affect how well and how long a child lives.[1] Notwithstanding the fact that children often die early regardless of whether they are obedient or disobedient, the general rule of life is that children who honor and obey their parents live longer and better.

There are several reasons for this. One is that a child who obeys his parents will regularly be warned from harm's way. He or she will experience less accidents and physical trauma from such things as high places and sharp objects. Remember the dangers and tight places you got yourself into while growing up because you disobeyed your parents' warning?

Another reason is that an obedient child will be spared the bad habits and bad friends which tend to ruin and shorten life. I well remember a dark night in my life when, in disregard of parental advice, I indulged in some things which eventuated in a black eye, an encounter with the police, and the vandalizing of my car.

The final reason a child who obeys and honors his or her parents will prosper is that such a person will be far more likely to develop healthy character traits, whereas a disobedient child is much more likely to develop harmful patterns. The Scriptures repeatedly state this principle: "Listen, my son, accept what I say, and the years of your life will be many" (Proverbs 4:10); "The fear of the Lord adds length to life, but the years of the wicked are cut short" (Proverbs 10:27); "The eye that mocks a father, that scorns obedience to a mother, will be pecked out by the ravens of the valley, will be eaten by the vultures" (Proverbs 30:17).

Thus we see that children ought to honor and obey their parents first because of *natural law* (it is "right"), and second because of *divine law* (God commands it — and in doing so, commands that which will make children live longer and better). For children, for teenagers, and for collegians, there is truth here which can only be ignored to their detriment. A conscious decision to respect and obey one's parents will change the direction of one's young life — for the better!

What is required to "obey your parents in the Lord"? The Greek word translated "obey" is very helpful because it comes from two words, *under* and *to listen* — so that it literally means *to listen under*. Obedience involves conscious listening. If you do not really listen, you cannot really obey. That is why parents are always saying, "Listen to me!" The idea is to *listen under* with the intent to understand and do it. This does not mean that a son or daughter is to obey if the parents ask him or her to do something that is morally wrong or goes against Scripture or Christian conscience. Children are to obey parents "in the Lord" — that is, in those things which are consistent with Christ and his Word.

Much of this is a matter of attitude. We are not to be like the little boy who misbehaved and was told by his teacher to sit in the corner, which he did with grudging obedience, all the while saying to himself, "I'm sitting down on the outside, but I'm standing up on the inside!" The call to honor our parents goes beyond mere outward obedience. To honor our parents means to love them, to regard them highly, to show them respect and consideration. While we may outgrow the call to obey our parents, we never outgrow the obligation to honor them. This is where our culture is fast failing. The aged are shelved and patronized, but not respected. Grown-up children dishonor their parents by forgetting them and neglecting them.

GOD'S WISDOM FOR PARENTS (v. 4)

Turning from advice for children, we come to wisdom for parents, which is in two parts. The first is negative, the second positive.

The prohibition is most clear: "Fathers, do not exasperate your children" (v. 4a). Literally this means, *do not provoke your children to anger* so that they begin to seethe with resentment and irritation like sap swelling in a tree on a hot day. Such "exasperation" can be done in a number of ways.

Unreasonableness is very common. Some parents ask things beyond the child's capability, or load the child with so many demands that frustration is inevitable.

Then there are *fault-finding* parents. Every year when we decorate our Christmas tree and I place a tiny red-and-green glass-beaded wreath on the tree, I think of the little boy who gave it to me when I coached soccer — and his sarcastic, demeaning father, the only parent I ever told to be quiet or leave the field. I wonder how that boy, now a man, has fared.

Another avenue to exasperation is *neglect.* This was King David's great sin, which drove Absalom to rebellion, treason, and attempted patricide (2 Samuel 14, 15).

Another common provocation is *inconsistency.* I recall one of my college friends, who had deep personal problems, telling me how when he was a child his father left his mother so that she became so destitute she placed my friend in an orphanage, where his father would periodically call to say he was coming to visit. My friend told how he would with welling expectancy climb up on the orphanage's iron gate and wait all day for his father, who never once came.

These are but a few of a thousand ways to exasperate our children to the point of swelling wrath.

What a fragile flower a child is. He (or she) can be so easily crushed by his parents, or he can be made to blossom beyond expectation, bringing untold joy to his parents and himself. Paul provides the formula for prospering a child with his positive, concluding admonition: "instead, bring them up in the training and instruction of the Lord" (v. 4b). There are three beautiful elements here which are especially beautiful in concert.

First, there is *gentleness.* The words "bring them up" means "to nourish or feed," as in 5:29 which says that a man "feeds and cares" for his own body. Calvin translates "bring them up" with the words, "let them be kindly cherished," and then goes on to emphasize that the overall idea is gentleness and friendliness.[2] We are to be tender in bringing up our children. Men are never more true men than when they are tender with their children, whether holding a baby in their arms, loving their grade-schooler, or hugging their teenager or a grown son or daughter.

Second, there is *"training."* This is a strong word which means "discipline, even by punishment." Pilate used the same word when he said of Jesus, "I will punish him and then release him" (Luke 23:16). I well remember in kindergarten having a dispute with another kindergartner and kicking my antagonist. When corrected by the teacher, I told her she was "stupid" and then ran away. I also remember my mother coming for me in her new pea-green 1947 Studebaker ("the styler and originator of the new look in motor cars") and giving me a spanking which forever turned me from a criminal path! Gentle as she normally was, she was in complete accord with the Scriptures: "Discipline your son, for in that there is hope; do not be a willing party to his death" (Proverbs 19:18). "He who ignores discipline despises himself, but whoever heeds correction gains understanding" (Proverbs 15:32). "No discipline seems pleasant at the time, but painful. Later on, however, it produces a harvest of righteousness and peace for those who have been trained by it" (Hebrews 12:11). Discipline produces practical "righteousness." It also produces "peace" — *shalom*, well-being, wholeness. That is what it did for me and my children.

Last, there is "*instruction*" — verbal instruction, verbal warning. The word "instruction" literally means "to place before the mind." Often it means to confront. This is precisely where the high priest Eli was such an abysmal domestic failure in raising his sons. First Samuel 3:11-13 tells us, "And the Lord said to Samuel: 'See, I am about to do something in Israel that will make the ears of everyone who hears of it tingle. At that time I will carry out against Eli everything I spoke against his family — from beginning to end. For I told him that I would judge his family forever because of the sin he knew about; his sons made themselves contemptible, and he failed to restrain them.'" (Note: the Greek word for "*restrain*" in the Septuagint is the same root as for "*instruction*" here in Ephesians 6:4.) Clear, forthright instruction is necessary for a proper upbringing! This takes time and thought — two elements so often neglected in today's busy domestic world.

What an enviable picture this positive instruction presents in concert: solid discipline — clear verbal instruction — all wrapped in nourishing tenderness. Notice that we are told to "bring them up in the training and instruction *of the Lord*." The Lord himself stands behind this kind of training and instruction, so that it is he who disciplines and instructs.[3] What an encouragement this is for Christian parents. Christ ministers through us through his divinely given *Haustafel*.

The raising of children can seem an eternity when you are in the midst of it, but when it is over it seems but a season. Growing up seems to take forever when you're twelve, but when you're forty it seems like the throb of a cocoon. Those of us who have raised children say, "Where did the time go?" But whatever your perspective, we need to understand that this is a time when lives are made and broken.

Children should live out God's direction so they can embrace life to its fullest. They ought to covenant to "obey your parents in the Lord," to "'Honor your father and mother . . . that it may go well with you and that you may enjoy long life on the earth.'"

"Fathers [and all parents], do not exasperate your children." That baby daughter will be having your grandson tomorrow. "Bring them up in the training and instruction of the Lord" now.

Slaves, obey your earthly masters with respect and fear, and with sincerity of heart, just as you would obey Christ. Obey them not only to win their favor when their eye is on you, but like slaves of Christ, doing the will of God from your heart. Serve whole-heartedly, as if you were serving the Lord, not men, because you know that the Lord will reward everyone for whatever good he does, whether he is slave or free. And masters, treat your slaves in the same way. Do not threaten them, since you know that he who is both their Master and yours is in heaven, and there is no favoritism with him. (6:5-9)

24

Slaves and Masters

EPHESIANS 6:5-9

As we come to the end of the Ephesian *Haustafel*, it is natural that advice regarding the conduct of masters and slaves be given, because nearly every household was affected (or even dominated) by master/slave relationships. It has been estimated that there were some 60,000,000 slaves in the Roman Empire,[1] and that as many as one third of the populations of large cities such as Rome, Corinth, and Ephesus were slaves.[2] Some in the Ephesian church were masters, as was Philemon in the Colossian church. Many in the church were either slaves or ex-slaves (called "freedmen"). And some were slaveless citizens who, because of their lack of servants, were often poor. So virtually everyone in the Ephesian church had an interest in the Christian *Haustafel* for masters and slaves.

In order to understand what the directions meant then, so we can apply them helpfully to today's relationships, we need to know what slavery was like in New Testament times. This will involve the exploding of some common misconceptions. The greatest of these is that the average slave was subject to extreme exploitation. This simply was not so! To be sure there was the traditional ancient teaching such as in Aristotle's *Nichomachian Ethics* that "A slave is a living tool, just as a tool is an inanimate slave," which rendered a slave a thing, although in his *Politics* Aristotle did concede that "a slave is a kind of possession with a soul."[3] It is also true that under Roman law, according to Gaius, a slave was a thing to be owned and bought and sold and not a legal person.[4] It is true, too, that some slaves had suffered terribly at the hands of their owners, such as the slave of Augustus who was crucified because he killed a pet quail.[5] It is also a fact that there had been major slave rebellions, such as that led by Spartacus, but those were pre-Christian (between the years 140-70 B.C.).[6]

The fact is, by the time of the Christian era and the writing of this Ephesian *Haustafel*, sweeping changes had been introduced which radically improved the treatment of slaves. Slaves under Roman law in the first century could generally count on eventually being set free. Very few ever reached old age as slaves. Slave owners were releasing slaves at such a rate that Augustus Caesar introduced legal restrictions to curb the trend. Despite this, inscriptions indicate that almost 50 percent of slaves were freed before the age of thirty.[7] What is more, while the slave remained his master's possession he could own property — including other slaves! — and completely controlled his own property, so that he could invest and save to purchase his own freedom. In fact, the *nouveaux rich* extravaganzas of ex-slaves scandalized the "old money" Bostonian Romans![8]

We also must understand that being a slave did not indicate one's social class. Slaves regularly were accorded the social status of their owners. Regarding outward appearance, it was usually impossible to distinguish a slave from free persons. A slave could be a custodian, a salesman, or a CEO. Many slaves lived separately from their owners. Finally, selling oneself into slavery was commonly used as a means of obtaining Roman citizenship and gaining an entrance into society. Roman slavery in the first century was far more humane and civilized than the American/African slavery practiced in this country much later. This is a sobering and humbling fact!

We have attempted to clarify the status of first-century slaves for two reasons. First, to answer those who criticize Christianity because the New Testament nowhere directly attacks or condemns slavery. The reasons it did not do so are: 1) because of the positive reforms then in effect in regard to Roman slavery; 2) because the institution of slavery was not generally considered evil by slaves or masters; 3) because to attack slavery would have wrongly labeled Christianity as economically subversive (besides, the immediate demise of slavery would have reduced both slaves and masters to poverty); and 4) because the radical brotherhood and equality explicit in the gospel would be a death knell to slavery (cf. Philemon 16, Galatians 3:28, and the entire Book of Ephesians).

The other reason we have dispelled some of the false conceptions about first-century slavery is to help us understand that parallels between the relationships of first-century slaves and masters and between twentieth-century employees and employers are closer than one might first think. The *Haustafel* for the Ephesian church is directly applicable to today's bosses and workers.

As we follow the order of our text, we see behavioral principles for slaves/employees in verses 5 to 8 and their counterparts for masters/employers in verse 9. What is the *Haustafel* for slaves?

I. HAUSTAFEL FOR SLAVES (vv. 5-8)

This comes in four consecutive bits of advice which are summarized in four adverbs. Slaves were to obey and serve their masters respectfully, sincerely, conscientiously, and pleasantly.

First, *respectfully*. "Slaves," says Paul, "obey your earthly masters with respect and fear" (v. 5a) — literally, *with fear and trembling*. This does not suggest servile respect — shaking in your boots lest you make a wrong move, or an obsequious, fawning "Yes, sir! Double yes, sir! Whatever you say, sir!" Rather, it suggests Christian reverence and respect for the master's position and authority.

The Christian slave being instructed here would probably have a non-Christian boss. Normally the slave would be an integral part of his boss's household, so that he would know him and his affairs inside out — a situation which easily bred contempt on the slave's part. Montaigne, the famous French philosopher and essayist, said that far from home he was considered a great man, in the neighboring town only a man of good business ability, and at home merely as a scribbling country lord.[9]

It's so true — "familiarity [especially that which is literally familial] breeds contempt." It was so natural for the slave in a household to resort to hypocritical patronizing and a sarcastic inner attitude: "I know I'm better and smarter than you, but I will feign inferiority. But if I ever get the upper hand, you're in trouble!" This is why Paul advised Timothy to instruct believing slaves that "All who are under the yoke of slavery should consider their masters worthy of full respect, so that God's name and our teaching may not be slandered" (1 Timothy 6:1). Evidently some disrespectful Christian slaves had tarnished the gospel's cause among non-Christian masters.

In the case where the slave had a Christian master, the temptation toward disrespect could be easily intensified by their spiritual equality as "brothers." In some situations this was inflamed because the slave was a teacher in the church and his master was actually instructed by him. This could produce a disrespectful malaise in their professional relationship. I have seen this in Christian organizations where familiar, spiritual equalitarianism has spawned a brooding, disrespectful lethargy which brings disgrace to Christ. That is also why Paul further addressed the problem in 1 Timothy 6:2 — "Those who have believing masters are not to show less respect for them because they are brothers. Instead, they are to serve them even better, because those who benefit from their service are believers, and dear to them."

There can be no place in the Christian employee's life for subtle insubordination toward his employer or for cleverly concealed contempt or sardonic humor. God's Word says that as employees we must conduct ourselves "with respect and fear" toward our earthly employers — not because

207

we think they have earned it, but because they are in that position. I once strolled through the Army War College with a colonel who was serving as Chief of Staff at that elite institution. As a civilian, I was amazed at the respect he was shown and quipped, "Now I know what God must feel like!" The respect, of course, was for his authoritative position, for many who so ceremoniously snapped to attention did not even personally know him. There are some good lessons here, I mused, for "the Lord's army" as it serves in this world.

Sincerely. Paul's next point — that we should conduct ourselves sincerely (v. 5, "and with sincerity of heart, just as you would obey Christ") — perfectly complements the call for respect. "Sincerity" literally means *singleness of heart*, the idea being that we ought to obey and serve with an undivided mind — with no ulterior motive or hypocrisy.

The key to this singleness of heart is its focus upon Christ — "just as you would obey Christ," says Paul. In fact, it is this focus on Christ which dominates all the advice to slaves/employees. Verse 6 says we are to be "like slaves of Christ." Verse 7 similarly says, "serving the Lord, not men." And in verse 8 we read, "the Lord will reward everyone for whatever good he does." That we are serving Christ as we serve those over us is to be the transforming realization and motivation behind our work. This is the great need of Christian workers everywhere!

> It is possible for the housewife to cook a meal as if Jesus Christ were going to eat it, or to spring-clean the house as if Jesus Christ were to be the honored guest. It is possible for teachers to educate children, for doctors to treat patients and nurses to care for them, for solicitors to help clients, shop assistants to serve customers, accountants to audit books and secretaries to type letters as if in each case they were serving Jesus Christ.[10]

A well-traveled parable tells of three workmen building a cathedral who were questioned by a visitor as to what they were doing. The first answered, "I am chipping these stones." The second answered, "I am earning wages." The third answered, "I am building a great cathedral." This third response is the attitude which is ours when we see lives as Christ's edifice being built to his glory, and this is what spawns our *respect* and *sincerity* toward those we serve here on earth.

Conscientiously. Next comes our call to serve conscientiously (v. 6, "Obey them not only to win their favor when their eye is on you, but like slaves of Christ, doing the will of God from your heart").

If you have ever observed a gym class doing push-ups, you will understand the sense of this verse. The coach orders everyone down and begins to intone, "up-down, up-down," and all are following until he looks to the side. In that moment the students go on "hold." There are employees who are all action when the boss is around, but otherwise loll around the watercooler. Out of his eye there is no industry, no enthusiasm, no heart.

This is apparently what happened in the Parable of the Talents in Matthew 25. The two servants who were given the five and two talents immediately got to work even though the master was gone on a journey. And when he returned he praised them with "'Well done, good and faithful servant!'" (v. 23). But to the slave who did nothing with his charge while the boss was gone (he buried it!), the master gave this withering epithet: "'You wicked, lazy servant!'" (v. 26). The Lord has no use for sloth. There is no such thing as a lazy-faithful servant.

If you are working at what you consider to be a "nothing" job, you are nevertheless called to work energetically all the time — whether the boss is there or not. This applies to students who work part-time summer jobs as well as to long-term employees. This kind of work makes a difference not only to God, but with men.

Dr. Harold John Ockenga, pastor of Park Street Church and founding president of both Fuller and Gordon-Conwell Seminaries, told how before the war when he was preaching in Poland he was invited to visit Prince Carol Radzevil on his thirteen-hundred-acre estate. Suddenly the prince pointed to an impressive young man standing by. The prince said, "You see that young man? He is the best worker on my estate. It was due to him that I invited you here today." He then went on to say that he was favorably disposed to a religion that could so affect a man's life.[11]

Pleasantly. Lastly, slaves/employees are charged to serve pleasantly: "Serve wholeheartedly [or better, with "good will," as the RSV and NASB translate this], as if you were serving the Lord, not men, because you know that the Lord will reward everyone for whatever good he does, whether he is slave or free" (vv. 7, 8). The idea is that we are to go about our tasks with cheerful goodwill, with pleasantness. We have all met Christian sourpusses (an admitted contradiction in terms, but they do exist) who bring unpleasantness to everything — even driving. As the little boy innocently said to his mother, "Mommy, why do all the idiots come out when Daddy drives?" I particularly remember a woman who handled accounts for a Christian organization and who obviously could barely tolerate the wretches (like me) she had to deal with. She seemed to be thinking, "How can I soar with the eagles when I have to work with turkeys like you?" Such people's negativeness sours what ought to be the proper deserts of their work — and certainly reduces their eternal benefits.

Rather, our work is to be rendered with good cheer because we know that "the Lord will reward everyone for whatever good he does, whether he is slave or free." What a motivation for pleasantness as we do the drudgeries of life. Perhaps you've seen the Norman Rockwell-style painting of the man asleep with a grand smile across his face, and above him in the sky a beautiful cherry pie — the focus of his dreams. There is a reward coming to those who serve God by serving others, and it is not "pie in the sky by and by." It is, rather, Heaven and all its attendant glories. The Spirit-filled first-century slaves knew this and held it close to their hearts, and the twentieth-century believers who hold it with similar wisdom will know the same pleasantness.

The *Haustafel* for all of us employees is wonderful when its dimensions are lived out because it gives divine proportion to our lives. We are to render our services *respectfully, sincerely, conscientiously,* and *pleasantly.*

How do our lives shape up?

II. HAUSTAFEL FOR MASTERS (v. 9)

Studs Terkel in his widely-acclaimed oral history, entitled *Working: People Talk About What They Do All Day and How They Feel About What They Do*, opens with these words:

> This book, being about work, is by its very nature, about violence — to the spirit as well as to the body. It is about ulcers as well as accidents. About shouting matches as well as fist fights. About nervous breakdowns as well as kicking the dog around. It is, above all (or beneath all), about daily humiliations.[12]

This is, of course, the way millions in our culture feel. But it would not be so if the Ephesian *Haustafel* were lived out, if the Bible triumphed over culture in our lives. What we have here are truly revolutionary social ethics.

First Paul states the *Managerial Golden Rule*: "And masters, treat your slaves in the same way." Just as the mutual submission invoked in 5:21 controls first husband-and-wife relationships, and then parent-and-child relationships while maintaining a divine order, so does the principle of mutual submission hold here, leaving the employer/employee relationship in proper order.

What Paul is telling those in authority is, treat your slaves/employees the way you want to be treated. If you want *respect*, show respect. If you want *sincerity*, be sincere. If you want *conscientiousness*, you be the same. If you want *pleasantness*, model pleasantness. "Promote the welfare of your slaves as you expect them to promote yours. Show the same interest in them and in their affairs as you hope they will show in you and your affairs."[13] Today this is what enlightened management is doing, and where it has been in effect for some time there is harmony and productivity.

Second, there is to be an understanding of the radical spiritual equality of both slave and master. "Do not threaten them, since you know that he who is both their Master and yours is in heaven, and there is no favoritism with him" (v. 9b). The master/employer, though he holds superior authority, must view himself and his charges as equal before God. It is not lip service that is required but an attitude of heart.

This will result in dramatic equity from God at the Judgment. It demands that the employer refrain from harshness and from using his superior position to bully. It introduces a sanctifying tension in the employer's life. Because God is his judge, he must be careful to pay fair wages and benefits, must care about his employees' illnesses, must be concerned for their marriages, for their children, for their education and future.

As with the preceding *Haustafel*, the living out of this is radical and redemptive. But it is not an option. God's Word to those of us who are employers is clear in its points and application, just as it is for employees.

As we noted when we began our study of the *Haustafel*, it is dominated and is given its enabling dynamic by the fullness of the Holy Spirit. Those who are full of the Spirit have hearts which make music to the Lord, and even minister to one another in music, and have a prayerful spirit of thanksgiving, and rejoice in mutual submission. And it is these who live out the *Haustafel* in all its beauty.

Ultimately the living out of the *Haustafel* by the power of the Holy Spirit will bring grace to a lost world. Justin Martyr wrote in the second century:

> Our Lord urged us by patience and meekness to lead all from shame and the lusts of evil, and this we have to show in the case of many who have come in contact with us who were overcome and changed from violent and tyrannical characters, either from having watched the constancy of their Christian neighbors . . . or from doing business with Christians.[14]

Finally, be strong in the Lord and in his mighty power. Put on the full armor of God so that you can take your stand against the devil's schemes. For our struggle is not against flesh and blood, but against the rulers, against the authorities, against the powers of this dark world and against the spiritual forces of evil in the heavenly realms. (6:10-12)

25

The View for Victory

EPHESIANS 6:10-12

As we have noted, Ephesians falls into two major divisions: Chapters 1 through 3 are *doctrine*, and chapters 4 through 6 have to do with *duty*. While this is helpful for a general understanding of Ephesians, there is also a final division which, though extremely practical and descriptive of our duty, can be regarded as a separate section: *spiritual warfare*. (Indeed some writers/commentators do divide Ephesians into three sections. For example, Ruth Paxson has it *Wealth* (1–3), *Walk* (4–6:9), and *Warfare* (6:10ff.). Likewise, Watchman Nee divides Ephesians as *Sit — Walk — Stand*.) We will now take up this intensely practical section on spiritual warfare — i.e., standing against the Enemy.

To the apostle's original readers, caught up in the beauty of his thought, this subject may have come as a jolt. In the course of his letter Paul had opened to them the "bright secrets of grace": the mystery of their election — the wonder of their salvation and spiritual resurrection — the celebration of divine power in their lives, of their heavenly position, of their peace, of their unity, of their giftedness — and then the call to live as light and be filled with the Spirit and live out the beautiful order of the *Haustafel* in mutual submission as husbands and wives, parents and children, and masters and servants.[1] These were such exalted thoughts — substance for dreamy reflection — and then slap! — the ugly blood and grime of war with the Devil! The fact is, a beautiful life is to be lived even while camped out on enemies' dismal territories.

This is spiritual reality and is necessary for those of us who want to live out the Ephesian vision in today's modern world. The prevailing materialistic, mechanistic thinking of our age leaves no room for the supernatural, or indeed anything without a physical cause. Sadly, many Christians are so influenced by this thinking that even though they give conscious voice to their belief in Satan and spiritual warfare, their lives show no evidence of this reality. They actually live in *unconscious disbelief*. For such persons, this passage provides a much-needed antidote.

Our study has its dangers. It is possible to move from practical disbelief in the Devil and his minions to a preoccupation with them — like the *New Yorker* cartoon which pictured a man pointing toward his car's transmission saying, "I think there is a demon in my bellhousing." We've probably all felt that way at times, but if we attribute every problem to demons we are in trouble!

At the same time Paul's worldview, the Biblical worldview, is that we are in a spiritual battle with evil in which there is no truce, no quarter. As we consider this view, we will first look at the perspective of verse 12, and then the preceding commands in verses 10 and 11.

PAUL'S COSMIC PERSPECTIVE

"For our struggle is not against flesh and blood, but against the rulers, against the authorities, against the powers of this dark world and against the spiritual forces of evil in the heavenly realms" (v. 12). In asserting that "our struggle is not against flesh and blood" the apostle makes three points.

First, the struggle is *supernatural* — supra flesh and blood.

Second, the struggle is *personal*. The word for "struggle" indicates a hand-to-hand fight (as the Spanish say, *mano a mano*). The root idea here is, swaying back and forth while locked in mortal battle. An exchange of arrows or artillery is not pictured here, but sweat against sweat, breath against breath.

Third, the struggle is *futile if fought in and by our own flesh*. As Calvin said:

> He means that our difficulties are far greater than if we had to fight against men. Where we resist human strength, sword is opposed to sword, man contends with man, force is met by force, and skill by skill; but here the case is very different, for our enemies are such as no human power can withstand.[2]

We are all involved in a superhuman battle in which conventional tactics will avail nothing.

Awareness that we are involved in a cosmic battle which is *supernatural, personal*, and *futile if fought with natural weapons* is the beginning of conquering wisdom. We must be convinced of these things if we are to succeed. We must go beyond evangelical lip service to a deep-souled conviction which bursts our simplistic religious shackles.

Paul is specific about the nature of our evil opponents: "our struggle is

... against the rulers, against the authorities, against the powers of this dark world and against the spiritual forces of evil in the heavenly realms" (v. 12). The fact that they inhabit "the heavenly realms" indicates that they have run of what we might call the "celestial sphere." They do not have run of the highest heaven where Christ is seated at the Father's right hand (1:20) and where believers are seated with Christ (2:6). But they do move freely about in the rest of creation, "the kingdom of the air" as it is called in 2:2. The Devil and his evil servants are hardly provincials!

The designation of these angels as "rulers," "authorities," "powers," and "spiritual forces of evil" indicates that they form a vast organized hierarchy. The word translated "powers," or "world rulers" (AV), is *kosmokratoras* or, in a recognizable anglicized rendering, *cosmocrats*, which professor F. F. Bruce thinks may refer to high-ranking fallen angels such as the angel-princes of Persia and Greece who hindered the archangelic messenger in his divine errand (as recorded in the Book of Daniel).[3] When the angel finally got to Daniel he explained, "Do not be afraid, Daniel. Since the first day that you set your mind to gain understanding and to humble yourself before your God, your words were heard, and I have come in response to them. But the prince of the Persian kingdom resisted me twenty-one days. Then Michael, one of the chief princes, came to help me, because I was detained there with the king of Persia" (Daniel 10:12, 13; cf. v. 20).

Whatever the exact designations of the angels, there is a great demonic enemy with a defined and disciplined chain of command. The evil described here is not the trivialized, pallid Satan of folklore commanding a gang of spirits that look like winged possums!

THE CHILLING IMPLICATIONS OF THESE COSMIC REALITIES

The immediate implication is that Satan is terribly powerful. To be sure he does not possess anything near the power of God, but in God's inscrutable arrangement he temporarily dominates and drives the world, which on the whole is separated from God's grace. Though the Devil can only be in one place at a time, with his myriads of malignant spirits he imitates God's omnipresence and omnipotence — for he desires to be God more than anything. His *cosmocrats* are strategically positioned in the world's culture, both secular and ecclesiastical. Their lieutenants are likewise well-schooled and well-placed so as to best spread their cancer.

The consensus of Scripture is that this world is the *cosmos diabolicus*. John tells us in 1 John 5:19, "We know that we are children of God, and that the whole world is under the control of the evil one." Paul writes in 2 Corinthians 4:4, "The god of this age has blinded the minds of unbelievers, so that they cannot see the light of the gospel of the glory of Christ, who is the image of God." In 2:2 the Devil is called "the ruler of the kingdom of the air, the spirit who is now at work in those who are disobedient." In Acts 26:18 we find that Jesus commissioned Paul "to open their eyes and turn them from darkness to light, and from the power of Satan to God." This is the Devil's world. That is why Satan could make a bona fide offer of the kingdoms of this world to Christ if he would but worship him (Matthew 4:8, 9).

In our own culture we see some of this in the amoral and immoral banter of the TV talk shows. The hosts and audiences are virtually all the same — a herd of morally desolate groupies committed to unthinking, doctrinaire relativism, regularly calling good evil and evil good (see Isaiah 5:20), approving of actions that dogs under full sway of their animal natures would never do! The "Evil Empire" is worldwide, sometimes showing itself in oppression, sometimes in license and debauchery, and both are typical of the *cosmos diabolicus*.

A parallel implication is the terrible total spiritual evil of Satan. Our verse alludes to this as we are told that we struggle against "the powers of this dark world" (or "this present darkness," as the RSV has it). We understand from Romans 1 – 3 that all of us are totally depraved. By this we mean that every part of our nature is tainted by sin. This does not mean we are as bad as we could be. There is always room for "deprovement." Some humans fall deeper in their depravity than others — say, serial murderers such as Ted Bundy or the Satanic murderers in Matamoros, Mexico, whose hideous work was shown in *Time* magazine — a caldron stuffed with dismembered human and animal parts. Yet even those who have gone so low have not equalled Satan's evil. Satan has no conscience, no compassion, no remorse, no morals. He feeds on pain and anguish and filth.

This chilling truth was dramatically illumined for me years ago when I first read C. S. Lewis's *Perelandra*, in which the hero, a Professor Ransom, encounters a Satan-figure, Dr. Weston, on a flawless planet. As Dr. Weston dispassionately ripped helpless creatures apart because he had nothing else to do at the moment, their eyes met, and

> It [Dr. Weston] looked at Ransom in silence and at last began to smile. We have all often spoken — Ransom himself had often spoken — of a devilish smile. Now he realised that he had never taken the words seriously. The smile was not bitter, nor raging, nor, in an ordinary sense, sinister; it was not even mocking. It seemed to summon Ransom, with horrible naiveté of welcome, into the world of its own pleasures, as if all men were at one in those pleasures, as if they were the most natural thing in the world and no dispute could ever have occurred about them. It did not defy goodness, it

ignored it to the point of annihilation. This creature was whole-hearted. The extremity of its evil had passed beyond all struggle into some state which bore a horrible similarity to innocence. It was beyond vice.[4]

Such is the spirit with whom we wrestle. There is nothing in Satan which is redeemable. There is no virtue, but only a dark, cannibal void.

Along with this, he is supremely cunning. Verse 11 refers to this ("the devil's schemes," or as the Greek says, *methodias* — methods). He has been honing his methods for millennia. His emissaries visited the church councils at Nicea and Chalcedon. He sat in on medieval faculty meetings. He is an accomplished philosopher, theologian, and psychologist. He has had thousands of years to study.

I am no genius at mathematics, but even with my limited capabilities I could be terrific at math if I worked at it for 100 years (maybe!). If I labored hard at it for a 1,000 years and read all the learned theories, I would be a Newton or an Einstein. Or what if I had 10,000 years? Given that time, any of us could become the world's greatest philosopher or psychologist or theologian or linguist (we could curse or preach in a thousand languages). Satan has had multiple millennia to study and master the human disciplines, and when it comes to human subversion, he is the ultimate manipulator.

One of his deadly methods is masquerading as an agent of God, as Paul records in 2 Corinthians 11:14, 15 — "And no wonder, for Satan himself masquerades as an angel of light. It is not surprising, then, if his servants masquerade as servants of righteousness. Their end will be what their actions deserve." Today his emissaries may don Brooks Brothers suits, flaunt Madison Avenue aplomb, and travel between Bonn, Berlin, New York, and Paris. He specializes in mixing enough truth with falsehood to make it seem plausible, just as he did with Eve in the garden. Heresy is truth out of proportion, and twisting the truth is his specialty.

Perhaps his most common method today is sensuality. How many have sold their souls to accommodate their slidden morality. Theological aberration is as often the result of moral declension as it is an intellectual process.

One of the Devil's most effectual methods is to instill doubts about God's goodness. This was his greatest tool against Martin Luther. Roland Bainton, Luther's great biographer, writes: "The content of his depressions was always the same, the loss of faith that God is good and that he is good to *me*. After the frightful *Anfechtung* of 1527 Luther wrote, 'For more than a week I was close to the gates of death and hell.'"[5]

Seldom does Satan ever attack openly. His strategies as ministered by his devils are nearly always unseen, shrewd, and perfectly tailored for the victim. What a terrible foe we face. He is immensely *powerful*, imitating

217

God's power and presence with his demonic hosts. He is evil beyond our comprehension and without conscience or principle. He is diabolically *cunning*. And he is after us!

"Our struggle is not against flesh and blood." This struggle is too much for the twentieth-century, one-dimensioned materialist and indeed for many who think themselves Christian. Our enemy is subtle and powerful. He hates Christ. He hates God's children. He hates the Church.

> *For still our ancient foe*
> *Doth seek to work us woe;*
> *His craft and power are great,*
> *And, armed with cruel hate,*
> *On earth is not his equal.*

These are the chilling realities Paul communicated in his letter to the Ephesians. All would be despair except that this is only part of the apostle's perspective, and the counterpart is correspondingly heartening.

THE HEARTENING REALITIES OF PAUL'S COSMIC PERSPECTIVE

On earth, among mortals, Satan has no equal, but in the heavenly realms he is far exceeded by the Triune God. The great Colossian hymn of the Incarnation reveals that Satan, and in fact the entire invisible spiritual realm, owes his existence to Christ: "For by him all things were created: things in heaven and on earth, visible and invisible, whether thrones or powers or rulers or authorities; all things were created by him and for him" (Colossians 1:16; cf. Colossians 2:10). There is no dualism here. Satan is not the counterpart of God. Because Satan is finite and God is infinite, our enemy is infinitely inferior! Satan's power is overwhelmed by that of God.

Consider the account in Exodus 7 (vv. 6-12), when Aaron, at God's command, threw down his staff before Pharaoh and it became a snake, demonstrating that God's power was with Moses and Aaron. And remember how Pharaoh's magicians did the same — there were snakes everywhere! But then Aaron's snake swallowed all the rest. Those grotesque moments, as Aaron's snake was vacuuming up the other serpents, said it all: God has power — Satan too has power — but God's power is far superior! Think how Aaron felt when he reached down and picked up his fat snake and it again became his staff. Think of the power he felt as he waved it before Pharaoh!

But there is more — Christ is not only more powerful by virtue of his being the spirits' Creator. He is also more powerful because he defeated

Satan at the cross, and as a result Satan and his minions are under Christ's feet. In fact, the apostle tells us in Colossians 2:15 that our Lord Jesus Christ has led them in a victory parade: "And having disarmed the powers and authorities, he made a public spectacle of them, triumphing over them by the cross." He has sealed their doom, although during the present over-lapping of the new age with the old, they still exercise control over those who have not found freedom in Christ.

As John Stott says: "They were defeated at the cross and are now under Christ's feet and ours. So the invisible world in which they attack us and we defend ourselves is the very world in which Christ reigns over them and we reign with him."[6] If we are filled with the Spirit (5:18), Satan's forces cannot subdue us. But those of us who neglect our resources, and especially those who give the enemies room in our lives, place ourselves in harm's way.

When we avail ourselves of Christ, there is always victory! Full of Christ, we can say with Luther:

> *The Prince of Darkness grim,*
> *We tremble not for him;*
> *His rage we can endure,*
> *For lo, his doom is sure;*
> *One little word shall fell him.*

A mere word from Christ is all that is needed.

So in respect to these cosmic realities about Satan's vast power, but Christ's transcending power, what must we do? Paul leaves two commands which dominate his advice to the end of this section. First: "Finally, be strong in the Lord and in his mighty power" (v. 10). This is a passive imperative: *be made strong in the Lord, find your strength in him.* We can-not fight Satan ourselves. All our own doing will be in vain. Nevertheless there is something we can do, and that is to avail ourselves of the Lord's strength. Paul says elsewhere, "But he said to me, 'My grace is sufficient for you, for my power is made perfect in weakness.' Therefore I will boast all the more gladly about my weaknesses, so that Christ's power may rest on me" (2 Corinthians 12:9). We are to acknowledge our weakness and invite his power. We must imitate Gideon's going from 32,000 warriors to 10,000 to 300 armed only with trumpets and lanterns (Judges 7). This divestment of natural strength enabled the putting on of God's power — and a mighty victory!

Next, we are to "put on the full armor of God so that you can take your stand against the devil's schemes" (v. 11). This armor includes: "truth" — "righteousness" — "the gospel of peace" — "faith" — "salvation" —

"the word of God" — "prayer." (We will examine these individually in the following studies.) But what is called for here is a breathing out of dependence upon self and a breathing in of God's mighty power.

Why not prayerfully do this right now? First, acknowledge the futility of fighting your spiritual battles with natural strength — exhale all self-dependence. Second, prayerfully inhale his mighty power, asking him to fill you with his fullness (3:19).

Therefore put on the full armor of God, so that when the day of evil comes, you may be able to stand your ground, and after you have done everything, to stand. Stand firm then, with the belt of truth buckled around your waist, with the breastplate of righteousness in place . . . (6:13, 14)

26

Armed for Battle (I)

EPHESIANS 6:13, 14

Paul's cosmic perspective, so eloquently stated in verse 12 — "For our struggle is not against flesh and blood, but against the rulers, against the authorities, against the powers of this dark world and against the spiritual forces of evil in the heavenly realms" — is life-changing when truly believed. Without it our theology is monochrome, colorless, faded like an old photograph. But truly believed and lived out, it becomes polychrome, technicolor, throbbing with light and reality. Even more, with this Biblical worldview in our hearts, we have the foundation for victorious spiritual warfare.

Paul's mind is full of unseen war, and as he reaches for metaphors to describe further realities necessary for the battle, a Roman soldier unwittingly sits for his portrait (very possibly the one to whom Paul was chained). That soldier's armor became the vehicle for teaching us what is necessary to win the invisible war.

Though a Roman soldier wore other essentials for war, such as protective greaves on his shins (like a baseball catcher), Paul focuses on six indispensable items: his *belt, breastplate, sandals, shield, helmet,* and *sword,* to which Paul adds a seventh non-clothing item, *prayer,* thus emphasizing the completeness of such an outfit for spiritual battle.

In presenting his charge to don these seven essentials for battle, Paul reiterates the commands of verses 10 and 11 in verse 13: "Therefore put on the full armor of God, so that when the day of evil comes, you may be able to stand your ground, and after you have done everything, to stand." The charge is both a command and a promise, the promise being that if we will really put on the full armor of God, *we will stand and be victorious.*

Those who have traveled through Tolkien's most imaginative Middle Earth perhaps remember that Bilbo Baggins passed on to his successor,

Frodo, a finely wrought coat of delicately woven mail which was secretly made under the mountains by dwarves and was virtually impenetrable, thus saving their Hobbit skins on several occasions. But here with Paul, in the context of ultimate spiritual reality, we are offered real armor wrought on the anvils of Heaven which will protect us in real war if we will but wear it. In this study we are going to examine the first two items on the list: the soldier's belt and his breastplate.

THE BELT OF TRUTH (v. 14a)

Paul says, "Stand firm then, with the belt of truth buckled around your waist" (v. 14a). When a soldier tightened his belt he was ready for combat, because in the process of tightening he drew up his tunic and cinched it so it could not impede him as he charged into battle. It also firmly fixed his sword in place. To get the feel here, we might think of a football player clenching his mouthpiece in his teeth, adjusting his pads, and hitching up his waist to get ready for the next play. But what the soldier did was even more crucial. His belt held everything in place. Without it, he would be powerless in battle.

Paul says that *truth* performs this crucial function in spiritual warfare. Truth holds the spiritual armor in place and safeguards against deadly entanglements. To what truth is he referring? Some commentators, especially ancient ones, think this is the eternal, Biblical truth revealed in the Scriptures. I believe they are correct — as far as they go. Jesus proclaimed to those in the bonds of false teaching, "You will know the truth, and the truth will set you free" (John 8:32; cf. John 8:43-45). Later he said, "Sanctify them by the truth; your word is truth" (John 17:17). Paul refers in 4:21 to "the truth that is in Jesus" (cf. 5:9). There is objective, spiritual truth in Jesus and his Scriptures: truth about God, ourselves, history, and the future. Without it we do not have a chance in the spiritual battles which come our way.

Without cinching ourselves tightly with the truth of Scripture, the other weapons of our warfare will clatter in disarray. Those who have stood firm as great warriors for Christ have been men and women of the Word and so were filled with the eternal truth of Scripture.

One can scarcely imagine a greater soldier than Martin Luther, standing *contra mundum*. It is not incidental that he had memorized virtually all the Bible (in his case, in Latin). Later, in the seventeenth century, the supreme soldier was John Wesley, and he bucked the religious establishment with such evangelistic power that he changed the course of English society and altered history. Significantly, Wesley had memorized most of the Greek New Testament. Effective Christian warriors are bound with God's truth.

Having this objective truth, those victorious in spiritual warfare go a step further and live out the truth, as later commentators, beginning with Calvin, have emphasized. Their lives were bound tightly for battle with an honest, truth-trafficking lifestyle. Paul's point is that truthful character, along with a knowledge of the truth, holds one together in the fight.

Though truthfulness is necessary for victory, it does not come easily to the human race. Consider the rejection notice a Chinese publisher sent to a British author in turning down his manuscript:

> We have read your manuscript with boundless delight. If we were to publish your paper it would be impossible for us to publish any work of a lower standard. And, as it is unthinkable that in the next thousand years we shall see its equal, we are, to our regret, compelled to return your divine composition, and beg you a thousand times to overlook our short sight and timidity.[1]

Charles Colson believes that our American society's constant, mindless engagement with the media, where trash is heaped upon trash and the bizarre is commonplace, has left us morally exhausted and without discernment.

> "The inability to make moral distinctions is the AIDS of the intellectuals: an acquired immune deficiency syndrome . . . moral blindness of this caliber requires practice. It has to be learned." [Charles Krauthammer, quoting Thomas Sowell] In a culture infected with moral AIDS, words lose all meaning; or, they are manipulated to obscure meaning. Thus taxes become "revenue assessment enhancements"; perversion is "gay"; murder of unborn children is "freedom of choice"; Marxism in the church is called "liberation theology." These are all good words (in the Nazi era "the final solution" had a nice ring to it also). And everyone just nods unquestioningly. But when words lose their meaning, it is nearly impossible for the Word of God to be received. If sin and repentance mean nothing, then God's grace is irrelevant. Our preaching falls on deaf ears. This moral deafness leads to disaster. The Scriptures tell us it was when people accepted King Ahab's gross evils as "trivial" that fearsome judgment befell ancient Israel.[2]

This is where we are right now as a culture. We hear almost daily of a new case of perjury by the prestigious. Many of our nation's icons have fallen due to their lies, but despite this they are placed back in the pantheon by their followers. We now have one truth for the elite and a separate truth for the people. Doctrinaire news reporting masquerades as objectivity. The

advertising industry has institutionalized deceit. We live in a foggy netherland of deception.

The tragic result is that many who claim to be "light in the Lord"
(5:8) traffic in untruth. I am not referring to the use of hyperbole to adorn a
good story, but unconscious and conscious lying. I have had professing
believers tell me bald-faced lies, and so have you! Moreover, they have
remained unrepentant and even aggressive purveyors of moral AIDS. Paul's
injunction, "Therefore each of you must put off falsehood and speak truthfully to his neighbor, for we are all members of one body" (4:25) is ignored.

The result of this is spiritual impotence. Those positionally seated
with Christ in the heavenly places are dominated by the Devil. Practically,
there is little that can be done for liars except to pray for them.

The opposite is true of those who walk in truth. Their armor is
cinched close by the objective truth of God and its subjective outworking in
their lives. Truth arms them with a clear conscience which makes it possible
to unflinchingly face the enemy. Paul told Timothy, "So fight gallantly,
armed with faith and a good conscience" (1 Timothy 1:19, NEB). When
you are filled with God's truth and living it, you will have a good conscience, and having that you can face anything.

How's the spiritual battle going? If you are having trouble, it may be
that you need to tighten your belt — to regird yourself with truth. We must
fill ourselves with the truth of God's Word and then consciously submit to
it, so we will be instinctively truthful. We must determine to be truthful,
honest, sincere people.

The great Dr. Samuel Johnson gave this advice for raising children,
which we can well apply to our own lives:

> Accustom your children constantly to this [the telling of the truth];
> if a thing happened at one window, and they, when relating it, say
> that it happened at another, do not let it pass, but instantly check
> them; you do not know where deviation from truth will end. . . . It
> is more from carelessness about truth than from intentional lying,
> that there is so much falsehood in the world.[3]

A truthful life is never an accident.

THE BREASTPLATE OF RIGHTEOUSNESS (v. 14b)

Following the war belt comes the breastplate: "Stand firm then . . . with the
breastplate of *righteousness* in place." Most likely the breastplate, the *tho-
rax*, was a metal piece which covered the front of the body, although
Marcus Barth argues that it was chain mail, because this is what the best-
outfitted soldiers of the day wore.[4] Whatever the exact style, its function

was to ward off the deadly thrusts of the popular short sword, thus protecting the vital organs, especially the heart. This is what righteousness does.

"The breastplate of righteousness" is God's own righteousness freely given to those who truly believe in Jesus Christ. It is not something which we generate on our own. Isaiah 64:6 says, "All of us have become like one who is unclean, and all our righteous acts are like filthy rags." Filthy rags form a futile breastplate. Paul says in Romans 3:10-12, "As it is written: 'There is no one righteous, not even one; there is no one who understands, no one who seeks God. All have turned away, they have together become worthless; there is no one who does good, not even one.'" "Worthless" literally means "rotten." And then in verses 22, 23, he adds the capper: "There is no difference, for all have sinned and fall short of the glory of God."

But there is "a righteousness from God" (Romans 1:17). Isaiah 59:17 tells us that "[God] put[s] on righteousness as his breastplate, and the helmet of salvation on his head" as he comes out to destroy his enemies. Here in Ephesians he gives us his shining armor of righteousness. Paul describes his experience of receiving God's righteousness in Philippians 3:7-9 —

> But whatever was to my profit I now consider loss for the sake of Christ. What is more, I consider everything a loss compared to the surpassing greatness of knowing Christ Jesus my Lord, for whose sake I have lost all things. I consider them rubbish, that I may gain Christ and be found in him, not having a righteousness of my own that comes from the law, but that which is through faith in Christ — *the righteousness that comes from God and is by faith.* (italics added)

The breastplate of righteousness is received and put on through faith as God gives us his righteousness. He clothes us through his Son, Jesus Christ — "God made him who had no sin to be sin for us, so that in him we might become the righteousness of God" (2 Corinthians 5:21). It is what theologians call *imputed righteousness*. If you do not have this righteousness, nothing can save you; but if you have it, you are safe for eternity!

When you have this righteousness from God, you begin to develop and manifest a righteous character in righteous living — "a devout and holy life," to borrow Calvin's description.[5] Such a life is not only secure in God's righteousness but is filled with power. R. C. Sproul explains:

> A few years ago one of the leading golfers on the professional tour was invited to play in a foursome with Gerald Ford, then President of the United States, Jack Nicklaus, and Billy Graham. The golfer was especially in awe of playing with Ford and Billy Graham (he had played frequently with Nicklaus before). After the round of

golf was finished, one of the other pros came up to the golfer and asked, "Hey, what was it like playing with the President and with Billy Graham?" The pro unleashed a torrent of cursing, and in a disgusted manner said, "I don't need Billy Graham stuffing religion down my throat." With that he turned on his heel and stormed off, heading for the practice tee. His friend followed the angry pro to the practice tee. The pro took out his driver and started to beat out balls in fury. His neck was crimson and it looked like steam was coming from his ears. His friend said nothing. He sat on a bench and watched. After a few minutes the anger of the pro was silent. He settled down. His friend said quietly, "Was Billy a little rough on you out there?" The pro heaved an embarrassed sigh and said, "No, he didn't even mention religion. I just had a bad round."

Astonishing. Billy Graham had said not a word about God, Jesus, or religion, yet the pro had stormed away after the game accusing Billy of trying to ram religion down his throat. How can we explain this? It's really not difficult. Billy Graham didn't have to say a word; he didn't have to give a single sideward glance to make the pro feel uncomfortable. Billy Graham is so identified with religion, so associated with the things of God, that his very presence is enough to smother the wicked man who flees when no man pursues. Luther was right: the pagan does tremble at the rustling of a leaf. He feels the hound of heaven breathing down his neck. He feels crowded by holiness even if it is only made present by an imperfect, partially sanctified human vessel.[6]

The song of the righteous is this: "For we are to God the aroma of Christ among those who are being saved and those who are perishing. To the one we are the smell of death; to the other, the fragrance of life" (2 Corinthians 2:15, 16).

Do you have a righteousness "which is through faith in Christ — the righteousness that comes from God and is by faith" (Philippians 3:9)? If not, all you have to do is renounce dependence upon the rags of your self-righteousness and humbly ask. His righteousness will guard your heart as effectively as the finest breastplate. Why not do this now? And with that righteousness comes a righteous life, a marvelous offensive weapon in the hands of Christ.

Do we believe in the polychrome reality of Paul's worldview: "For our struggle is not against flesh and blood, but against the rulers, against the authorities, against the powers of this dark world and against the spiritual forces of evil in the heavenly realms" (v. 12)? If so, then we must obey his command: "Therefore put on the full armor of God, so that when the day of evil comes, you may be able to stand your ground, and after you have done everything, to stand" (v. 13). How do we do this? Not in our own strength, for "the armor of God" is *his* armor. Therefore it is not by self-reliance, but by *dependence upon him.*

In ancient times, before a squire was knighted he would spend the night in vigil in the castle chapel, with his armor spread before him as he offered up his soul to God. This is the way to don the armor of God, for he is the one who teaches us the ways of war and fights the battle through our hands and feet. It is in communion with Christ that the armor is set and reset for battle. We must allow him to cinch the belt tight and to lower over us the breastplate of righteousness. Thus armed, we may ask that his truth and righteousness permeate our speech and life.

In conscious dependence we must cultivate truth through reading his Word and truthing life in love. In conscious dependence, we must revel in the breastplate of his righteousness and allow what clothes us to fill our souls, so that we become instruments of wonderful spiritual aggression.

. . . and with your feet fitted with the readiness that comes from the gospel of peace. In addition to all this, take up the shield of faith, with which you can extinguish all the flaming arrows of the evil one. (6:15, 16)

27

Armed for Battle (II)

EPHESIANS 6:15, 16

No one ever faced a more formidable human opponent than did David when he squared off with Goliath. The giant was well over nine feet tall (about 9'6"). If he was as well-proportioned as Wilt Chamberlain, the great seven-foot NBA center of past years, he must have weighed at least 400 pounds, for Chamberlain weighed 275 though he was two feet shorter! His torso was fitted with "scale armor of bronze weighing five thousand shekels" (1 Samuel 17:5), which is to say, in today's terms, that he wore metal underwear weighing 125 pounds. Goliath's spear was like a weaver's rod (some fourteen feet long), and its iron point weighed "six hundred shekels" (v. 7), which is about fifteen pounds, almost the weight of a college shot put. Some point! The entire spear probably weighed thirty pounds. What an awesome sight the giant made in full armor.

How should anyone approach him for battle? Conventional wisdom suggested equally full armor, which is exactly what Saul gave David when he volunteered to take on the Philistines' Mega-Man. Remember what happened? David tried on the king's oversized armor (Saul was a head taller than any other of the Israelites, 1 Samuel 9:2) and "tried walking around" (v. 39). But David was a 42 and Saul was size 50, so no go. If David had faced Goliath in Saul's garb, he would have been skewered like a shish kebab, armor and all. So he politely returned the armor to Saul, saying, "I cannot go in these . . . because I am not used to them" (v. 39) — or, roughly translated, "You can have your royal tin cans."

We all know the rest of the story. Young David, in refusing Saul's armor, kept himself fleet-footed to charge into battle and chose five smooth stones as ammunition for his deadly sling (v. 40). According to General Moshe Dayan, the one-eyed mastermind behind Israel's victory in the Six

Day War, David had the perfect strategy and equipment. That day saw one very surprised — and very dead — Philistine.

David was victorious that day because of two things: He set aside conventional armament, and he chose dress and weaponry suitable for battling his unique foe. May the lesson not be wasted on us. We fight an enemy whose troops are far more capable and lethal than the Philistine giant. If for sixty seconds we could see their size and ranks — General Satan, his *cosmocrats*, their lieutenants and foot soldiers — we would forever reject reliance on conventional methods and would flee to God's armory for instruction and outfitting. As we take up our text again with verses 15 and 16, which describe pieces three and four of the Christian's full armor, this is precisely what we are doing. May the divine wisdom, here so vividly given, equip us for victory.

THE WAR BOOTS: THE GOSPEL OF PEACE (v. 15)

Having instructed us in the necessity of being belted with truth and sheathed with the breastplate of righteousness, Paul continues to challenge us to "stand firm . . . with your feet fitted with the readiness that comes from the gospel of peace" (vv. 14, 15).

The image Paul has in mind comes from the Roman soldier's war boot, the *caliga* or half-boot which the legionnaire regularly wore while on duty. It was an open-toed leather boot with a heavily nail-studded sole which was tied to the ankles and shins with straps. These were not shoes for running — for example, fleeing or pursuing an enemy. In fact, Josephus tells of a centurion who, because he was running after his enemies while wearing "shoes thickly studded with sharp nails," slipped and fell on his back on the stone pavement, where he was duly dispatched.[1]

These boots served for marching, especially in battle. Their function was like today's cleated football shoe. They gave the foot traction and prevented sliding.[2] Much ancient battle was hand-to-hand and foot-to-foot, like on the line of scrimmage, so these boots gave the Roman soldier an advantage over ill-equipped foes. The "readiness" of our text pictures us being ready with our *caliga* firmly planted on solid ground. Thus established, the enemy is not going to be able to push us back. Rather, we are set to advance.

The spiritual lesson here is perfectly clear. It is "the gospel of peace" — the peace that comes to us in and through the gospel and makes us immovable in battle.[3] The Scriptures present two aspects of this peace.

First, it is peace *with* God. Romans 5:1 says, "Therefore, since we have been justified through faith, we have peace with God through our Lord Jesus Christ." Life apart from Christ has no deep peace, and all people are aware of this cosmic discomfort to some degree. For some it manifests itself in a general sense of alienation. With others it is a raging awareness that their life is not right. Some pursue peace with passive desperation, longing for it to somehow come. They may go wild in pursuit of it, hoping it will come through money or sex or the accumulation of knowledge or religious exploration — but all they ever find is temporary relief. Peace is an ever-receding mirage.

But when a person finds peace with God through Christ, it is ineffably wonderful. Knowing that one's sins are forgiven and forgotten through Jesus Christ is the grandest knowledge one can have. The solid awareness that one is reconciled to God is joyfully sublime.

Personally, my initial experience of this is fixed in my memory as the greatest, most joyful day of my life. I had such relief at having my sins lifted that I felt as if I had lost my gravity and could float up to God. There was nothing between me and God but peace.

This is the point: when our feet are shod and planted in this peace, we can stand firm against the greatest assaults of the enemy.

Second, in addition to having peace with God, there comes, as the holy sequel, the peace *of* God. In the upper room on the final night of his earthly life Jesus told his disciples, and indeed all who follow him, "Peace I leave with you; my peace I give you" (John 14:27). *He gives us His personal peace.* It was the peace he knew as he lay fast asleep in the boat amidst a storming sea (Matthew 8:23-27). It is the peace which so unnerved the fearful Pilate as he interrogated Christ (John 19:5-12). It is from above, and thus rises above the difficulties around it.

The word behind this is *shalom*: "completeness, soundness, welfare."[4] The great German Old Testament scholar Gerhard Von Rad, in an oft-quoted essay, says it means "well-being."[5] Thus we can paraphrase Jesus' words as, "Peace and well-being I leave to you; my peace and my well-being I give to you." Paul refers to this in Philippians 4:7 when he says that "the peace of God, which transcends all understanding, will guard your hearts and minds in Christ Jesus." His peace and well-being literally garrisons (as with a platoon of soldiers) the lives of faithful believers. His peace super-surpasses all understanding.

Those who first have peace *with* God, and then the corollary peace *of* God girding their feet are powerful soldiers in the spiritual battle. No matter what the enemy throws at them, no matter what move the enemy makes, they hold their ground.

A common epigram — "the cobbler's children have no shoes" — expresses the irony of missing that which so surely ought to be ours because of our relationship and position. If we are Christians, we have peace *with* God because of the work of Christ. But the tragic irony is that many of us do not have the peace *of* God because we have pushed it away through rebellion and neglect. And as a result we are ever falling in battle.

When the going gets rough we panic. Sometimes we even bolt. Our fellow warriors find us a burden rather than a blessing.

If this is so, we need to reopen the lines of communication and ask for his peace. "Do not be anxious about anything, but in everything, by prayer and petition, with thanksgiving, present your requests to God. And the peace of God, which transcends all understanding, will guard your hearts and your minds in Christ Jesus" (Philippians 4:6, 7). Then you will stand in the battle!

THE WAR SHIELD: FAITH (v. 16)

The next item of armor that Paul delineates is the shield: "In addition to all this, take up the shield of faith, with which you can extinguish all the flaming arrows of the evil one" (v. 16). The shield indicated here, in distinction to the small round shield worn on the forearm in battle, was a large shield about four feet high and two and a half feet wide, very much like a door (from which the word is actually derived). It must have been the kind of shield the Spartan mother had in mind when she charged her son, "Take care that you return with your shield, or on it." His shield would either be his protection or his bier.

The Roman *scutum* or shield was made of two layers of laminated wood, covered first with linen and then with hide, and then bound top and bottom with iron, with an iron ornament decorating the front of it.[6] A man could put his entire body behind it as it absorbed the javelins and arrows of the enemy. In the case of flaming arrows, very often the arrow would snuff out as it buried itself in the thickness of the shield. During battles these great shields would often bristle with smoking arrows like roasted porcupines.

This is the picture Paul presents us: As we are battling in warfare, the enemy launches repeated volleys of blazing arrows — temptations, strategies, deceptions — to inflame us and bring our demise. But up come our shields of faith (*as we trust God and his Word*) into which hot arrows thud harmlessly.

We all have lusts within us which are easy to ignite. All that is needed is the tiniest flame and we are a roaring fire. So we are assaulted with hot shafts of sensuality — foul, diseased arrows of degrading passions — smoking arrows of materialism.

We burn so easily! As the arrows fly toward us, our rationalizations come so naturally: "If God didn't want me to have this, then why did he make me with such a desire for this thing, this person, this pleasure? My neighbor has it. He does it. And he is doing so well . . ." But then comes God's Word: "You shall not covet your neighbor's house. You shall not covet your neighbor's wife, or his manservant or maidservant, his ox or donkey, or anything that belongs to your neighbor" (Exodus 20:17). "It is God's will that you should be holy; that you should avoid sexual immorality; that each of you should learn to control his own body in a way that is holy and honorable . . . For God did not call us to be impure, but to live a holy life. Therefore, he who rejects this instruction does not reject man but God, who gives you his Holy Spirit" (1 Thessalonians 4:3-8). "Finally, brothers, whatever is true, whatever is noble, whatever is right, whatever is pure, whatever is lovely, whatever is admirable — if anything is excellent or praiseworthy — think about such things" (Philippians 4:8).

As we believe God's Word, the shield flies up and the arrows fall to ashes. It is as Lewis said: "We must pray for the gift of Faith, for the power to go on believing not in the teeth of reason but in the teeth of lust."[7]

Then there are the fiery trials awaiting all of us in this life — illness, tragedies, maybe even persecution. Along with this, Satan's emissaries will launch arrows of doubt about God's goodness, the truth of the gospel, even his existence. But the shield of faith cools them again as we believe God's Word: "'For I know the plans that I have for you,' declares the Lord, 'plans for welfare and not for calamity to give you a future and a hope'" (Jeremiah 29:11, NASB). From this we understand by faith that even the apparent tragedies we suffer will eventuate in our welfare. By faith we see the unseen.

Some of the most lethal arrows come from within our own camp. Unseen hands grasp the hands of our brothers and sisters, take their bows, dip them in tar, and with evil synergism send them flaming toward our hearts — arrows of rejection and criticism and hypocrisy. But the shield of faith goes up again. The Word of God has not left us ignorant of the human condition, but rather informs us about those "who sharpen their tongues like swords and aim their words like deadly arrows. They shoot from ambush at the innocent man; they shoot at him suddenly, without fear" (Psalm 64:3, 4). Some of the arrows strike us, and they hurt, but the incendiary pain can be snuffed by the shield of faith. Through belief in God's Word we forgive. "Do not be overcome by evil, but overcome evil with good" (Romans 12:21).

There are also delectable arrows which bring pleasurable fire to the furnaces of our hearts — shafts of pride and vanity and false self-love. This age of narcissism encourages us to open ourselves to these deadly arrows, but we trust God's Word. "'God opposes the proud but gives grace to the humble.' Submit yourselves, then, to God. Resist the devil, and he will flee from you" (James 4:6, 7). "Blessed are the poor in spirit, for theirs is the kingdom of heaven" (Matthew 5:3).

It is no exaggeration to say that during earthly life multiple thousands of deadly blazing arrows are launched at the Christian warrior by demons and by demon-oppressed culture. But the answer is faith. The Apostle John wrote, "And this is the victory that has overcome the world — our faith" (1 John 5:4, NASB). Why? Because faith binds us in vital, deep union with God. Faith is not just belief; it is belief plus trust. It is resting in the person of God and his Word to us.

There is battle and confusion all around. The sky rains glowing shafts. But the Christian raises his shield, and the arrows, though they be a thousand, are caught in victory. His shield is from God and to God, and he raises it, smoking, up to God, and the savor is sweet to Heaven.

When David battled Goliath, he came to victory because he rejected conventional wisdom and chose weaponry suited to defeat his foe. The conventional wisdom of this world says that we fight fire with fire, violence with violence, hate with hate, spite with spite, pride with pride. But the wisdom from above says we fight with "peace" and "faith."

How awesome is the soldier whose feet are shod with "peace." He has peace *with* God and the peace *of* God. His heart is at rest before God, and he is filled with a sense of well-being. He sings from the heart, "It is well, it is well with my soul." The "shield of faith" is ever before him. The burning arrows fly — sensuality, trials, jealousy, criticism, hypocrisy, vanity — but he stands victorious.

Ultimately the proper armor and weapons produced in young David a mighty, God-honoring aggression:

> David said to the Philistine, "You come against me with sword and spear and javelin, but I come against you in the name of the Lord Almighty, the God of the armies of Israel, whom you have defied. This day the Lord will hand you over to me, and I'll strike you down and cut off your head. Today I will give the carcasses of the Philistine army to the birds of the air and the beasts of the earth, and the whole world will know that there is a God in Israel. All those gathered here will know that it is not by sword or spear that the Lord saves; for the battle is the Lord's, and he will give all of you into our hands" (1 Samuel 17:45-47).

And with that David took off in a dead run at the lumbering giant, his sling fiercely whirling over his head, and with one great heave dealt death to the blaspheming enemy!

Here is the divine wisdom: "For our struggle is not against flesh and blood, but against the rulers, against the authorities, against the powers of this dark world and against the spiritual forces of evil in the heavenly realms. Therefore put on the full armor of God, so that when the day of evil comes, you may be able to stand your ground, and after you have done everything, to stand" (Ephesians 6:12, 13).

Take the helmet of salvation and the sword of the Spirit, which is the word of God. (6:17)

28

Armed for Battle (III)

EPHESIANS 6:17

Most of us are probably aware that John Bunyan, the author of *Pilgrim's Progress*, wrote another famous allegory entitled *The Holy War*. But most of are probably not aware of its full title: *The Holy War made by King Shaddai upon Diabolus for the Regaining of the Metropolis of the World or the Losing and Taking Again of the Town of Mansoul.*[1] It was typical for seventeenth-century titles to tell the potential reader exactly what the book was about, and Bunyan's title leaves us in no doubt.

He believed that God and Satan are locked in a titanic war in which the souls of humanity are at stake — that we are the principal players in a *real war*. There is nothing of the anti-supernatural, flat-sided theology of today's avant-garde theologians in Bunyan, but rather the full-blooded realities of Biblical theology — that "our struggle is not against flesh and blood."

Bunyan sought, by the powerful use of allegory, to instruct believers in the subtleties of this warfare, and to reinforce the reality that *every true believer is a warrior*. Bunyan knew from Biblical revelation and repeated personal persecution that life is one long battlefield in which there can be no retreat, no surrender, and no quarter if we are to be faithful to Jesus Christ. It is significant that most of Bunyan's work was done while in prison. The Christian soldier must never expect to find rest in this world. He will never hear orders to relax his guard or put his armor aside.

God's Word in Ephesians 6:10-18, the *locus classicus* on The Holy War, tells us there are seven items which must be worn if we are to wage successful warfare. They are best appreciated if we imagine putting them on with a view to impending hand-to-hand combat. Ancient warfare was singularly horrifying. The experienced soldier knew that soon he would be facing a phalanx of razor-sharp spears thrusting and jabbing at his vitals, followed by foot-to-foot, hand-to-hand, breath-to-breath hacking and stabbing and bloody wrestling set to the terrible music of the howls and moans of battle. Trembling, the soldier begins to dress.

First, he takes his thick leather war belt to which is attached his sword and cinches it tightly about him, drawing his sword close for battle and tucking in his tunic for mobility. Girt tight with God's Word, his whole person is bound in truth, so that his character and life exude truth. He has "truth in the inner parts" (Psalm 51:6). As a result he is "armed with . . . a good conscience" (1 Timothy 1:19, NEB). With truth holding his life together within and without, he can confidently face any spiritual enemy.

Second, he reaches, still trembling, for his metal breastplate, shaped to protect his chest and abdomen, his vital organs. A comrade helps cinch it in place. This is righteousness which first comes from God through faith in Christ — *imputed righteousness* (Philippians 3:9). As this righteousness is properly worn, it produces holy living. Thus outwardly sheathed and inwardly infused with righteousness, the warrior's heart is impervious to the attacks of the enemy. God's righteousness protects his life. He cannot die in battle. And more, his righteous life allows him fearlessly to face the foe.

Third, he bends over and methodically laces the straps of his nail-studded legionnaire boots to his ankles and shins. His feet will be secure as he stands his ground in battle. He will not slip and will not retreat. The boots are peace *with* God (Romans 5:1) and the peace *of* God (John 14:27) — *shalom*. Whereas there had been enmity with God, there is now peace, well-being, and a sense of his presence. This is *Christ's personal peace* — "my peace," says Christ (John 14:27). Thus grounded, the Christian warrior faces all onslaughts, never stepping back. Under the fiercest spiritual attacks, he simply regards his peace and, in the strength of his well-being in Christ, digs in.

Fourth, after tying the last boot thong, he picks up his great oblong shield, which he will use to catch the enemies' barrages of flaming arrows. The shield is faith in God and his Word. Through faith, the warrior binds himself close to the heart and purpose of God. And when those burning shafts of doubt come flying toward him, up comes the shield of faith, into which they harmlessly thud. "This is the victory that has overcome the world, even our faith" (1 John 5:4). Truth, righteousness, peace, faith — what awesome armament! What is to be added to this? We now consider the final two pieces, before the ultimate equipping of prayer, which we will see in our next study.

THE HELMET OF SALVATION (v. 17a)

Paul says in verse 17: "Take the helmet of salvation . . ." Roman military helmets were of two types: the *galea* (made of leather) or the *cassis* (metal).

The helmet had a band to protect the forehead and plates for the cheeks, and extended down in back to protect the neck. When the helmet was strapped in place, it exposed little besides the eyes, nose, and mouth.[2] The metal helmets, due to their weight, were lined with sponge or felt. Virtually the only weapons which could penetrate a metal helmet were hammers or axes.[3] No soldier's uniform was complete without a proper helmet.

Paul presents the helmet as a metaphor for salvation — "the helmet of salvation" — and in doing so borrows from the beautiful words of Isaiah's prophetic vision (59:17). In that Old Testament passage God donned the breastplate of righteousness, positioned on his brow the helmet of salvation, and then went on to defeat his enemies and save his people as the resplendent Divine Warrior. But Paul changes the image. In Isaiah, God's helmet of salvation is what he *does*; in Ephesians, it is what he *gives*.

"The helmet of salvation" is the assurance of salvation and the resulting confidence it brings. A helmet is a confidence-builder. Put a football helmet on an eight-year-old and he will typically swell with overweening confidence and turn into a sixty-pound kamikaze attack — at least until he's been knocked down a few times. Nevertheless, a good helmet is valid ground for confidence. Properly worn and used, it affords remarkable protection. This was especially true on the field of ancient war, where the sky was filled with arrows and javelins, and swords and axes were hacking and chopping. The helmet enabled a man to stand where otherwise he would have been long gone.

Now consider "the helmet of salvation" placed on our heads by the nail-pierced hands of Christ at our conversion. The helmet assures us that *whatever happens we will be saved and experience victory in Christ*. "For it is by grace you have been saved" (perfect passive participle — *you have been saved, and the results continue on*) (2:8, 9). The helmet infuses optimism about the course of the battle in this world. "Being confident of this, that he who began a good work in you will carry it on to completion until the day of Christ Jesus" (Philippians 1:6). The helmet also instills an irrepressible hope — "the hope of salvation as a helmet," as Paul terms it in 1 Thessalonians 5:8 — a bounding hope of future salvation and glory with Christ.

The transcending effect of all of this is an imperial confidence amidst the smoke of battle in this life. We have no doubt that we are victors, and we show this in battle. In July 1988 I watched a television videotape of the heavyweight championship "fight" between Mike Tyson and Michael Spinks, and I remember two things in particular: 1) Mike Tyson's calm, determined demeanor before the fight. His massive muscles augmented his lethal confidence. He knew he was going to win (and I think Michael Spinks knew it too — he looked terrified); 2) the horrifying punching power of Mike Tyson which put Michael Spinks down in ninety-one seconds!

On a vastly more elevated level, "the helmet of salvation" is to bring this confidence to our lives so we can fight "without being frightened in any way by those who oppose you. This is a sign to them that they will be destroyed, but that you will be saved — and that by God" (Philippians 1:28). I have personally witnessed this spiritual confidence in the lives of mature Christians over the years. The nobility of their lives is a lingering grace as it challenges me to fully don my helmet. Confidence in battle is a sign of our salvation and the enemies' destruction.

Are you embattled? If so, are you fearful and lacking confidence? Then reach for your helmet, pull it down hard over your ears, fasten the strap, and stand tall. It is *his* helmet, so nothing can fell you. You are victor!

THE SWORD OF THE SPIRIT (v. 17b)

Up to this point all the recommended equipment has been defensive, but now the apostle puts forth a weapon which is primarily offensive (though it aids in defense). It is the *machaira*, the Roman legionnaire's double-edged short sword, a most effective weapon for hand-to-hand fighting. The last part of verse 17 enjoins us to "Take . . . the sword of the Spirit, which is the word of God." The Holy Scriptures are originated by the breath of the Spirit of God (2 Timothy 3:16) and thus are "the sword of the Spirit." In reference to this text, Oliver Cromwell's soldiers, his "Ironsides," fought with a sword in one hand and a Bible in the other.[4] This was a pious gesture, but hardly what the Scripture suggests!

What we are to understand is that when we take up God's Word to fight spiritual warfare, we have the weapon *par excellence* for defensive and offensive battle. During the duel between Christ and Satan in the desert, recorded in Matthew 4, when Satan three times tempted Christ, Christ parried each of the three temptations with quotations from the Scriptures (Deuteronomy 8:3, 6:16, 6:13). Christ, the Divine Warrior, is the Master Swordsman. His final thrust sent the Devil scurrying, and Christ was left alone in the desolation as victor (Matthew 4:11).

May the lesson not be wasted: if Christ, the Divine Man, in battling Satan while here on earth did so with the sword of the Word, how much more do we frail men and women need to wield that same sword if we are to be victorious? In this respect, it is significant that in Deuteronomy 32:46, 47 (the very same book which Christ three times quoted in defeating Satan) Moses says of God's words, "Take to heart all the words I have solemnly declared to you this day, so that you may command your children to obey carefully all the words of this law. They are not just idle words for you — they are your life." We must heed the example of the Psalmist: "I have hidden your word in my heart that I might not sin against you" (Psalm 119:11). How does this work? God's Word reveals God's mind. God's mind cannot be subject to sin. Therefore if we fill our heart with his Word, sin and temptation cannot dominate us. Bunyan says:

> Then Apollyon, espying his opportunity, began to gather up close to Christian, and wrestling with him, gave him a dreadful fall; and with that Christian's sword flew out of his hand. Then said Apollyon, "I am sure of thee now," and with that he had almost pressed him to death, so that Christian began to despair of life. But as God would have it, while Apollyon was fetching of his last blow, thereby to make a full end of this good man, Christian nimbly reached out his hand for his sword, and caught it, saying, "Rejoice not against me, O mine enemy! When I fall I shall arise"; [Micah 7:8] and with that, gave him a deadly thrust, which made him give back, as one that has received his mortal wound. Christian, perceiving that, made at him again, saying, "Nay, in all these things we are more than conquerors through him that loved us." [Romans 8:37] And with that, Apollyon spread forth his Dragon's wings, and sped away, that Christian saw him no more.[5]

The Word of God draws the blood of Satan himself! "I write to you, young men, because you are strong, and the word of God lives in you, and you have overcome the evil one" (1 John 2:14b).

So the Word of God is an awesome defensive weapon, but it is especially effective in taking the offense. The writer of Hebrews tells us that the Word slices through the human spirit like a hot knife through butter — "The word of God is living and active. Sharper than any double-edged sword, it penetrates even to dividing soul and spirit, joints and marrow; it judges the thoughts and attitudes of the heart" (Hebrews 4:12).

> Then said Mr. Great-heart to Mr. Valiant-for-truth, "Thou has worthily behaved thyself. Let me see thy sword." So he showed it him. When he had taken it into his hand and looked thereon awhile, he said, "Ha! It is a right Jerusalem blade." Then said Mr. Valiant-for-truth, "It is so. Let a man have one of these blades, with a hand to wield it and skill to use it, and he may venture upon an angel with it. He need not fear its holding if he can but tell how to lay on. Its edges will never blunt; it will cut flesh, and bones, and soul, and spirit, and all."[6]

God's Word wounds terribly. It will cleave a man or woman from north to south with never a pause. It is all edge. It goes to the very center of human personality.

Somehow Christians manage to believe this and not believe it at the same time. For example, it is a mystery to me that many evangelical ministers say they believe in the inerrancy of the Scriptures, but when they preach there is no serious attempt to open them, but rather a chain of illustrations lengthened to support a life-situation story with an allegedly Scriptural moral. Sometimes I suspect this is from sloth, because preaching the Word takes work. But I also think it is often because they do not truly believe in the power of the Word. They really do not believe it is a sword. The irony is, if they truly are Christians, they were at one time laid open by the Word — given a terrible wound. And it was this wound which laid bare the condition of their hearts so they would believe and repent and be made alive. God's Word is a laser beam which kills to make alive. What a weapon!

Face the truth — we are at war, and our razor-sharp weapon is God's Word, and we are fools to keep it in the scabbard simply because our culture says it cannot cut. That is what the enemy wants us to believe, that it is "irrelevant" and "archaic" and "not understandable," so keep it in the sheath, where it is, of course, harmless.

How much better it is to obey God. Our text says we are to "Take . . . the sword of the Spirit, which is the word of God." This is, in fact, a command. How do we do this?

First, by *reading* it! It is amazing that a Christian can imagine that he or she can live a Christian life without regularly reading the Bible, for that is impossible! Our minds are such that we do not retain what we need to know. They need to be refreshed again and again. My experience is that though I have studied whole books of the Bible word for word, I soon forget so much. In fact, reading the same book a year later not only refreshes me to what I have forgotten, but rewards me with new truths!

Some who have been believers for years have never read the Bible through once. There are truths God has for us that we have not inconvenienced ourselves enough to discover. No wonder we are empty. What a difference reading the Word can make in the war.

Dr. Harry Ironside, a man of little formal education but great power, read the Bible fourteen times by the age of fourteen.[7] His mark is still on Chicago and indeed the entire world. Five pages a day is a good place to begin. Within a year you will have read the entire Bible. We begin to take up the sword by reading it.

Second, we take up the sword by *meditating* on it. This is the secret of God's great warriors. Hudson Taylor, the founder of China Inland Mission, conquered immense hardships by daily meditation on God's Word. Dr. and Mrs. Howard Taylor record this in his biography:

> It was not easy for Mr. Taylor, in his changeful life, to make time
> for prayer and Bible study, but he knew that it was vital. Well do

the writers remember traveling with him month after month in northern China, by cart and wheelbarrow with the poorest of inns at night. Often with only one large room for coolies and travelers alike, they would screen off a corner for their father and another for themselves, with curtains of some sort; and then, after sleep at last had brought a measure of quiet, they would hear a match struck and see the flicker of candlelight which told that Mr. Taylor, however weary, was poring over the little Bible in two volumes always at hand. From two to four a.m. was the time he usually gave to prayer; the time he could be most sure of being undisturbed to wait upon God.[8]

Meditating upon the Word brings victory, but too few pay the price. "Blessed is the man who does not walk in the counsel of the wicked or stand in the way of sinners or sit in the seat of mockers. But his delight is in the law of the Lord, and on his law he meditates day and night. He is like a tree planted by streams of water, which yields its fruit in season and whose leaf does not wither" (Psalm 1:1-3).

Third, the sword is grasped for effective battle through *memorization*. Mrs. Barnhouse said of her famous preacher husband:

Someone once asked him how long it had taken him to prepare a certain sermon. His answer was "Thirty years and thirty minutes!" He had immersed himself in the Bible from the time he was fifteen years old, when he memorized the Book of Philippians a verse a day until he knew the entire book by heart, then went on to other passages. He felt it was not enough to learn by rote — it had to be by heart; because you loved and believed it.[9]

Why not begin with a verse — perhaps a verse a week — fifty-two in one year!

Fourth, we become mighty with the sword by *studying* it. Paul told Timothy, "Do your best to present yourself to God as one approved, a workman who does not need to be ashamed and who correctly handles the word of truth" (2 Timothy 2:15).

When my family was visiting Cambridge, England, we saw a notice that a tour of Jesus College was to be conducted by one of the don's wives to benefit charity. Only two others responded, so we were virtually given a private glimpse of the college's treasures. In the sixteenth-century library we were shown a copy of the first Bible printed in America, Jesus College graduate John Eliot's translation of the Scriptures into Massachusetts Algonkian (1661-1663). We also saw the original edition of Thomas Malthus's landmark *Essay on Population* (1798), which gave rise to the

245

Malthusian theory. But best of all, to me, was the original edition of Thomas Cranmer's *Book of Common Prayer* (1549). Cranmer, one-time fellow of Jesus College, went on to become Archbishop of Canterbury (1553) and a martyr of the Church.

Cranmer was a man of the Word. This is his collect for the second Sunday of Advent:

> Blessed Lord, who has caused all holy Scriptures to be written for our learning: Grant that we may in such wise hear them read, mark, learn, and inwardly digest them, that by patience and comfort of thy holy Word we may embrace, and ever hold fast, the blessed hope of everlasting life, which thou hast given us in our Saviour Jesus Christ.[10]

Let us grip the sword firmly through diligent study!

We are at war, and there is a sense in which warfare is to be our occupation, avocation, and preoccupation. We must always be in armor. We must sleep in it and, though wearing it, still put it on daily: the belt of *truth* — the breastplate of *righteousness* — the gospel boots of *peace* — the shield of *faith*. Are they in place? Then we must reverently and joyfully take the helmet of *salvation* from our Savior's pierced hand. Slip it on. Straighten up. Stand tall with imperial confidence — "without being frightened in any way by those who oppose you . . . a sign to them that they will be destroyed, but that you will be saved" (Philippians 1:28).

Now we must reach out our hand and "Take . . . the sword of the Spirit, which is the *word of God*" and raise it to him in worshipful salute.

> Valiant-for-truth: "I fought till my sword did cleave to my hand. And then they were joined together as if a sword grew out of my arm, and when the blood run through my fingers, then I fought with most courage."

> Great-heart: "Thou hast done well; thou hast resisted unto blood, striving against sin. Thou shalt abide by us, come in and go out with us; for we are thy companions."[11]

Soldiers of Christ, arise and put your armor on!

And pray in the Spirit on all occasions with all kinds of prayers and requests. With this in mind, be alert and always keep on praying for all the saints. Pray also for me, that whenever I open my mouth, words may be given me so that I will fearlessly make known the mystery of the gospel, for which I am an ambassador in chains. Pray that I may declare it fearlessly, as I should. (6:18-20)

29

Armed for Battle (IV)

EPHESIANS 6:18-20

Recently I stood with my sons in the armory of Cambridge University's great Fitzwilliam Museum and wondered at the ancient helmets and shields and bucklers and swords. Though these armaments were dark with the patina of centuries, we easily imagined the day when shining swords rang from their scabbards and steel crashed against steel in awful combat. The reason for this, of course, was that every piece of armament suggested action — pounding, desperate, life-and-death action.

The same is true when we pause to reflect upon the formidable picture of the Christian warrior dressed in "the full armor of God" (6:10-17). Everything about it says *action*. As he readies himself he adjusts his war belt. His heart pounds under his breastplate so that it almost rings. He scuffs at the earth like a football player with his nail-studded boots, testing his traction. He repeatedly draws his great shield across his body in anticipation of the fiery barrages to come. Reflexively he reaches up and repositions his helmet. He gingerly tests the edge of his blade.

The enemy approaches. A thousand swords ring from their scabbards in dreadful symphony. The warriors stand motionless, breathing heavily. And then the Christian soldier does the most amazing thing — he falls to his knees in deep, profound prayer! To be sure, there will be action. He will rise, and his steel will flash, but all will be done in prayer, for prayer is primary.[1]

This is the precise form of the Ephesian picture, for after the Christian warrior's armament is in place we read: "And pray in the Spirit on all occasions with all kinds of prayers and requests. With this in mind, be alert and always keep on praying for all the saints" (v. 18). Those who would engage in spiritual warfare, regardless of how well they wear *truth* and *righteousness* and *faith* and *salvation*, regardless of how well they are grounded in *peace*, regardless of how well they wield the *Word*, must make *prayer* the first thing. The Christian soldier fights on his knees! As Edward Payson said: "Prayer is the first thing, the second thing, the third thing necessary to minister. Pray, therefore, my dear brother, pray, pray, pray."[2] This is what the apostle wanted us to see by making prayer the seventh item of armament, for seven is the Biblical number for perfection and completion.

John Bunyan called this weapon "All-Prayer," thus giving it a memorable designation.[3] Prayer is the supreme weapon to use "against the rulers, against the authorities, against the powers of this dark world and against the spiritual forces of evil in the heavenly realms" (v. 12). Verse 18 lists five aspects of "All-Prayer" which are necessary to fully don this awesome armament.

SPIRIT-DIRECTED PRAYER

The first element of *"All-Prayer"* is that it is *Spirit-directed*. "And pray in the Spirit . . ." begins Paul. How does prayer in the Spirit take place? The principal text which answers this is Romans 8:26, 27 where we are told, "the Spirit helps us in our weakness. We do not know what we ought to pray, but the Spirit himself intercedes for us with groans that words cannot express. And he who searches our hearts knows the mind of the Spirit, because the Spirit intercedes for the saints in accordance with God's will." So we see that the Holy Spirit prays for us and also joins us in our praying, infusing his prayer into ours so that we "pray in the Spirit." Jude 20 refers to this same phenomenon: "But you, dear friends, build yourselves up in your most holy faith and pray in the Holy Spirit."

When we pray in the Spirit, two supernatural things happen to our prayers. First, the Holy Spirit tells us what we ought to pray for. Apart from the Holy Spirit's assistance, our prayers are limited to our own reason and intuition, but with the Holy Spirit's help they move to a higher level. As we seek his help he will speak to us through his Word, which conveys his will regarding every matter of principle. Further, he will settle certain things in our hearts to pray for with the conviction that they are God's will — so that we are praying in faith.

Oswald Sanders, a former director of Overseas Missionary Fellowship (formerly China Inland Mission), has said in this regard:

> The very fact that God lays a burden of prayer on our hearts and keeps us praying is prima facie evidence that He purposes to grant the answer. When asked if he really believed that two men for whose salvation he had prayed for over fifty years would be con-

verted, George Müller of Bristol replied, "Do you think God would have kept me praying all these years if He did not intend to save them?" Both men were converted, one shortly before, the other after Müller's death.[4]

Such confident direction in one's prayer life is not unusual. I had a similar conviction regarding my brother, who came to Christ after I had been praying for him over thirty years! When God's people "pray in the Spirit," they receive similar direction and conviction not only about people, but about events and projects and even whole nations.

The second thing that praying in the Spirit provides is the energy of the Holy Spirit for prayer, energizing tired, even infirm bodies, elevating the depressed to pray with power and conviction for God's work.

How the Church of Christ needs to learn to pray in the Spirit! To help myself do this, I have written "Pray in the Spirit" at the top of my prayer list as a constant reminder to wait on the Lord in silence, asking him to give me prayers to pray. Of course, I have a list of long-standing regular petitions which I pray, but I also want to be open to the Spirit, so that as he wishes he will invade my openness with his direction and energy. "Prayer," says Bunyan, "is a sincere, sensible, affectionate pouring out of the heart or soul to God, through Christ, in the strength and assistance of the Holy Spirit, for such things as God has promised, or according to the Word of God, for the good of the church, with submission in faith to the will of God."[5] Let us learn to pray in the Spirit!

CONTINUAL PRAYER

The second ingredient in *"All-Prayer"* is that it is *continual* — "on all occasions." This was the experience of the Apostolic Church. Acts 1:14 says, "They all joined together constantly in prayer, along with the women and Mary the mother of Jesus, and his brothers" (cf. 2:42). Paul told the Thessalonians to "pray continually" (1 Thessalonians 5:17). Is this possible, we ask? Yes and no. It is impossible to carry on a running verbal dialogue while we do our business, but prayer is not so much the articulation of words as the posture of the heart.

Thomas Kelley says in his *Testament of Devotion*:

> There is a way of ordering our mental life on more than one level at once. On one level we can be thinking, discussing, seeing, calculating, meeting all the demands of external affairs. But deep within, behind the scenes, at a profounder level, we may also be in prayer and adoration, song and worship, and a gentle receptiveness to divine breathings.[6]

251

The irrepressible medieval monk Brother Lawrence records his experience of this in the classic *The Practice of the Presence of God*: "The time of business does not differ with me from the time of prayer; and in the noise and clatter of my kitchen, while several persons are at the same time calling for different things, I possess God in as great tranquillity as if I were on my knees."[7]

This was also John Wesley's experience, who wrote of it in the third person:

> [H]is heart is ever lifted up to God, at all times and in all places. In this he is never hindered, much less interrupted, by any person or thing. In retirement or company, in leisure, business, or conversation, his heart is ever with the Lord. Whether he lie down or rise up, God is in all his thoughts; he walks with God continually, having the loving eye of his mind still fixed upon Him, and everywhere "seeing him that is invisible."[8]

Thus we see that a life of continual prayer is possible and that some live it out. Paul challenges us to see that this life is not meant just for some but for all of us. This is God's will for every Christian, no exceptions. I can do it, you can do it — business people, housewives, students, young mothers — all can do it. We can have a secret dialogue with God, we can always be looking up even when mowing the lawn or washing the dishes.

VARIED PRAYER

The third aspect of the *"All-Prayer"* way of life is that it is *varied* — "with all kinds of prayers and requests." This grows out of what we have just seen about continual prayer, because if we pray continually, the various situations we encounter will demand variety in prayer. Think of the variety appropriate to life's unfolding situations: *confession — thanksgiving — intercession — adoration — meditation — humility before God — song*. We are to be skilled in all these types of prayer — and constantly exercising them.

Floyd Pierson, a retired Africa Inland Mission worker, was a man who literally prayed "on all occasions with all kinds of prayers and requests." So habitual was this that in his seventies, when he went to take a driver's test, he said to the examiner, "I always pray before I drive — Let's bow our heads together." The official likely wondered what kind of ride he was in for! I can see him checking his seat belt and settling his hand on the door handle. Pierson passed! But apart from the humor, there is something quite beautiful here — the unaffected witness of a vibrant inner spiritual reality which bubbles up "with all kinds of prayers and requests."

PERSISTENT PRAYER

The fourth aspect of a life of *"All-Prayer"* is *persistence in prayer* — "With this in mind, be alert and always keep on praying."

One February my wife and I vacationed with my brother and his wife in Northern Maine. I had been praying for him for over thirty years, since we were boys, that he would come to know Christ and be born again. We journeyed to our snowbound vacation with great expectations, which were not to be disappointed. The second night together he broached the subject, saying in essence, "Let's talk about my soul," and all of us talked long into the night about our journeys to Christ. On the following morning I said I would like to talk some more alone. He replied that was just what he was going to suggest. So in the leather-chaired ambience of an old 1920s, wainscot-paneled library we reviewed the essentials of the faith, then got on our knees together as he repented, asking Christ into his life. We stood and hugged and walked to the other end of the house where he announced, "If I die tonight, I'll beat you all there," then embraced his lovely wife for several minutes while we stood around and wiped our tears.

I tell this story to emphasize that there is a mysterious efficacy to persistent prayer. Put another way, the Lord delights to honor perseverance in prayer. This is not to suggest that God regards prayer as a meritorious work — when there are enough prayers, he answers. Rather, he sovereignly chooses to encourage persistence in prayer and to answer it to his everlasting glory.

In one of his prayer parables in the Gospel of Luke, the Lord dramatized what he wants from all believers:

> "In a certain town there was a judge who neither feared God nor cared about men. And there was a widow in that town who kept coming to him with the plea, 'Grant me justice against my adversary.' For some time he refused. But finally he said to himself, 'Even though I don't fear God or care about men, yet because this widow keeps bothering me, I will see that she gets justice, so that she won't eventually wear me out with her coming!'" (Luke 18:2-5)

The cultivation of persistence was a recurring motif in Jesus' teaching on prayer. At the end of the Sermon on the Mount he enjoined his followers to the tenacious pursuit of spiritual things: "Ask and it will be given to you; seek and you will find; knock and the door will be opened to you" (Matthew 7:7). The Lord's language is unusually compelling because the three verbs (*ask*, *seek*, and *knock*) indicate an ascending intensity. *"Ask"* implies requesting assistance for a conscious need. We realize our lack and thus ask for help. The word also suggests humility in asking, for it is commonly used of one asking a superior. The next step, "*seek*," involves asking, but adds action. The idea is not just to express our need, but to get up and look around for help. It involves effort. The final step, "*knock*," includes asking plus persevering — like someone who keeps pounding on a closed door! The stacking of these words is extremely forceful, and the fact that they are present imperatives gives them even more punch. The text actually reads: "Keep on asking, and it shall be given to you; keep on seeking, and you shall find; keep on knocking, and it shall be opened to you." The picture is of a man who will not stop knocking. This tenacity is exactly what Paul has in mind here in our passage on spiritual warfare as he calls us to "be alert and always keep on praying."

Do we pray this way for spiritual work? Are there individuals or ministries or groups for which we persist in prayer? There ought to be. We are in an invisible war, and those who persist in prayer prevail.

INTERCESSORY PRAYER

The fifth and final aspect of *"All-Prayer"* is *intercessory prayer* — "for all the saints."

> Some years ago the record of a wonderful work of grace in connection with one of the stations of the China Inland Mission attracted a good deal of attention. Both the number and spiritual character of the converts had been far greater than at other stations where the consecration of the missionaries had been just as great. This rich harvest of souls remained a mystery until Hudson Taylor, on a visit to England, discovered the secret. At the close of one of his addresses a gentleman came forward to make his acquaintance. In the conversation which followed, Mr. Taylor was surprised at the accurate knowledge the man possessed concerning this China Inland Mission station. "But how is it," Mr. Taylor asked, "that you are so conversant with the conditions of that work?" "Oh!" he replied, "the missionary there and I are old college mates; for years we have regularly corresponded; he has sent me names of enquirers and converts, and these I have daily taken to God in prayer." At last the secret was found — a praying man, praying definitely, praying daily.[9]

There are many worthy things to pray for, but *believers*/"saints" are to have a large part of our prayers. Sure, we are to pray for those without Christ, but high on our list should be fellow Christians, "all the saints" — even great saints like Paul himself.

Imagine with me for a moment the aged Apostle Paul — with gray flowing beard and a thinning gray mane falling askew around his weathered face. His sinewy old body bears the marks of war. The bow of his legs has increased because of his repeated marches across the Roman Empire. Scar tissue covers his torso as he has five times received thirty-nine stripes (some 195 lashes). He is bent by the gravity not only of time but of the cosmic burdens of apostleship — "Who is weak, and I do not feel weak? Who is led into sin, and I do not inwardly burn?" (2 Corinthians 11:29).

Can you see him? Now imagine him in his well-worn armor. He has worn his war belt so long that it is sweat through and salt-stained and comfortable like an old horse's bridle, and it holds everything perfectly in place. The "*belt of truth*," God's truth, has girt him tight for years, so that it has permeated his life and reigns within. He is armed with the clear eyes of a clean conscience. He can face anything. His torso is sheathed with a battle-tarnished breastplate. It is crisscrossed with great lateral grooves from slicing sword blows and dented from enemy artillery. The "*breastplate of righteousness*" has preserved his vitals intact. His holy life has rendered his heart impervious to the spiritual assaults of Satan. His gnarled legs are comfortable in his ancient war boots. He has stood his ground on several continents. The boots are the "*gospel of peace*," the peace *with* God that comes through faith in him, and the resultant peace *of* God — the sense of well-being and wholeness — *shalom*. He stands in peace, and being rooted in peace he cannot be moved.

Paul's great shield terrifies the eyes, for the broken shafts and the many charred holes reveal him to be the victor of many fierce battles. The "*shield of faith*," held up as he has repeatedly believed God's Word, has caught and extinguished every fiery dart of doubt and sensuality and materialism. None has as much as touched him. On his old gray head he wears a helmet which has seen better days. Great dents mar its symmetry, reminders of furtive blows dealt him by the enemy. Because the "*helmet of salvation*," the confidence of knowing that he is saved and will be saved, has allowed him to stand tall against the most vicious assaults, his imperial confidence gives him a regal bearing. And then there is his sword. He was equal to a hundred when his sword flashed. The "*sword of the Spirit*, which is the word of God*," the ultimate offensive weapon, cut through everything — armor, flesh, glistening bone, and running marrow — even the soul.

What an awesome figure the apostle was. He had stood before Felix and Agrippa, the legates and officials of Rome — and had not given an inch. He was the consummate warrior. He could do it himself! But could he? Listen to the warrior's plea: "*Pray* also for me, that whenever I open my mouth, words may be given me so that I will fearlessly make known the mystery of the gospel, for which I am an ambassador in chains. Pray that I may declare it fearlessly, as I should" (6:19, 20). "I cannot do it without your prayers!" says Paul. "I fear that I may lose courage and fail under the stress. Pray that I will have the courage to declare the gospel fearlessly. I need your prayers!"

Was Paul putting them on? Was this a self-conscious attempt at humility? We know that it was not. "Prayer is the first thing, the second thing, the third thing. Pray, therefore, my dear brother, pray, pray, pray." Paul challenges us to "always keep on praying for all the saints" (v. 18).

In September 1978 John Alexander, then president of Inter-Varsity Christian Fellowship, sent this communication to his staff:

> *Saturday Night.* While a leader must be careful about talking about his prayer life lest he appear to be "lengthening his tassels and broadening his phylacteries" (i.e., parading spirituality), there is one aspect I'd like to mention in hopes some of you will join in it.
>
> Every Saturday night I pray through a list of pastors — thanking God for them, for their ministry, for their personal friendship. I then intercede that, on this eve of another Lord's Day, the Spirit of Christ will give them a good night's rest and anoint them with wisdom, power, and joy for the morrow. On Sunday morning I go through the list again, interceding as they step to their pulpits, that their proclamation of the whole counsel of God will be simple, clear, tender where it should be gentle, bold where it should be courageous — that it will be straight and true to the minds and hearts of listeners who say, "Sir, we would see Jesus." I pray that the Lord will bind Satan from attacking pastor and laymen (especially through loveless criticism) and that Christ will touch the congregation to hear, see, understand and obey God's proclaimed truth. I invite you to join me in this Saturday night and Sunday morning discipline of intercession. Ask God to indicate those pastors He wants on your list.
>
> I hope that IVCF staff will train our chapter leaders in this ministry of prayer so that as students today and church leaders tomorrow they'll help lay a deepening prayer foundation beneath the shepherds of our nation's churches. The goal is an undergirding of prayer for pastors Sunday mornings.
>
> Any volunteers?
>
> John W. Alexander

On May 31, 1985, I received this letter from John Alexander:

Dear Kent:
Just a note to say thanks for the worship service you provided last Sunday. . . . Enjoyed meeting both you and

Barbara. . . . Enclosed is a page from Inter-Varsity InterCom explaining what I had in mind when I told you I pray for you every Saturday night. There are several pastors on my list for such a prayer session; the automatic ones are those who minister to my children each Sunday morning. Since _____ has no parents, I include you as her pastor as one of the "automatics" on my list. May the Lord continue to keep His good hand upon you.

    Cordially in Christ,

    John

John Alexander lives out the Scriptural call to "keep on praying for all the saints." Do we intercede for others? Do we have a prayer list for our brothers and sisters in Christ, and do we use it?

We are in a cosmic spiritual battle: "For our struggle is not against flesh and blood, but against the rulers, against the authorities, against the powers of this dark world and against the spiritual forces of evil in the heavenly realms" (v. 12). The spiritual weapons of our warfare are: *truth, righteousness, peace, faith, confidence, the Word, and prayer* — prayer which is: *Spirit-directed* ("pray in the Spirit"); *continual* ("on all occasions"); *varied* ("with all kinds of prayers and requests"); *persistent* ("be alert and always keep on praying"); *intercessory* ("for all the saints") (v. 18).

We close with these fitting words from Dr. John Piper's book *Desiring God*:

Unless I'm badly mistaken, one of the main reasons so many of God's children don't have a significant life of prayer is not so much that we don't want to, but that we don't plan to. If you want to take a four-week vacation, you don't just get up one summer morning and say, "Hey, let's go today!" You won't have anything ready. You won't know where to go. Nothing has been planned.

But that is how many of us treat prayer. We get up day after day and realize that significant times of prayer should be part of our life, but nothing's ever ready. We don't know where to go. Nothing has been planned. No time. No place. No procedure. And we all know that the opposite of planning is not a wonderful flow of deep, spontaneous experiences in prayer. The opposite of planning is the rut. If you don't plan a vacation you will probably stay home and watch TV! The natural unplanned flow of spiritual life sinks to the lowest ebb of vitality. There is a race to be run and a fight to be fought. If you want renewal in your life of prayer you must plan to see it.

Therefore, my simple exhortation is this: Let us take time this very day to rethink our priorities and how prayer fits in. Make some new resolve. Try some new venture with God. Set a time. Set a place. Choose a portion of Scripture to guide you. Don't be tyrannized by the press of busy days. We all need mid-course corrections. Make this a day of turning to prayer — for the glory of God and for the fullness of your joy.[10]

Tychicus, the dear brother and faithful servant in the Lord, will tell you everything, so that you also may know how I am and what I am doing. I am sending him to you for this very purpose, that you may know how we are, and that he may encourage you. Peace to the brothers, and love with faith from God the Father and the Lord Jesus Christ. Grace to all who love our Lord Jesus Christ with an undying love. (6:21-24)

30

Glad Benedictions

EPHESIANS 6:21-24

From the time we were young teenagers in Southern California, Dave MacDonald and I were inseparable buddies. We did everything together. As, for example, on the May day that we decided to "do" Southern California. We began the day at 4:30 A.M. when we eased his old 1949 Plymouth (pinstriped *El Chabasco, The Whirlwind*) from the driveway and headed for Laguna Beach, where we bodysurfed and shivered ourselves dry in the dawn. Then we climbed into the old Plymouth and drove back across the Los Angeles basin and over the Cajon Pass to the high desert where we found a dry lake bed and spun donuts with *El Chabasco*. Tiring of that, we broke out our rifles and shot up some tin cans. Next we drove up the backside of the San Bernardino Mountains and tossed snowballs in Big Bear, snacked, and headed back to the ocean (Ocean Boulevard in Long Beach to be exact, where, with a theatre full of sailors, we watched *War of the Worlds*). Some day!

When Dave and I graduated from high school, we arranged to be college roommates and continued to wear the wheels off our cars with midnight visits to Greenblatt's Delicatessen in Hollywood, various Christian events on the West Coast, and always the beach. My first date with Barbara was a double date with Dave and his wife-to-be, Judy. He was best man at my wedding, and I at his. Years later when we both had young families we all rendezvoused in Colorado, where one evening I recall David saying to me, "If anything happens to you, Judy and I will take care of Barbara and the kids."

The shared experiences of life over a long period of time have made David and me truly *soul brothers*. There is unshakable mutual esteem and love between us that has not diminished one whit though we rarely see each other today.

I have related this personal account in order to warm us to the subject of the profound friendship of Paul and Tychicus and their apostolic band. For the truth is, though Dave and I are close because of what we experienced as friends, we have hardly anything to match the mutual experience of Paul and Tychicus and company in their epic lives. What soul brothers Paul and Tychicus were!

The Scriptures briefly mention Tychicus five times.[1] Though the mentions are brief, we can draw some revealing conclusions about his experiences and place in life. Tychicus first appears at the end of Paul's missionary work in Ephesus, and since he was a native of the Province of Asia (Acts 20:4), of which Ephesus was the major city, we surmise that he was almost surely a convert of Paul's long ministry in Ephesus. Thus, he likely witnessed the great Ephesian silversmiths' riot against Paul, which prompted the apostle to leave Ephesus for Macedonia (Acts 19:35 — 20:1), and as an ardent supporter of Paul shared his danger and bravery.

A short time later, when Paul decided to return to Jerusalem where he would ultimately be arrested, Tychicus was one of the seven who accompanied him as traveling companions (Acts 20:4). Tychicus was probably the one who actually carried the offering for the poor in Jerusalem. When Paul was arrested, Tychicus, along with Dr. Luke and others, stayed with Paul through his epic journey to Rome, which included his arrest and imprisonment in Caesarea, his dramatic appearances before kings and governors, his miserable voyage and shipwreck en route to Rome, and his residence (under house arrest) in Rome awaiting trial.

Tychicus shared an immense mutuality of experience and of soul with Paul. When Paul said, "I have been constantly on the move. I have been in danger from rivers, in danger from bandits, in danger from my own countrymen, in danger from Gentiles; in danger in the city, in danger in the country, in danger at sea; and in danger from false brothers. I have labored and toiled and have often gone without sleep; I have known hunger and thirst and have often gone without food; I have been cold and naked" (2 Corinthians 11:26, 27). Paul was saying it for Tychicus too!

With this in mind, we come to the writing of the Letter to the Ephesians, this prison epistle which we surmise Tychicus was taking down in dictation from Paul. Paul has come to the end of the letter, having laid out the mystery of the Church (the new order, the "third race," the new humanity), having given massive *theological* foundations in chapters 1 — 3 and matching *practical* implications in chapters 4 — 6. Now, content with his writing, Paul takes the stylus from Tychicus, as was his habit at the end of such letters,[2] and begins his glad *benedictions* — first regarding Tychicus (vv. 21, 22) which we will briefly consider, and then over his brothers and sisters in Ephesus (vv. 23, 24).

SINGULAR BENEDICTIONS (vv. 21, 22)

Smiling with satisfaction, Paul glances at Tychicus and writes, "Tychicus, the dear brother and faithful servant in the Lord, will tell you everything, so that you also may know how I am and what I am doing. I am sending him to you for this very purpose, that you may know how we are, and that he may encourage you" (vv. 21, 22). These opening words beautifully frame Tychicus for the rest of history — "Tychicus, the dear [literally beloved] brother and faithful servant in the Lord." Paul calls him *the beloved brother* because he was greatly loved by Paul and by the church in Rome. This alone is no small thing. Many kings and presidents and senators never experience this in their entire life. It is a sublime benediction from a soul brother. The other benediction, "faithful servant in the Lord," celebrates Tychicus' character, for he was faithful *par excellence.*

As such, Paul charged Tychicus with two duties. First, to deliver this letter, along with letters to the Colossians (Colossians 4:7, 8), Philemon, and the mysterious lost letter to the Laodiceans (Colossians 4:16). His second responsibility was simply to tell the churches in Asia about Paul's situation and how he was doing — as only a soul brother with a servant's heart could do. Later references in the Pastoral Epistles confirm that Tychicus maintained this character and function throughout Paul's life and ministry (Titus 3:12; 2 Timothy 4:11, 12).

Tychicus was not a "somebody" in human terms. He left no writing that survives. He did no feats which Dr. Luke thought worthy of preserving in the Book of Acts. But where would Paul have been without him?

> *For the loss of a nail, lose a horseshoe;*
> *for the loss of a horseshoe, lose a horse;*
> *for the loss of a horse, lose a soldier;*
> *for the loss of a soldier, lose a battle;*
> *for the loss of a battle, lose a kingdom.*

Low-profile Tychicus was someone to celebrate with glad benedictions like "dear brother . . . faithful servant." Every time this letter is read there is implicit thanksgiving for his faithfulness to the Church universal.

GLAD BENEDICTIONS (vv. 23, 24)

Now we turn to Paul's glad benedictions, his final four wishes for the Church, which indeed are wishes for us as well. As we consider them, we must reflect on this: there is nothing more revealing about us than what we wish for those we love most.[3] What do we wish for our children or for our long-time friends? If what we are wishing for can only be categorized under headings like *education, profession,* or *possessions,* that is what we value most — and we are a long way from Paul's mind, perhaps even an eternity away. Paul's glad wishes for us center around four words given in an unusual order: *peace, love, faith,* and *grace.* "Peace to the brothers, and love with faith from God the Father and the Lord Jesus Christ. Grace to all who love our Lord Jesus Christ with an undying love" (vv. 23, 24). As we ponder these glad benedictions, we must keep before us the fact that they are the greatest blessings we could wish for, and we must learn to wish them for ourselves and for all we love.

First, there is *peace* — "Peace to the brothers."

Some time ago now a retired couple, alarmed by the threat of nuclear war, began a serious study of all the inhabited places on the globe. Their purpose was to determine where in the world would be the place to be least likely affected by nuclear war — a place of ultimate security. They studied and traveled and traveled and studied. Finally they found The Place. And at Christmas they sent a card from their new home to their friends in the States. It was the Falkland Islands — the soon-to-be battleground between Britain and Argentina!4 What a way to learn the unchangeable truth that there is no place on earth, or indeed in the universe, that will ensure us mortals peace. People will look from now to the Second Coming for inner and outer peace apart from Christ, but will never find it. What does this glad wish, "Peace to the brothers," mean?

As we have seen in our study of the armor of God and "the gospel of peace" (6:15), this is initially *reconciliation with God.* Through believing faith we find peace *with* God through Jesus Christ (Romans 5:1). Along with this, we receive the peace *of* God — "my peace I give you," says Jesus (John 14:27). It is his personal peace which he has lived out here on earth and perpetuated in Heaven. This is not just the absence of conflict, but well-being, wholeness — what the Scriptures call *shalom.* A major distinctive of this is a pervasive sense of his presence, as is so beautifully seen in the Aaronic benediction:

> "'The Lord bless you and keep you;
>   the Lord make his face shine upon you
>   and be gracious to you;
> the Lord turn his face toward you
>   and give you peace.'"
> (Numbers 6:24-26)

The promise and experience of this is an anchor to one's heart. "'For I know the plans that I have for you,' declares the Lord, 'plans for welfare

[literally *shalom*] and not for calamity to give you a future and a hope'"
(Jeremiah 29:11, NASB).

But having this in place, Paul's glad benediction is for us to have the
fruit of this peace, i.e., *reconciliation with one another* — "Peace to the
brothers." Earlier in 2:14 he says, "For he himself is our peace," and then in
2:15 he says that Christ miraculously effected peace between bitter enemies
(Jews and Gentiles) by creating in himself "one new man out of the two,
thus making peace." Thus he gives us peace with our brothers and sisters.

This is so sweet when experienced, for it comes when the Holy Spirit
has equally free course in each other's lives. "What is the best thing I could
wish?" says Paul, and the answer comes: "Peace to the brothers." May I
suggest that we stop right now and pray this for ourselves and for the first
person God brings to mind?

The second element of the benediction is *love* — "Peace to all the
brothers and love . . ." This has certainly been a big word in Ephesians, for
it is used some fourteen times, seven of which have the emphasis, as here,
of love among the brothers and sisters in the Church.

The March 1978 *Reader's Digest* carried this little vignette from a
Sunday school teacher:

> For St. Patrick's Day, I asked the five-year-olds in my Sunday
> School class to bring "something green that you love." The next
> Sunday they brought the usual green hats, green sweaters and green
> books. But one boy entered with an especially big grin. Behind
> him, wearing a green dress, came his four-year-old sister.[5]

This is literally a *primary lesson* on the mutual esteem and love that
ought to permeate the adult body of Christ. "Here is someone red that I love
. . . and yellow . . . and black . . . and white."

And here the Ephesian church shone, for they loved all the brothers
and sisters. "For this reason," wrote Paul in 1:15, "ever since I heard about
your faith in the Lord Jesus and your love for all the saints, I have not
stopped giving thanks for you, remembering you in my prayers." It is easy
to love *some* of the saints, but *all* the saints — that is another matter. But
the Ephesians did so! Nevertheless, the wise apostle did not take this for
granted. Hence his glad benediction and charge.

Theologically everything is in place for us to love the brothers. Peace
has been made in Christ. "God has poured out his love into our hearts by
the Holy Spirit" (Romans 5:5). We now have the ability to love "because he
first loved us" (1 John 4:19). All that remains is for us to do it. As with so
many things which rest on deep spiritual realities, it comes down practically
to the human will. In his sister epistle to the Colossians Paul says, "[P]ut on

love" (3:14). Is it hypocritical to act lovingly toward someone we don't "like"? No! It is never hypocrisy to bend our wills to the Scriptural mandate. And the glorious fact is that as we continue to put on love, we will begin to wear it unconsciously. Is there someone we need to will to love now? Who does the Spirit bring to mind? Let us covenant to love this person — in fact, all the saints.

The third word is *faith* — ". . . love with faith." This word appears seven other times in our small letter.[6] Paul has in mind both saving faith and practical day-to-day faith. There is so much talk about faith that for many it has become like an old dime in our pocket. It circulates from hand-to-hand and pocket-to-pocket and purse-to-purse so much that the lettering has worn off. Many other people who use the word "faith" have only a dim idea what it means.

Real faith has two elements: *belief* and *trust*. To have true faith we must believe what is revealed about God in the Scriptures and what is said about us. Faith begins with belief, but belief alone is not faith. There must, along with belief, be trust — trusting God on the basis of what we believe. Paul wants the Ephesians to "button up intellectually" in relation to the deep truths he has given them, and then he wants them to trust those truths in the living out of life.

What a glad benediction is trust! "Ease back and rest on what you believe. Put your whole weight on it" — that's what Paul is saying. So many go through the Christian life the way some people ride in airplanes. Intellectually they believe the plane will get them to their location, but in flying they never quite put their full weight down. Their belief is not matched by trust. Trust is one of the most beautiful qualities we could wish for anyone. Let us pray now for belief plus trust.

Lastly, Paul wishes *grace* upon the Church — "Grace to all who love our Lord Jesus Christ with an undying love" (v. 24). "Grace" is the very first word of the formal greeting of the letter, and here it is the final thought of the closing — its twelfth occurrence in the letter.[7]

The story is told of a man who appeared at Heaven's gate and was met there by an angel who told him, "It will take 1,000 points to get in. Tell me about yourself so that I will know how many points to give you." The man smiled and said, "Well, I've been going to church almost every Sunday all my life." "Excellent," the angel said. "That will give you three points. What else?" The man was shocked. "Only three points?" he gasped. "Well, I was a Sunday school superintendent for a while, and I tithed, and I tried to be a good neighbor." "Very good," the angel said. "That will give you ten points." The man gasped again. "At this rate," he said, "I'll never get in except by the grace of God!"

Grace is God's free gift. It cannot be earned or deserved. The illustration is excellent except that all the man's works would not earn even ten points, but rather zero! The condition of saving grace is faith — "For it is by grace you have been saved, through faith — and this not from yourselves, it is the gift of God — not by works, so that no one can boast" (2:8, 9). It is totally of God — even the faith.

But after receiving saving faith there is a condition to maintaining its undisturbed flow, and that is to "love our Lord Jesus Christ with an undying love." A mighty, surging, growing love for the Savior keeps wide the floodgates of his grace and spiritual riches.

Loving him is of foremost importance. "One of them [the Pharisees], an expert in the law, tested him with this question: 'Teacher, which is the greatest commandment in the Law?' Jesus replied: '"Love the Lord your God with all your heart and with all your soul and with all your mind." This is the first and greatest commandment'" (Matthew 22:35-38). We have it from the lips of Jesus himself — there is nothing of greater importance than loving him.

For those who love him, life becomes a torrent of grace. As John says, "For of His fulness we have all received, and grace upon grace" (John 1:16, NASB) — literally, "grace instead of grace." The idea is, "grace following grace" — "grace heaped on grace."

The quintessential question for each one of us is, do we love Christ? Do we delight in him? Is he dear to us? Is our love alive and growing? Do we love him more than when we first came to him? Do we love him more than we did a year ago? Is the river of grace growing deeper and wider with the passage of time?

The aged Apostle Paul, having laid out the magisterial doctrines of the Church and their wondrous effects, lovingly wishes us the very best he could wish:

Peace — "Peace to the brothers" — reconciliation with God and with our brothers and sisters.

Love — "Peace to the brothers and love" — love for all the saints, a love rich and comfortable with our brothers and sisters.

Faith — "love with faith" — belief and trust, resting all upon him.

Grace — "Grace to all who love our Lord Jesus Christ with an undying love" — grace upon grace flowing in the conduit of our love.

These are glad benedictions indeed!

Soli Deo gloria!

Notes

CHAPTER ONE: CELEBRATION OF BLESSING

1. John A. Mackay, *God's Order* (New York: Macmillan, 1953), p. 14.
2. *Ibid.*, p. 12.
3. F. F. Bruce, *The Epistles to the Colossians, to Philemon, and to the Ephesians* (Grand Rapids, MI: Eerdmans, 1984), p. 229.
4. Mackay, p. 14, who quotes J. Scott Lidgett, *God in Christ Jesus: A Study of Paul's Epistle to the Ephesians*, p. 2.
5. Bruce, p. 230, quoting S. T. Coleridge, *Table Talk*, May 25, 1830; see H. N. Coleridge (ed.), *Specimens of the Table Talk of the Late Samuel Taylor Coleridge* (London, 1835), p. 88.
6. Mackay, p. 11.
7. *Ibid.*, p. 17.
8. *Ibid.*, pp. 7, 8.
9. Bruce M. Metzger, *A Textual Commentary on the Greek New Testament* (New York: United Bible Societies, 1975), p. 601.
10. Ruth Paxson, *The Wealth, Walk and Warfare of the Christian* (Old Tappan, NJ: Revell, 1939), pp. 9, 10.
11. Watchman Nee, *Sit Walk Stand* (London: Witness and Testimony, 1958), pp. x, xi.
12. Marcus Barth, *Ephesians, Introduction, Translation, and Commentary on Chapters 1 — 3* (New York: Doubleday, 1974), p. 66.
13. John Calvin, *The Epistles of Paul and the Apostles to the Galatians, Ephesians, Philippians and Colossians*, trans. T. H. L. Parker (Grand Rapids, MI: Eerdmans, 1974), p. 123.
14. F. F. Bruce, *The Epistle to the Ephesians* (London: Pickering and Inglis, 1973), p. 26.
15. J. Armitage Robinson, *St. Paul's Epistle to the Ephesians* (London: Macmillan, 1904), p. 21.
16. C. H. Spurgeon, *The Metropolitan Tabernacle Pulpit*, Sermon No. 1,738, "Glory Be Unto the Father," Volume 29 (Pasadena, TX: Pilgrim Publications, 1973), p. 486.
17. *Ibid.*, p. 487.
18. William MacDonald, *Ephesians the Mystery of the Church* (Wheaton, IL: Harold Shaw, 1968), p. 17 attributes this quotation to Lewis Sperry Chafer.
19. The Greek words for "Holy Spirit" mean that it is the operation of the Holy Spirit which is in view.
20. Mackay, pp. 9, 10.

CHAPTER TWO: CELEBRATION OF ELECTION

1. *Calvin's Commentaries, The Epistles of Paul the Apostle to the Galatians, Ephesians, Philippians and Colossians*, David W. Torrance and Thomas F. Torrance, eds., T. H. L. Parker, trans., Volume III (Grand Rapids, MI: Eerdmans, 1974), p. 125.

2. John A. Mackay, *God's Order* (New York: Macmillan, 1953), p. 67.
3. Marcus Barth, *Ephesians, Introduction, Translation and Commentary on Chapters 1 — 3* (New York: Doubleday, 1974), p. 125.
4. F. F. Bruce, *The Epistles to the Colossians, to Philemon, and to the Ephesians* (Grand Rapids, MI: Eerdmans, 1984), pp. 254, 255.
5. John R. W. Stott, *God's New Society* (Downers Grove, IL: InterVarsity Press, 1979), p. 37.
6. Harold J. Ockenga, *Faithful in Christ Jesus* (New York: Revell, 1948), p. 33.
7. J. I. Packer, *Knowing God* (Downers Grove, IL: InterVarsity Press, 1973), p. 182.
8. *Reader's Digest.*
9. Bruce, p. 258.
10. Barth, pp. 81, 82 says:

A literal translation of the whole clause under review has to take its start from analogous Greek and Hebrew idioms: the Greek uses the cognate expression 'begracing with grace,' and means exclusively an abundant demonstration of grace; of 'grace upon grace.' (John 1:16)

CHAPTER THREE: CELEBRATION OF REDEMPTION

1. J. Armitage Robinson, *St. Paul's Epistle to the Ephesians* (London: Macmillan, 1904), p. 19, says:

At first we marvel at the wealth of his language: but soon we discover, by the very repetition of the phrases which have arrested us, the poverty of all language when it comes to deal with such topics as he has chosen. He seems to be swept along by his theme, hardly knowing whither it is taking him. He begins with God, — the blessing which comes from God to men, the eternity of His purpose of good, the glory of its consummation. But he cannot order his conceptions, or close his sentences. One thought presses hard upon another, and will not be refused. And so this great doxology runs on and on: 'in whom . . . in Him . . . in Him, in whom . . . in whom . . . in whom . . .'

2. William Barclay, *The Letters to the Galatians and Ephesians* (Philadelphia: Westminster Press, 1958), p. 94.
3. Charles Colson, *Who Speaks for God?* (Westchester, IL: Crossway Books, 1985), pp. 76, 77.
4. Charles Hodge, *An Exposition of Ephesians* (Wilmington, DE: Sovereign Grace, 1972), p. 16.
5. F. F. Bruce, *The Epistle to the Ephesians* (London: Pickering and Inglis, 1973), pp. 31, 32 says:

But here it is more likely that the 'wisdom and prudence' are gifts which the believer receives in consequence of the divine grace. Not only are redemption and forgiveness bestowed on us, but spiritual wisdom (Gk. *sophia*) and discernment (Gk. *phronesis*) are imparted as well, so that we may grasp something of the divine purpose of the ages and of the place which we occupy therein.

6. Allan Bloom, *The Closing of the American Mind* (New York: Simon and Schuster, 1987), p. 60.
7. Robinson, p. 30.
8. Hodge, p. 17.
9. Barclay, p. 98.
10. John R. W. Stott, *God's New Society* (Downers Grove, IL: InterVarsity Press, 1979), pp. 41, 42 argues convincingly:

The context of Ephesians 1 certainly seems to suit the notion of "gathering together" better than that of "condensing." For a little later, in verse 22, Paul will be affirming that God has made Jesus Christ "the head (*kephale*) over all things for the church." So here he seems to be saying that "the summing up of the totality takes place in its subjection to the Head." Already Christ is head of his body, the church, but one day "all things" will acknowledge his headship. At present there is still discord in the universe, but in the fullness of time the discord will cease, and that unity for which we long will come into being under the headship of Jesus Christ.

11. *Calvin's Commentaries, The Epistles of Paul the Apostle to the Galatians, Ephesians, Philippians and Colossians*, David W. Torrance and Thomas F. Torrance, eds., T. H. L. Parker, trans., Volume II (Grand Rapids, MI: Eerdmans, 1974), p. 130.

12. H. Dermot McDonald, *Commentary on Colossians and Philemon* (Waco, TX: Word, 1980), p. 49:

For him: He is the Goal unto which all things have their direction. For, or "toward" (*eis*) him the total cosmic order moves. The phrase, "toward" or "to him" indicates the end for which the universe was created. It "finds its goal in no one save Christ alone" (Lohse). "As all creation passed out from Him, so does it all converge again towards Him" (Lightfoot). The preexisting Son is, then, the goal of the universe, as he is its starting point. He is the End as he is the Beginning — both the Alpha and the Omega. As all things sprang forth at his command, so all things will return to him at his bidding.

CHAPTER FOUR: CELEBRATION OF SALVATION

1. Edward Hickman, ed., *The Works of Jonathan Edwards*, Volume 1 (Edinburgh: The Banner of Truth Trust, 1974), pp. xii, xiii.
2. John A. Mackay, *God's Order* (New York: Macmillan, 1953), p. 97.
3. Gerhard Kittle, ed., *Theological Dictionary of the New Testament*, Volume 2 (Grand Rapids, MI: Eerdmans, 1968), p. 541.
4. Mackay, p. 99.
5. Alexander Maclaren, *Expositions of Holy Scripture*, Volume 10 (Grand Rapids, MI: Baker, 1974), pp. 227, 228.
6. Frank S. Mead, *Handbook of Denominations in the United States*, Sixth Edition (New York: Abingdon Press, 1975), pp. 7-16.
7. Malcolm Muggeridge, *Living Water* (Edinburgh: The Saint Andrew Press, 1968), p. 6.
8. Regarding the promise of the Holy Spirit, see Joel 2:28; John 14:16, 17; 15:26; 16:13; Acts 1:4; 2:16ff.
9. T. K. Abbott, *The Epistles to the Ephesians and to the Colossians* (Edinburgh: T. & T. Clark, 1968), p. 23, who quotes Lightfoot as saying: "The actual spiritual life of a Christian is the same in kind as his future glorified life; the kingdom of heaven is a present kingdom; the believer is already seated at the right hand of God."
10. Charles Hodge, *An Exposition of 1 and 2 Corinthians* (Wilmington, DE: 1972), p. 23 says: "Those influences of the Spirit which believers now enjoy are at one a prelibation or antepast of future blessedness, the same in kind though immeasurably less in degree; and a pledge of the certain enjoyment of that blessedness."

CHAPTER FIVE: A PRAYER FOR ENLIGHTENMENT

1. William Barclay, *The Letters to the Galatians and Ephesians* (Philadelphia: Westminster Press, 1958), p. 104.

2. *Calvin's Commentaries, The Epistles of Paul the Apostle to the Galatians, Ephesians, Philippians and Colossians*, David W. Torrance and Thomas F. Torrance, eds., T. H. L. Parker, trans., Volume II (Grand Rapids, MI: Eerdmans, 1974), p. 133.

3. Henry Fairlie, *The Seven Deadly Sins* (Notre Dame, IN: University of Notre Dame Press, 1979), p. 79.

4. Harold J. Ockenga, *Faithful in Christ Jesus* (New York: Revell, 1948), p. 85 says:

   It is true, however, that only those who are thankful for spiritual achievements of believers can truly intercede for them. Note your own prayers, whether you thank God for His grace in others and intercede for them that they may know greater blessing, or whether your prayers are entirely confined to yourself. Then you will know something of your spiritual achievement in prayer.

5. Marcus Barth, *Ephesians*, Volume 1 (New York: Doubleday, 1974), p. 149 says: "The composite noun, as well as the corresponding verb, may denote a real, deep and full knowledge, as distinct from first awareness, a superficial acquaintance."

6. H. C. G. Moule, *The Epistle to the Ephesians*, in the *Cambridge Bible for Schools and Colleges* (Cambridge: University Press, 1899), p. 58.

7. E. W. Bullinger, *Selected Writings* (London: The Lamp Press, 1960), p. 227.

8. F. F. Bruce, *The Epistles to the Colossians, to Philemon, and to the Ephesians* (Grand Rapids, MI: Eerdmans, 1984), p. 271.

CHAPTER SIX: THE FULLNESS OF HIM

1. This story was told by Dr. Howard Hendricks on March 4, 1982 at the International Congress on Biblical Inerrancy in San Diego, California.

2. R. M. L. Waugh, *The Preacher and His Greek Testament* (London: The Epworth Press, 1953), pp. 39-41.

3. Peter Toon, *The Ascension of Our Lord* (Nashville, TN: Nelson, 1984), p. 6:

   (a) the presentation of the Ascension as not merely a physical departure into the sky but also an assumption into heaven (Luke 24:51b and Acts 1:11); (b) the hint that Jesus departed slowly, conveyed by the use of the imperfect tense in both Luke 24:51, "He was (slowly) carried up" and in Acts 1:10, "as He was (slowly) going" (NIV). (In contrast, on earlier occasions when Jesus left, his disappearance was sudden — for example, Luke 24:31, "He vanished").

4. *Ibid.*, p. 12:

   In this book we are adopting the position that there was a secret ascension on Easter morning, and then on the fortieth day there was a symbolic demonstration of that ascension by Jesus for the benefit of his disciples. This approach does greatest justice to the biblical evidence.

5. *Ibid.*, pp. 17-19.

6. J. Armitage Robinson, *St. Paul's Epistle to the Ephesians* (London: Macmillan, 1904), p. 41.

7. William H. Goold, ed., *The Works of John Owen*, Volume 2 (Edinburgh: Banner of Truth Trust, 1980), pp. 70, 71.

8. D. M. Lloyd-Jones, *God's Ultimate Purpose, An Exposition of Ephesians 1:1 to 23* (Grand Rapids, MI: Baker, 1979), p. 426.

9. Charles Hodge, *An Exposition of 1 and 2 Corinthians* (Wilmington, DE: Sovereign Grace, 1972), p. 32, says:

But in every other case in which it occurs in the New Testament, it is used actively — that which does fill. Matt. 9, 16, The piece put into an old garment is called its fulness. i. e. "that which is put in to fill it up." Mark 6, 43, The fragments which filled the baskets are called their fulness. John 1, 16, "Of his fulness," means the plenitude of grace and truth that is in him. Gal. 4, 4, The fulness of the time, is that which renders full the specified time. Col. 2, 9, The fulness of the Godhead, is all that is in the Godhead. Eph. 3, 19, The fulness of God, is that of which God is full — the plenitude of divine perfections. 1 Cor. 10, 26, The fulness of the earth, is that which fills the earth. The common usage of the word in the New Testament is therefore clearly in favour of its being taken in an active sense here. The church is the fulness of Christ — in that it is the complement of his mystic person. He is the head, the church is his body.

10. Lloyd-Jones, p. 431.
11. William Hendriksen, *Exposition of Ephesians* (Grand Rapids, MI: Baker, 1967), p. 104.
12. *Calvin's Commentaries: The Epistles of Paul the Apostle to the Galatians, Ephesians, Philippians and Colossians*, Volume II, trans. T. H. L. Parker (Grand Rapids, MI: Eerdmans, 1974).

CHAPTER SEVEN: FROM DEATH TO LIFE

1. *Calvin's Commentaries: The Epistles of Paul the Apostle to the Galatians, Ephesians, Philippians and Colossians*, Volume II, trans. T. H. L. Parker (Grand Rapids, MI: Eerdmans, 1974), p. 139.
2. John R. W. Stott, *God's New Society* (Downers Grove, IL: InterVarsity Press, 1979), p. 72.
3. See also Ford Lewis Battles, *Calvin: Institutes of the Christian Religion*, Volume 2 (Philadelphia: The Westminster Press, 1975), p. 251, who says: "Original sin, therefore, seems to be a hereditary depravity and corruption of our nature, diffused into all parts of the soul, which first makes us liable to God's wrath, then also brings forth in us those works which Scripture calls 'works of the flesh' [Gal. 5:19]."
4. James Montgomery Boice, *Foundations of the Christian Faith* (Downers Grove, IL: InterVarsity Press, 1986), pp. 200, 201.
5. Marcus Barth, *Ephesians, Introduction, Translation, and Commentary on Chapters 1 — 3* (Garden City, NY: Doubleday, 1974), pp. 219, 220.
6. *Illustration Cornucopia*, Summer 1984, Number 1, Archives of the Billy Graham Center, Wheaton College, Wheaton, IL.
7. William Hendriksen, *Exposition of Ephesians* (Grand Rapids, MI: Baker, 1970), p. 119.
8. F. F. Bruce, *The Epistle to the Ephesians* (London: Pickering & Inglis, 1973), p. 51.
9. Hendriksen, pp. 119, 120.

CHAPTER EIGHT: ALL OF GRACE

1. John R. W. Stott, *God's New Society* (Downers Grove, IL: InterVarsity Press, 1979), p. 83. See also Calvin, *Commentary*: "He does not mean that faith is the gift of God, but that salvation is given to us by God, or, that we obtain it by the gift of God" (p. 145). Also Bruce: "It is the whole concept of salvation by grace through faith that is described as the gift of God" (p. 51).
2. W. H. Auden and Louis Kronenberger, *The Viking Book of Aphorisms* (New York: Dorset Press, 1966), p. 89.

CHAPTER NINE: GOD'S AMAZING WORK

1. James Hastings, ed., *The Speaker's Bible, Ephesians*, Volume 1 (Grand Rapids, MI: Baker, 1974), p. 92.
2. F. F. Bruce, *The Epistle to the Ephesians* (London: Pickering & Inglis, 1973), p. 52.
3. Annie Dillard, *Pilgrim at Tinker Creek* (New York: Bantam Books, 1978), p. 35.
4. Clyde E. Fant, Jr., and William M. Pinson, Jr., eds., *Twenty Centuries of Great Preaching*, Volume 3 (Waco, TX: Word, 1976), p. 74, which quotes from Jonathan Edwards' sermon "God Glorified the Man's Dependence."
5. Bruce, p. 52.
6. John A. Mackay, *God's Order* (New York: Macmillan, 1953), pp. 120, 121.
7. J. D. Douglas, ed., *The New International Dictionary of the Christian Church* (Grand Rapids, MI: Zondervan, 1979), p. 210.
8. R. Kent and Barbara Hughes, *Liberating Ministry from the Success Syndrome* (Wheaton, IL: Tyndale House, 1987), pp. 133, 134.

CHAPTER TEN: ALIENATION TO RECONCILIATION

1. William Barclay, *The Letters to the Galatians and Ephesians* (Philadelphia: Westminster Press, 1958), p. 125.
2. *Ibid.*, p. 132.
3. *Ibid.*, p. 129. Note: I paraphrased Barclay's quotation, which is as follows:

   I rejoice and disport me in my youth; long enough beneath the earth shall I lie, bereft of life, voiceless as a stone, and shall leave the sunlight which I loved; good man though I am, then shall I see nothing more. "Rejoice, O my soul, in thy youth; soon shall other men be in life, and I shall be black earth in death.
   "No mortal is happy of all on whom the sun looks down."

4. F. F. Bruce, *1 & 2 Thessalonians* (Waco, TX: Word, 1982), p. 96, who also gives the Latin:

   > *soles occidere et redire possunt:*
   > *nobis, cum semel occidit breuis lux,*
   > *nox est perpetua una dormienda.*

   > *The sun can set and rise again*
   > *But once our brief light sets*
   > *There is one unending night to be slept through.*

   (Catullus 5.4-6)

5. James Hastings, ed., *The Epistle to the Ephesians*, Volume 16 in *The Speaker's Bible* (Grand Rapids, MI: Baker, 1971), p. 103.
6. H. Lewis, *Modern Rationalism* (London: Society for Promoting Christian Knowledge, 1913), p. 390.
7. *The Orange County Register*, Sunday, July 6, 1986, pp. A1, A2.
8. H. St. J. Thackaray, trans., *The Jewish War*, Books IV-VII (Cambridge, MA: Harvard University Press, 1979), pp. 257, 258 which reads:

   Proceeding across this towards the second court of the temple, one found it surrounded by a stone balustrade, three cubits high and of exquisite workmanship; in this at regular intervals stood slabs giving warning, some in Greek, others in Latin characters, of the law of purification, to wit that no foreigner was permitted to enter the holy place, for so the second enclosure of the temple was called.

9. William Hendriksen, *Exposition of Ephesians* (Grand Rapids, MI: Baker, 1967), p. 133.
10. Bruce, p. 296.
11. John R.W. Stott, *God's New Society* (Downers Grove, IL: InterVarsity Press, 1979), p. 104.
12. F. C. Cook, ed., *Speaker's Commentary* (New York: C. Scribner's, 1878-1896), p. 30.

CHAPTER ELEVEN: THE THIRD RACE

1. *Calvin's Commentaries: The Epistles of Paul the Apostle to the Galatians, Ephesians, Philippians and Colossians*, Volume II, T. H. L. Parker, trans. (Grand Rapids, MI: Eerdmans, 1974), p. 154.
2. James Montgomery Boice, *Philippians, An Expositional Commentary* (Grand Rapids, MI: Zondervan, 1971), pp. 101-103, where the author gives excellent background on the meaning of citizenship in Greek and Roman culture.
3. Charles Hodge, *An Exposition of Ephesians* (Wilmington, DE: Associated Publishers and Authors Inc., 1972), p. 52 says:

That the prophets here mentioned are those of the new dispensation, is evident — first from the position of the terms. It would more naturally be prophets and apostles if the Old Testament prophets had been intended. As God has set in the church, "first apostles, and second, prophets," it is obvious that these are the classes of teachers here referred to. 2. The statement here made that the apostles and prophets are, or have laid, the foundation of that house of which the Gentiles are a part, is more obviously true of the New, than of the Old Testament prophets. 3. The passage in ch. 3,5, in which it is said, "The mystery of Christ is now revealed to holy apostles and prophets by the Spirit," is also strongly in favour of this interpretation."

4. J. Armitage Robinson, *St. Paul's Epistle to the Ephesians* (London: Macmillan, 1904), p. 69.
5. F. F. Bruce, *The Epistles to the Colossians, to Philemon, and to the Ephesians* (Grand Rapids, MI: Eerdmans, 1984), p. 305.
6. F. F. Bruce, *The Epistle to the Ephesians* (London: Pickering & Inglis, 1973), p. 58 says:

And the fact that Paul uses the biological verb 'groweth' when speaking of the Church as a building suggests that the conception of the Church as a living organism, the body of Christ, is uppermost in his mind, whatever other figure he may be employing at the moment.

CHAPTER TWELVE: MYSTERY OF CHRIST

1. W. E. Vine, *An Expository Dictionary of New Testament Words* (Old Tappan, NJ: Revell, 1966), p. 51.
2. F. F. Bruce, *The Epistles to the Colossians, to Philemon, and to the Ephesians* (Grand Rapids, MI: Eerdmans, 1984), p. 316.
3. D. Stuart Briscoe, *Let's Get Moving* (Glendale, CA: Regal Books, 1978), p. 67.
4. John R. W. Stott, *God's New Society* (Downers Grove, IL: InterVarsity Press, 1979), p. 119.

5. John R. W. Stott, *Between Two Worlds* (Grand Rapids, MI: Eerdmans, 1982), p. 43.
6. Stott, *God's New Society*, p. 120.
7. *Ibid.*, pp. 123, 124, who quotes Mackay, p. 84 regarding the graduate school of the angels.
8. *Ibid.*, p. 124.
9. *Ibid.*, pp. 126-130.

CHAPTER THIRTEEN: A PRAYER FOR THE THIRD RACE

1. F. W. Boreham, *A Casket of Cameos* (New York: Abingdon, 1924), pp. 225-237.
2. D. Stuart Briscoe, *Let's Get Moving* (Glendale, CA: Regal Books, 1978), p. 75 says: "Anyone who has been to Jerusalem will have been strangely moved by the crowds of men standing at the Wall swaying and rocking on the balls of their feet, all the time reading their prayers."
3. *Ibid.*, p. 70.
4. Handley C. G. Moule, *Ephesians Studies* (London: Pickering & Inglis, n.d.), p. 129.
5. James S. Hewett, ed., *Illustrations Unlimited* (Wheaton, IL: Tyndale, 1988), p. 321.
6. *Calvin's Commentaries: The Epistles of Paul the Apostle to the Galatians, Ephesians, Philippians and Colossians*, Volume II, T. H. L. Parker, trans. (Grand Rapids, MI: Eerdmans, 1974), p. 168 says:

   What follows is sufficiently clear in itself, but has hitherto been obscured by a variety of interpretations. Augustine is very pleased with his subtlety, which has nothing to do with the subject. For he seeks here I know not what mystery in the figure of the cross; he makes the breadth to be love, the height, hope, and length, patience, and the depth, humility. All this pleases us with its subtlety, but what has it to do with Paul's meaning? No more, certainly, than the opinion of Ambrose, that it denotes the shape of a sphere.

7. Charles H. Spurgeon, *The Metropolitan Tabernacle Pulpit*, Volume 12 (Pasadena, TX: Pilgrim Publications, 1973), p. 478.
8. A. W. Tozer, *The Knowledge of the Holy* (New York: Harper & Row, 1961), p. 105.
9. G. Abbot-Smith, *A Manual Greek Lexicon of the New Testament* (New York: Charles Scribner's Sons, n.d.), p. 235 indicates that the root idea of *katalambano* is "to lay hold of, seize, appropriate" and thus a picture of mental action, "to apprehend, comprehend."
10. Hugh Martin, ed., *Selected Letters of Samuel Rutherford* (London: SCM Press, 1957), p. 43.
11. F. F. Bruce, *The Epistles to the Ephesians* (London: Pickering & Inglis, 1973), p. 71.
12. *Ibid.*

CHAPTER FOURTEEN: BUILDING THE CHURCH'S UNITY

1. G. Abbott-Smith, *A Manual Greek Lexicon of the New Testament* (New York: Charles Scribner's Sons, n.d.), p. 43.
2. Brian Morgan, *Discovery Papers*, Number 624, Ephesians 4:1-10, "God's Design for Community," August 31, 1986, p. 1.
3. John A. Mackay, *God's Order* (New York: Macmillan, 1953), p. 141. I have borrowed terms from Mackay, an ardent ecumenicist whose dreams of an adequate theology were never realized. Mackay said:

   But to repeat words which I have written elsewhere, never must the Church of Christ sponsor a blanched, eviscerated, spineless statement of confessional theology. It must give birth in this revolutionary transition time to a full-blooded, loyally Biblical, unashamedly ecumenical, and strongly vertebrate system of Christian belief.

4. William Barclay, *The Letters to the Galatians and Ephesians* (Philadelphia: Westminster Press, 1958), p. 159.

5. Whit Burnett, ed., *The World's Best* (New York: The Dial Press, 1950), "The Snows of Kilimanjaro," Ernest Hemingway, p. 35.

6. William Barclay, *A New Testament Wordbook* (New York: Harper and Brethren, n.d.), p. 103.

7. Hugh Evan Hopkins, *Charles Simeon of Cambridge* (Grand Rapids, MI: Eerdmans, 1977), p. 111.

8. J. Dwight Pentecost, *The Joy of Living* (Grand Rapids, MI: Zondervan, 1973), p. 55.

9. F. F. Bruce, *The Epistles to the Colossians, to Philemon and to the Ephesians* (Grand Rapids, MI: Eerdmans, 1984), pp. 336, 337 says:

> As for the "one baptism," it is beside the point to ask whether it is baptism in water or the baptism of the Spirit: it is Christian baptism — baptism "into the name of the Lord Jesus" (Acts 8:1; 6; 19:5; cf. 1 Cor. 1:13-15) — which indeed involved the application of water, as John's baptism had done, but (as its inauguration on the day of Pentecost indicates) was closely associated with the gift of the Spirit.

10. John R. W. Stott, *God's New Society* (Downers Grove, IL: InterVarsity Press, 1979), p. 151.

CHAPTER FIFTEEN: GROWING THE CHURCH

1. F. F. Bruce, *The Epistles to the Colossians, to Philemon, and to the Ephesians* (Grand Rapids, MI: Eerdmans, 1984), pp. 342, 343 says:

> An early targumic rendering is found in the Peshitta:
> "Thou hast ascended on high;
> thou hast led captivity captive;
> thou hast given gifts to men."
> A later amplification appears in the traditional Targum on the Psalter, which provides the text with a life-setting far removed from Jerusalem under the monarchy:
> "Thou hast ascended to the firmament, prophet Moses;
> thou hast led captivity captive;
> thou hast taught the words of the law;
> thou hast given gifts to men."
> Paul and other NT writers occasionally give evidence of using targumic renderings (or renderings known to us nowadays only from the Targums), especially where such renderings are better suited to the argument to which they are applied than the Hebrew or Septuagint wording would be. Even when a written Targum is quite late, the renderings it presents often had a long oral prehistory. However far "thou hast given gifts to men" deviates from "thou hast received gifts among (from) men," it circulated as an acceptable interpretation in the first century A.D.

2. John R. W. Stott, *God's New Society* (Downers Grove, IL: InterVarsity Press, 1979), p. 1957.

3. Bruce, p. 343. See also Charles Hodge, *An Exposition of Ephesians* (Wilmington, DE: Associated Publishers and Authors Inc., 1972), p. 77 who writes:

Perhaps the majority of commentators take this last to be the meaning of the passage before us. They suppose the reference is to the *descensus ad inferos*, or to Christ's "descending into hell." But in the first place this idea is entirely foreign to the meaning of the passage in the Psalm on which the apostle is commenting. In the second place, there as here, the only descent of which the context speaks is opposed to the ascending to heaven. "He that ascended to heaven is he who first descended to earth." In the third place, this is the opposition so often expressed in other places and in other forms of expression, as in John 3,13, "No man hath ascended up to heaven, but he that came down from heaven, even the Son of Man who is in heaven." John 6,38, "I came down from heaven." John 8,14, "I know whence I came and whither I go." John 16,28, "I came forth from the Father and am come into the world; again, I leave the world, and go to the Father." The expression of the apostle therefore means, "the lower parts, viz. the earth." The genitive . . . is the common genitive of apposition. Compare Acts 2,19, where the heaven above is opposed to the earth beneath; and John 8, 23.

4. *Ibid*, pp. 346, 347.
5. Stott, pp. 164, 165.
6. *Ibid*, p. 167.
7. *Ibid*.

CHAPTER SIXTEEN: THE DIVINE WARDROBE

1. John R. W. Stott, *God's New Society* (Downers Grove, IL: InterVarsity Press, 1979), p. 177 writes:

   If we put Paul's expressions together noting carefully their logical connections (especially because of and due to both translating *dia*), he seems to be depicting the terrible downward path of evil, which begins with an obstinate rejection of God's known truth. First comes their hardness of heart, then their ignorance, being darkened in their understanding, next and consequently they are alienated from the life of God, since he turns away from them, until finally they have become callous and have given themselves up to licentiousness greedy to practice every kind of uncleanness. NEB has "They stop at nothing to satisfy their foul desire." Thus hardness of heart leads first to darkness of mind, then to deadness of soul under the judgment of God, and finally to reck-lessness of life. Having lost all sensitivity, people lose all self-control. It is exactly the sequence which Paul elaborates in the latter part of Romans 1.

2. Handley C. G. Moule, *Ephesians Studies* (London: Pickering & Inglis, n.d.), p. 215.
3. *Christianity Today*, September 18, 1987, p. 25.
4. Moule, p. 212.
5. F. F. Bruce, *The Epistles to the Colossians, to Philemon, and to the Ephesians* (Grand Rapids, MI: Eerdmans, 1984), p. 356.
6. Bruce Buursma, *Chicago Tribune*, Tuesday, October 12, 1982, Section 1, p. 3.
7. Stott, p. 179.
8. Max Zerwick and Mary Grosvenor, *A Grammatical Analysis of the Greek New Testament* (Rome: Biblical Institute Press, 1981), p. 586 argue that the use of *manthano* with a direct object is unknown and suggest that "Paul thus emphasizes that what the Christian learns is the living Christ."
9. F. F. Bruce, *The Epistle to the Ephesians* (London: Pickering & Inglis, 1973), p. 93.

CHAPTER SEVENTEEN: LIVING UNDER THE SMILE

1. C. H. Spurgeon, *The Metropolitan Tabernacle Pulpit*, Volume 13 (Pasadena, TX: Pilgrim Publications, 1974), p. 121.

2. Mortimer J. Adler, *How to Read a Book* (New York: Simon and Schuster, 1972), p. 165.
3. *Calvin's Commentaries: The Epistles of Paul the Apostle to the Galatians, Ephesians, Philippians and Colossians*, Volume II, trans. T. H. L. Parker (Grand Rapids, MI: Eerdmans, 1974), p. 191.
4. John A. Mackay, *God's Order* (New York: Macmillan, 1953), p. 174.
5. Thomas Boston, *The Complete Works of the Late Rev. Thomas Boston*, Volume 4, ed. Samuel McMillan (Wheaton, IL: Richard Owen Roberts, 1980), p. 357.
6. Frederick Buechner, *Wishful Thinking: A Theological ABC* (New York: Harper & Row, 1973), p. 2.
7. James Hastings, ed., *The Speakers' Bible*, Volume 16 (Grand Rapids, MI: Baker, 1971), p. 271.
8. Marcus Barth, *Ephesians* (New York: Doubleday, 1974), p. 518 writes:

> No foul talk whatsoever shall pass your lips. The adjective "foul" can designate anything that is rotten, putrid, filthy, and therefore, unsound or bad. In the NT the term is used to describe bad trees, foul fruit, rotten fish. Paul's metaphoric application of the term to a certain sort of talk or voice has scarcely any parallels in Greek writings. But it has a positive counterpart in the reference to "salted" (i.e. well-seasoned and well-preserved) speech in Col 4:6. In Eph. 4:28, each "good" word is the alternative to "foul" talk.

CHAPTER EIGHTEEN: THE COOKIE JAR SYNDROME

1. Marcus Barth, *Ephesians 4 – 6* (New York: Doubleday, 1974), p. 561.
2. F. F. Bruce, *The Epistles to the Colossians, to Philemon, and to the Ephesians* (Grand Rapids, MI: Eerdmans, 1984), p. 370 says:

> The injunction, "let such things not even be named among you," does not imply a mealy-mouthed refusal to call a spade a spade after the fashion of some modern Bible versions (else the vices would not be named so plainly as they are in this and similar lists); it means rather that such unholy things should not be acceptable subjects of conversation among people whom God has called to be holy. Fornication, impurity, and covetousness are included in the fiefold catalogue of vices in Col. 3:5.

3. Henry W. Boynton, ed., *The Complete Poetical Works of Alexander Pope* (Boston: Houghton Mifflin Company, 1903), p. 144.
4. Robert Brody, "Anatomy of a Laugh," *American Health*, November/December 1983, pp. 43-47.
5. Barth, p. 562 says, "A line from Plantus' *miles gloriosus* suggests that Ephesus was especially known for producing facetious orators: 'I am a facetious cavalier, because I was born in Ephesus, not Apulia or Amimula.'"
6. Thomas Manton, *The Complete Works of Thomas Manton*, Volume 19 (Worthington, PA: Maranatha Publications, n.d.), p. 202.
7. John R. W. Stott, *God's New Society* (Downers Grove, IL: InterVarsity Press, 1979), p. 197.

CHAPTER NINETEEN: SHADES OF LIFE

1. Herbert Danby, trans., *The Mishnah* (London: Oxford University Press, 1974), p. 180, *Sukkah* 5:2-3.
2. James M. Boice, *The Sermon on the Mount* (Grand Rapids, MI: Zondervan, 1972), p. 80.
3. C. S. Lewis, *The Weight of Glory* (Grand Rapids, MI: Eerdmans, 1965), p. 374.
4. Corrie ten Boom, "Trust the Lord," *Guideposts* Magazine (August 1976), p. 7.

5. F. F. Bruce, *The Epistles to the Colossians, to Philemon, and to the Ephesians* (Grand Rapids, MI: Eerdmans, 1984), p.374.
6. *Calvin's Commentaries: The Epistle of Paul the Apostle to the Galatians, Ephesians, Philippians and Colossians*, Volume II, , trans. T. H. L. Parker (Grand Rapids, MI: Eerdmans, 1974), p. 200.
7. Bruce, p. 376.
8. C. H. Spurgeon, *The Metropolitan Tabernacle Pulpit*, Volume 12 (Pasadena, TX: Pilgrim Publications, 1973), pp. 578, 579, which provides the homiletical ideas regarding sleeping while appearing awake.

CHAPTER TWENTY: THE FULLNESS OF THE SPIRIT

1. Marguerite Michaels and James Willworth, "How America Has Run out of Time," *Time* Magazine, April 24, 1989, p. 58.
2. Lewis Carroll, *Alice's Adventures in Wonderland: Authoritative Text of Alice's Adventures in Wonderland, Through the Looking Glass, the Hunting of Snark, Backgrounds, Essays and Criticisms*, ed. Donald Gray (New York: W. W. Norton, 1971), p. 127.
3. John R. W. Stott, *God's New Society* (Downers Grove, IL: InterVarsity Press, 1979), pp. 204, 205.
4. D. Martyn Lloyd-Jones, *Life in the Spirit in Marriage, Home and Work* (Grand Rapids, MI: Baker, 1975), p. 15.
5. F. F. Bruce, *The Epistle to the Ephesians* (London: Pickering & Inglis, 1973), p. 111, quoting Epistle to Trajan. x.96.
6. *Ibid.*, quoting *Apology*, 39.
7. John A. Mackay, *God's Order* (New York: Macmillan, 1953), p. 181.
8. Stott, p. 207.

CHAPTER TWENTY-ONE: THE MYSTERY OF MARRIAGE (I)

1. Geoffrey W. Bromiley, *God and Marriage* (Grand Rapids, MI: Eerdmans, 1980), p. 60:

   Within marriage the differentiation of men and women, or husbands and wives, takes the form of order, of an ordered equality in which there is no superiority or inferiority but in which one is first and the other second. All the relevant passages make this point. According to Ephesians 5:23f., the husband is the head of the wife and the wife is to be subject to her husband. According to Colossians 3:18, wives are to be subject to their husbands. According to 1 Peter 3:1ff, wives are to be submissive to their husbands.

   Cf. pp. 72, 73.
2. Wayne Grudem, *The Role Relationship of Men and Women*, "Does *Kephale* ('Head') Mean 'Source' or 'Authority Over' in Greek Literature? A Survey of 2,336 Examples," ed. George W. Knight III (Chicago: Moody Press, 1985), p. 50.
3. *Ibid.*, pp. 65-68.
4. John Piper, *Desiring God* (Portland: Multnomah, 1982), p. 179, quoting *The Special Laws*, III, 184, Loeb Classical Library, Volume 8, p. 591.
5. F. F. Bruce, *The Epistle to the Colossians, to Philemon, and to the Ephesians* (Grand Rapids, MI: Eerdmans, 1984), p. 384.
6. John Stott, *God's New Society* (Downers Grove, IL: InterVarsity Press, 1979), pp. 218, 219 says:

   We have to be very careful not to overstate this biblical teaching on authority. It does not mean that the authority of husbands, parents and masters is unlimited, or that wives, children and workers are required to give unconditional obedience. No, the submission required is to God's authority delegated to human beings. If, therefore they misuse their God-given authority (e.g. by commanding what God forbids or forbidding what God commands), then our duty is no longer conscientiously to submit, but conscientiously to refuse to do so. For to submit in such circumstances would be to disobey God. The principle is clear: we must submit right up to the point where obedience to human authority would involve disobedience to God.

7. Dietrich Bonhoeffer, *Letters and Papers From Prison* (New York: Macmillan, 1973), p. 45.
8. Stott, p. 218, who quotes from Yoder's, *The Politics of Jesus*, p. 177, note 23.
9. Piper, p. 182.
10. *The Danvers Statement*, Affirmation 4, published by the Council on Biblical Manhood and Womanhood, P.O. Box 1173, Wheaton, IL 60189.

CHAPTER TWENTY-TWO: THE MYSTERY OF MARRIAGE (II)

1. James Humes, *Churchill, Speaker of the Century* (Briarcliff Manor, NY: Stein and Day/Scarborough House, 1980), p. 291.
2. William Barclay, *The Letter to the Galatians and Ephesians* (Philadelphia: Westminster Press, 1958), pp. 201-203.
3. *Ibid.*, p. 200.
4. Dante Alighieri, *The Inferno*, trans. John Ciardi (New York: New American Library, 1954), p. 42, quoting Canto III, which reads,

> *I am the way into the city of woe.*
> *I am the way to a forsaken people.*
> *I am the way into eternal sorrow.*
> *Sacred justice moved my architect.*
> *I was raised here by divine omnipotence,*
> *Primordial love and ultimate intellect.*
> *Only those elements time cannot wear*
> *Were made before me. and beyond time I stand.*
> *Abandon all hope all ye who enter here.*

5. William Alan Sadler, Jr., ed., *Master Sermons Through the Ages* (New York: Harper & Row, 1963), p. 116.
6. F. F. Bruce, *The Epistles to the Colossians, to Philemon, and to the Ephesians* (Grand Rapids, MI: Eerdmans, 1984), p. 387. Cf. Ezekiel 16:6-14.
7. N. G. L. Hammond and H. H. Scullard, eds., *The Oxford Classical Dictionary* (London: Oxford University Press, 1978), p. 722.

CHAPTER TWENTY-THREE: INSTRUCTIONS TO CHILDREN AND PARENTS

1. Here we note that Paul changes the final phrase of Deuteronomy 5:16, "so that you may live long and that it may go well with you in the land the Lord your God is giving you" to read, "that it may go well with you and that you may enjoy long life in the earth," because whereas the hearers of Deuteronomy 5:16 were exclusively Jews, the audience here is Jewish and Gentile believers.
2. *Calvin's Commentaries: The Epistles of Paul the Apostle to the Galatians, Ephesians, Philippians and Colossians*, trans. T. H. L Parker (Grand Rapids, MI: Eerdmans, 1974), p. 213.
3. John R. W. Stott, *God's New Society* (Downers Grove, IL: InterVarsity Press, 1979), p. 249 says:

The discipline and instruction in which parents are to bring up their children, Paul writes, are "the Lord's." This has been taken by some to mean simply that the kind of instruction and discipline intended "belong to a Christian upbringing" (NEB), and that Paul is specifying Christian as opposed to secular education. But I think it means more than this, namely that behind the parents who teach and discipline their children there stands the Lord himself. It is he who is the chief teacher and administrator of discipline.

CHAPTER TWENTY-FOUR: SLAVES AND MASTERS

1. William Barclay, *The Letters to the Galatians and Ephesians* (Philadelphia: The Westminster Press, 1958), p. 213.
2. Geoffrey W. Bromiley, ed., *The International Standard Bible Encyclopedia* (Grand Rapids, MI: Eerdmans, 1988), p. 544.
3. John R. W. Stott, *God's New Society* (Downers Grove, IL: InterVarsity Press, 1979), p. 251, who quotes *Nichomachian Ethics*, viii.11.6, and *Politics*, 1.2,4.
4. Bromiley, p. 544.
5. Barclay, p. 213.
6. Bromiley, p. 544.
7. *Ibid.*, p. 545.
8. *Ibid.*, p. 544.
9. Arthur John Gossip, *From the Edge of the Crowd* (New York: Charles Scribner's Sons, n.d.), p. 22.
10. Stott, p. 252.
11. Harold John Ockenga, *Faithful in Christ Jesus* (New York: Revell, 1948), p. 237.
12. Studs Terkel, *Working: People Tell About What They Do All Day and How They Feel About What They Do* (New York: Pantheon, 1974), p. xi.
13. William Hendriksen, *Exposition of Ephesians* (Grand Rapids, MI: Baker, 1970), p. 265.
14. R. E. O. White, *In Him the Fulness* (Old Tappan, NJ: Revell, 1973), p. 127.

CHAPTER TWENTY-FIVE: THE VIEW FOR VICTORY

1. Handley C. G. Moule, *Ephesian Studies* (London: Pickering & Inglis, n.d.), p. 321 says: "So this last passage gathers up the whole precious matter of the Epistle in the sense of an urgent reminder of the infinitely serious conditions under which the bright secrets of grace are to be lived out."
2. *Calvin's Commentaries: The Epistles of Paul the Apostle to the Galatians, Ephesians, Philippians and Colossians*, Volume II, trans. T. H. L. Parker (Grand Rapids, MI: Eerdmans, 1974), p. 218.
3. F. F. Bruce, *The Epistle to the Ephesians* (London: Pickering & Inglis, 1973), p. 128.
4. C. S. Lewis, *Perelandra* (New York: Macmillan, 1968), pp. 110, 111.
5. Roland H. Bainton, *Here I Stand* (New York: New American Library, n.d.), p. 282.
6. John R. W. Stott, *God's New Society* (Downers Grove, IL: InterVarsity Press, 1979), p. 266.

CHAPTER TWENTY-SIX: ARMED FOR BATTLE (I)

1. William F. Buckley. *Atlantic High* (Boston: Little, Brown & Company, 1982), p. 195.
2. Charles Colson, *Who Speaks for God?* (Westchester, IL: Crossway Books, 1985), p. 68.

3. William Barclay, *The Letters to the Galatians and Ephesians* (Philadelphia: Westminster Press, 1958), p. 183.
4. Marcus Barth, *Ephesians 4 — 6* (New York: Doubleday, 1974), p. 769, writes:

> The diction of Eph. 6:14 does not permit us to decide which material form or weight of the thorax Paul has in mind. However, since the context probably describes the equipment of a Roman infantryman of Paul's time, translators and commentators usually assume that the apostle was thinking of the frontal metal piece, which is mentioned by Polybius, appears on contemporary images, reliefs and statues of soldiers, and is properly translated by "breastplate." Indeed this part of a soldier's equipment was useful — but it was only the second-best protection of a man's chest. Whoever could afford it used the very best available: a scale or chain mail that covered chest and hips. Since elsewhere Paul has depicted the saints as rich heirs and noblemen, he would be negligent and self-contradictory if at this point he insinuated that God provides them with no more than a breastplate, rather than with a mail as worn by the rich and by officers. The translation of the ambiguous thorax by "cuirass" permits the reader to think of the best protection rather than only of armor mediocre in quality and effectiveness.

5. *Calvin's Commentaries: The Epistles of Paul the Apostle to the Galatians, Ephesians, Philippians and Colossians*, trans., T. H. L. Parker (Grand Rapids, MI: Eerdmans, 1974), p. 220.
6. R. C. Sproul, *The Holiness of God* (Wheaton, IL: Tyndale, 1985), pp. 91-93.

CHPATER TWENTY-SEVEN: ARMED FOR BATTLE (II)

1. Josephus, *War*, VI.1.8:

> Yet, after all, he too was to be dogged by Destiny, whom no mortal man may escape. For, wearing, like any other soldier, shoes thickly studded with sharp nails, while running across the pavement he slipped and fell on his back, with a loud clash of armour, which made the fugitives turn. A cry of concern for the hero went up from the Romans in Antonia, while the Jews crowding around him struck at him from all sides with spears and swords.

2. Marcus Barth, *Ephesians 4 — 6* (New York: Doubleday, 1974), p. 798.
3. *Ibid.*, p. 799:

> Despite the allusion to Isa 52:7 with the words "gospel of peace," Eph 6:15 belongs to the same pattern of military metaphors as is found in vss. 14, 16-17. This verse does not use the messenger imagery of Rom 10:14-18; rather, Paul speaks here of the equipment provided by God which makes Christians able to "stand" and "resist." They can say, "We shall not be moved."

4. Francis Brown, S. R. Driver, and Charles A. Briggs, *A Hebrew and English Lexicon of the Old Testament* (London: Oxford University Press, 1974), p. 1022.
5. Gerhard Kittel, ed., *Theological Dictionary of the New Testament*, Volume 2, trans. Geoffrey W. Bromiley (Grand Rapids, MI: Eerdmans, 1968), p. 402.
6. J. Armitage Robinson, *St. Paul's Epistle to the Ephesians* (London: Macmillan, 1904), p. 215.
7. C. S. Lewis, *Christian Reflections*, "Religion: Reality or Substitute" (Grand Rapids, MI: Eerdmans, 1941), p. 43.

CHAPTER TWENTY-EIGHT: ARMED FOR BATTLE (III)

1. John Bunyan, *The Holy War made by King Shaddai upon Diabolus for the*

Regaining of the Metropolis of the World or the Losing and Taking Again of the Town of Mansoul (Swengel, PA: Reiner Publications).

2. James Hastings, ed., *A Dictionary of the Bible*, Volume 2 (Edinburgh: T. & T. Clark, 1910), p. 347.

3. Marcus Barth, *Ephesians 4 — 6* (New York: Doubleday, 1974), p. 775.

4. William Barclay, *The Letters to the Galatians and Ephesians* (Philadelphia: Westminster Press, 1958), p. 218.

5. John Bunyan, *The Pilgrim's Progress* (New York: Dodd, Mead & Company, 1979), p. 59.

6. *Ibid.*, p. 283.

7. Warren W. Wiersbe, *Listening to the Giants* (Grand Rapids, MI: Baker, 1980), p. 198.

8. John Piper, *Desiring God* (Portland, OR: Multnomah, 1986), pp. 124, 125, quoting *Hudson Taylor's Spiritual Secret* (Chicago, IL: Moody Press, n.d.), p. 235.

9. Margaret N. Barnhouse, *That Man Barnhouse* (Wheaton, IL: Tyndale, 1983), pp. 250, 251.

10. *The Christian Century*, December 2, 1987, p. 1090.

11. Bunyan, p. 283.

CHAPTER TWENTY-NINE: ARMED FOR BATTLE (IV)

1. Kent and Barbara Hughes, *Liberating Ministry from the Success Syndrome* (Wheaton, IL: Tyndale, 1987), p. 77. See "Success Is Prayer," pp. 71-81.

2. E. M. Bounds, *Power Through Prayer* (Grand Rapids, MI: Zondervan, 1982), p. 28.

3. John Bunyan, *The Pilgrim's Progress* (Philadelphia: Universal Book and Bible House, 1933), p. 66:

   About the midst of this valley I perceived the mouth of hell to be, and it stood also hard by the wayside. Now thought Christian, what shall I do? And ever and anon the flame and smoke would come out in such abundance, with sparks and hideous noises (things that cared not for Christian's sword, as did Apollyon before), that he was forced to put up his sword, and betake himself to another weapon, called "All-Prayer."

4. J. Oswald Sanders, *Spiritual Leadership* (Chicago, IL: Moody Press, 1978), p. 83. Sanders's chapter "The Leader and His Praying," pp. 75-84, is very helpful.

5. John Bunyan, Bedford Prison, 1662.

6. Thomas Kelly, *Testament of Devotion* (New York: Harper, 1941), p. 35.

7. Brother Lawrence, *The Practice of the Presence of God* (New York: Revell, 1958), pp. 30, 31.

8. John Wesley, *Works*, VIII (Grand Rapids, MI: Zondervan, 1959), p. 343.

9. E. M. Bounds, *Purpose in Prayer* (Grand Rapids, MI: Baker, 1984), p. 131.

10. John Piper, *Desiring God* (Portland, OR: Multnomah, 1986), pp. 150, 151.

CHAPTER THIRTY: GLAD BENEDICTIONS

1. Acts 20:4; Ephesians 6:21; Colossians 4:7, 8; 2 Timothy 4:12; and Titus 3:12.

2. For Paul's custom of concluding with his own hand see 1 Corinthians 16:21; Galatians 6:11; Colossians 4:18; and 2 Thessalonians 3:17.

3. Alexander Maclaren, *Ephesians*, Volume 13 in *Expositions of Holy Scripture* (Grand Rapids, MI: Baker, 1974), pp. 381, 382 writes:

   There is no better test of a man than the things that he wishes for the people that he loves most. He desires for them, of course, his own ideal of happiness. What do you desire most for those that are dearest to you? You parents, do you train up your children, for instance, so as to secure, or to do your best to secure, not outward prosperity, but these loftier gifts; and for yourselves, when you are forming your wishes, are these the things that you want most? "Set your affections on things above," and remember that whoso has that trinity of graces, peace, love, faith, is rich and blessed, whatsoever else he has or needs. And whoso has them not is miserable and poor.

4. James S. Hewett, ed., *Illustrations Unlimited* (Wheaton, IL: Tyndale, 1988), pp. 402, 403.
5. Vickie Lucas, *Reader's Digest*, March 1978. Originally appeared in *Catholic Digest*.
6. For *faith* see 1:15; 2:8; 3:12, 17; 4:5, 13; and 6:16.
7. For *grace* see 1:2, 6, 7; 2:5, 7, 8; 3:2, 7, 8; 4:7, 29; and 6:24.

Scripture Index

Genesis

1:27	67, 83
2:24	189
4:1	51
12:2ff.	90
13:14ff.	90
15:1ff.	90
17:1ff.	90
22:15ff.	90
37:3, 23, 32	109

Exodus

7:6-12	218
19:5	46
20:17	235
40:34, 35	101

Leviticus

19:18	193

Numbers

6:24-26	264

Deuteronomy

5:16	280
6:7	46
6:13	242
6:16	242
8:3	242
14:2	46
26:18	46
28:1-14	19
32:46, 47	242

Judges

7	219

1 Samuel

3:11-13	201
9:2	231
17:5	231
17:7	231
17:39	231
17:40	231
17:45-47	236

2 Samuel

14, 15	200

1 Kings

8:10, 11	101

2 Kings

6:15-17	54

2 Chronicles

6:13	114

Job

1:5	184
4:4	153
38:7	109

Psalms

1:1-3	245
4:4	150
8:3-9	61
8:6	61
19:1	82
22	26
51:6	240
64:3, 4	235
68	132

68:7	132
68:8	132
68:11-14	132
68:16, 17	132
68:18	132
103:12	34
110:1	59
118:22	100
119:11	242
148:14	91
150	47

Proverbs

4:10	199
8:22-31	83
10:27	199
12:18	153
15:2	157
15:32	201
17:22	157
19:18	201
23:29-35	173
24:26	193
30:17	199

Ecclesiastes

3:4	157

Isaiah

5:20	141, 216
8:14-16	100
9:6	93
28:16	100
43:21	46
44:22	34
49:1	91
52:7	283
57:17	91
57:19	91, 93
59:17	227, 241
64:6	227

Jeremiah

2:13	174
6:14	126
29:11	235, 265
31:31-34	19
31:34	34

Ezekiel

13:10	126
13:10, 11	126
16:6-14	280
36:27	148
37	68
37:1-3	68
37:1-10	70

Daniel

10:12, 13	215

Micah

7:8	243
7:19	34

Malachi

3:17	46

Matthew

4	242
4:8, 9	216
4:11	242
5:3	75, 235
5:9	94
5:14	166, 168
5:17	92
5:21, 22	150
5:23, 24	94
5:27-30	155
6:9	99
6:14	94
6:25-34	19
7:7	253
7:22	74
7:22, 23	51
8:23-27	233
9:16	273
9:34	67
11:29	123
12:36, 37	158
13:43	164
18:10	109
19:28	37
21:42	100
22:35-38	267
25	74, 209
25:23	209
25:26	209
25:37-39	74
25:40-46	74
25:46	74
26:28	34

Mark

3:5, 6	140
6:43	273
7:21	158
10:45	32, 183
11:15	150
14:35, 36	114

Luke

2:14	93
11:13	20, 52, 67
18:2-5	253
18:11	74
22:26	183
23:16	201
24:50-53	59

John

1:12	26, 77
1:16	27, 267, 270, 273
3:13	132, 278
3:16	117
3:36	67
4:14	174
6:35	44
6:38	278
6:44	24
7:37, 38	174
7:37-39	45
8:12	163, 164
8:18	278
8:23	278
8:32	224
8:43-45	224
10:16	142
12:31	67
13:14-16	177
13:34, 35	50, 108
14–16	60
14:1-6	99
14:16	160
14:16, 17	148
14:27	93, 233, 240, 264
15	63
15:16	24
16:12, 13	148
16:28	278
17:3	51
17:11	44
17:17	224
17:21-23	127
17:24	60
19:5-12	233
20:19, 20	93
21:15-17	133
24:31	272
24:51	272

Acts

1:8	59
1:9-11	59
1:10	272
1:11	272
1:14	251
2	60
2:13	173
2:19	278
2:42	251
4:11	100
6	277
7	17
8:1	277
8:16	125
9:4, 5	17
9:22	17
11:26	42
11:27ff.	133
13:1ff.	133
13:39	77
16:31	77, 79
19:5	125, 277
19:35–20:1	262
20:4	262, 284
20:28	46, 133
20:36-38	114
21:4, 9	133
26:18	216
26:28	42

Romans

1	278
1–3	216
1:9	50
1:16	58
1:17	74, 227
1:18	141
1:21	141
1:22	141
1:28	198
1:30	198
3	67
3:10, 11	68
3:10-12	74, 227
3:11	90
3:13-18	74
3:10-18	74

3:20	52
3:21	74
3:22, 23	227
4:5	77
5:1	232, 240, 264
5:2	53
5:5	50, 265
5:12-14	67
6:3, 4	58
6:4	73
8:15	99
8:15, 16	26
8:16, 17	45
8:17	53
8:18-30	60
8:19	27
8:19-21	37
8:26, 27	148, 250
8:34	60
8:37	243
9:5	90
9:11	23
10:14-18	283
11:6	77
11:36	115
12	25
12:1	25, 121, 176
12:2	143
12:4, 5	150
12:6	131
12:6-8	132
12:18	127
12:21	235
14:19	127

1 Corinthians

1:4	50
1:13-15	125, 277
1:23-25	107
2:9, 10	46
2:10, 11	52
6:9, 10	159
6:11	160
6:19	148
8:3	51
8:6	124
9:16	17
10:26	273
11:10	109
12:3	125
12:4-6	124
12:8-10	132
12:13	124, 148, 173
12:14-26	150

12:28-30	132
13:8	117
13:12	52
14:1	133
15:9, 10	107
15:15, 20, 23	60
15:22	42
16:21	284

2 Corinthians

2:15, 16	228
3:6-15	92
4:4	67, 215
4:5	177
4:7	17
4:16	115
5:17	42, 83
5:21	24, 132, 227
8:1-5	152
11:14, 15	217
11:26, 27	262
11:29	255
12:1-6	20
12:8-10	
12:9	219
12:28-30	

Galatians

1:4	66
3:13	24
3:28	43, 184, 206
4:4	273
4:6	99
4:6, 7	26
4:9	51
5:19	273
5:19-21	159
5:22	19, 116, 144
5:22, 23	173
6:11	284

Ephesians

1	271
1–3	16, 121, 181, 213, 262
1:1	17
1:1-3	14 (Chapter 1)
1:2	18
1:2, 6, 7	285
1:3	19, 23, 31, 37, 47
1:3-6	22 (Chapter 2)
1:3-14	19, 41, 54
1:4	23, 25, 53

1:4, 5	23	2:13	105
1:4-6	23, 31, 37, 41	2:13, 14	91
1:4-14	23	2:14	93, 265
1:5	23, 26	2:15	92, 105, 265
1:6	27, 47	2:15, 16	92
1:7	31, 33	2:16	93, 173
1:7, 8	31, 35, 37	2:17	93
1:7-10	30 (Chapter 3)	2:17, 18	93
1:9, 10	36, 38, 109	2:18	93
1:11	23	2:19	98, 99
1:11, 12	41	2:19-22	96 (Chapter 11), 105
1:11-14	40 (Chapter 4)	2:20	100, 133
1:12	47	2:21, 22	101
1:13	42, 45, 148, 173	2:22	101
1:13, 14	45	3	105
1:14	46, 47, 53, 174	3:1	105, 113
1:15	265, 285	3:2-6	106
1:15, 16	49, 54	3:2-13	105, 113
1:15-19	48 (Chapter 5)	3:1-13	104 (Chapter 12)
1:16	50	3:4, 5	100
1:17	51, 54, 60	3:5	133, 275
1:18	52, 69, 125	3:6	106
1:18, 19	53, 54	3:7, 8	106, 131
1:18-23	56 (Chapter 6)	3:8	107
1:19	54	3:9	108
1:19, 20	56, 69	3:10-12	108
1:20	19, 20, 54, 215	3:10, 15	37
1:20, 21	58	3:12, 17	285
1:21	60	3:13	110
1:22	60, 61, 271	3:14	105, 113
1:22, 23	62	3:14, 15	99
2	37, 65, 105	3:14-21	112 (Chapter 13)
2:1	65, 66	3:16	115
2:1-3	65, 73, 81	3:16, 17	115
2:1-7	64 (Chapter 7)	3:17	116
2:1-10	89	3:17, 18	116
2:2	66, 67, 215, 216	3:17-19	116
2:2, 3	66	3:19	118, 220, 273
2:3	66, 67	3:20	58
2:4, 5	69	3:20, 21	118
2:4-7	65, 73, 81	3:21	119
2:5	42	4	121, 181
2:5, 7, 8	285	4–5	16
2:6	19, 20, 43, 69, 215	4–6	16, 93, 181, 213, 262
2:7	69	4–6:9	213
2:8	75, 76, 77, 78, 285	4:1	121
2:8, 9	49, 73, 81, 84, 92, 241, 267	4:1-6	120 (Chapter 14)
2:8-10	72 (Chapter 8)	4:1-16	121
2:9	74	4:2	122, 123, 124
2:10	80 (Chapter 9), 93, 105	4:3	122, 124, 125, 126, 127
		4:4	124
2:11	89	4:4, 5	124
2:11-18	88 (Chapter 10)	4:4-6	122, 124
2:11-22	41	4:5	124
2:12	90	4:5, 13	285

4:6	124, 125	5:20	175
4:7	131	5:21	176, 182, 210
4:7-10	59	5:21-24	180 (Chapter 21)
4:7-16	121, 130 (Chapter 15)	5:21–6:9	181, 182
4:7, 29	285	5:22	182, 194
4:8-10	131, 132	5:22-24	181
4:11	100, 132, 133	5:22-33	181
4:12	134	5:23	182, 183, 184, 185
4:12-14	135	5:23ff.	280
4:15	136, 193	5:24	184
4:15, 16	136	5:25	190, 192, 194
4:17	142	5:25-33	181, 188 (Chapter 22)
4:17ff.	121	5:25-27	192
4:17-19	140, 143	5:26, 27	190, 192
4:17-24	138 (Chapter 16)	5:28-30	190, 193
4:18	140, 141	5:29	200
4:19	141	5:31	189
4:20	142	5:32	15, 189
4:20, 21	142	6:1-3	198
4:21	142, 143, 224	6:1-4	181, 196 (Chapter 23)
4:22	143	6:2, 3	198
4:22-24	143	6:4	200, 201
4:23	143	6:5	207, 208
4:24	143, 144	6:5-8	206
4:25	153, 226	6:5-9	181, 204 (Chapter 24)
4:25-32	146 (Chapter 17)	6:6	208
4:26, 27	150, 153	6:7	208
4:28	151, 152, 153, 279	6:7, 8	209
4:29	152, 153	6:8	208
4:30	45, 147, 148	6:9	206, 211
4:30-32	153	6:10	219
5	181	6:10ff.	16, 213
5:1	150	6:10, 11	214, 223
5:1, 2	160	6:10-12	212 (Chapter 25)
5:1-7	154 (Chapter 18)	6:10-17	249
5:3	156	6:10-18	239
5:3-7	156	6:11	217, 219
5:4	157, 158	6:12	214, 215, 223, 228, 250, 257
5:6	160		
5:7	160	6:12, 13	236
5:8	164, 168, 226	6:13	223, 229
5:8-10	165	6:13, 14	222 (Chapter 26)
5:8-14	162 (Chapter 19)	6:14	224, 283
5:9	224	6:14, 15	232
5:11	166	6:14, 16, 17	283
5:11-14	166	6:15	232, 264, 283
5:12	166	6:15, 16	230 (Chapter 27)
5:13, 14	166	6:16	234, 285
5:14	167, 168	6:17	238 (Chapter 28)
5:15-21	170 (Chapter 20)	6:18	249, 256, 257
5:15, 16	172	6:18-20	248 (Chapter 29)
5:17, 18	172	6:19, 20	255
5:18	173, 219	6:21	284
5:18-21	176, 182, 186	6:21, 22	262, 263
5:19	174		

6:21-24	260 (Chapter 30)
6:23, 24	262, 264
6:24	266, 285

Philippians

1:3, 4	50
1:6	241
1:21	42
1:27	99
1:28	242, 246
2:3	177
2:5-8	182
2:8	117
2:11	125
2:12, 13	144
3:4-6	17
3:7-9	227
3:9	228, 240
3:10	52, 58
3:20	99
3:20, 21	20
4:6, 7	234
4:7	233
4:8	235

Colossians

1:3	50
1:10	85
1:15, 18	60
1:15-18	37, 60
1:16	37, 218
1:16, 17	83
1:16-18	24
1:17-22	109
1:19	118
1:23, 27	125
1:26	105
2:9	273
2:9, 10	118
2:10	218
2:15	219
3:1, 2	20
3:1-4	20
3:4	53
3:5	121, 279
3:9, 10	149
3:14	266
3:16	174, 177, 192
3:18	280
4:6	153, 279
4:7, 8	263, 284
4:16	263
4:18	284

1 Thessalonians

1:2	50
1:4-7	24
4:3-8	235
5:8	241
5:17	251

2 Thessalonians

1:3	50
2:13	24
2:16, 17	85
3:17	284

1 Timothy

1:15	107
1:19	226, 240
3:16	59
4:7	144
5:1, 2	99
6:1	207
6:2	207

2 Timothy

1:7	173
2:15	245
3:16	242
4:2	100
4:11, 12	263
4:12	284

Titus

2:13	125
3:12	263, 284

Philemon

4	50
16	206

Hebrews

1:2, 3	37
1:13	59
4:12	243
4:15	60
9:12	32
12:11	201
13:20, 21	85

James

3:17, 18	127

4:6, 7	235

1 Peter

1:2	24
1:10-12	32, 109
1:12	109
1:18, 19	32
1:22	123
2:4, 5	101
2:9	46
2:17	124
3:1ff.	280
3:8	124
4:8	124
4:11	132
4:16	42
5:2	133

2 Peter

1:4	164
3:10-13	37

1 John

1:3	106, 126, 127

1:3, 4	92, 127
1:9	34
2:14	243
2:20	148
2:27	148
3:1, 2	117
3:2	53, 125
3:7-10	159
4:19	265
5:4	236, 240
5:14, 15	119
5:19	215

Jude

20	250

Revelation

4, 5	175
5:9-12	33
12:1-6	59
22:17	174, 178

General Index

Aaron, 109, 218
   Aaronic benediction, 264
Abba, Father, 26, 28, 66, 99
Abraham, 97
Absalom, 200
Adam, 51, 67, 190
Adler, Mortimer, 149
Adoption, 19, 20, 26, 27, 28, 37
Agrippa, 255
Ahab, 225
Alexander, John, 256, 257
Alice in Wonderland, 171
Alienation, 91, 92, 93, 98, 99, 122, 127, 233, 278
Ambrose, 117, 276
Ames, William, xii
Angels, 18, 32, 33, 37, 38, 59, 60, 61, 62, 83, 84, 93, 97, 108, 109, 110, 215, 217
   angel of light, 217
Apartheid, 44
Apostles' Creed, the, 34, 147
Aquila, 183
Aristides, 140
Aristotle, 205
Armor of God, 219, 223, 224, 226, 228, 229, 232, 234, 236, 239, 246, 249, 255,264
Augustine, 24, 74, 83, 117, 126, 133, 153, 276
Augustus Caesar, 205, 206

Baggins, Bilbo, 223
Baggins, Frodo, 224
Bainton, Roland, 217
Baptism, 58, 124, 125, 192, 277
Barnhouse, Dr.Donald Grey, 116, 164, 245
Barth, Marcus, 18, 23, 69, 156, 226
Bayly, Joe, 167
Belgium, 108
Bentham, Jeremy, 66
Bernard of Clairvaux, 126
Bethge, Eberhard, 183
Blake, William, 139
Blessedness, 17, 19, 20, 25, 27, 31, 35, 36, 37, 38, 47, 49, 54, 75, 90, 115, 121, 173, 175, 245, 264, 270, 272, 285
Blondin (Jean Francois Gravalet), 77, 78
Bloom, Allan, 35
Bonhoeffer, Dietrich, 183

Boston, Thomas, 150
Briscoe, Stuart, 115
Brooks, Phillips, xi
Brother Lawrence, 252
Bruce, F. F., 53, 100, 133, 142, 183, 215
Buechner, Frederick, 150
Bullinger, E. W., 52
Bundy, Ted, 216
Bunyan, John, 17, 239, 243, 250, 251
Bush, President, 51

Cain, 51
Calvin, John, 18, 23, 24, 34, 37, 50, 63, 97, 126, 150, 200, 214, 225, 227
Catullus, 90
Chalmers, Thomas, 85
Chamberlain, Wilt, 231
Children, 182, 183, 184, 186, 198, 199, 200, 201, 202, 210, 211, 226, 281, 284
Christie, Agatha, 105
Chrysostom, 133
Church, the, see esp.
   Body of Christ, 15, 20, 37, 43, 45, 62, 63, 99, 124, 131, 134, 148, 149, 150, 182, 186, 193, 265, 270, 273, 275
   bride, 190, 192
   building (temple), 97, 100, 101, 102, 275
   city, 97, 99, 101
   family, 97, 99, 100, 102, 125
Churchill, Winston, 189
Clark, G. N., 37
Clement of Alexandria, 93
The Closing of the American Mind (Allan Bloom), 35
Coleridge, Samuel Taylor, 15
Colson, Charles, 17, 33, 225
Cranmer, Thomas, 246
Cromwell, Oliver, 61, 242

Daniel, 215
Dante, 191
David, King, 84, 200, 231, 232, 236
Davies, John J., 122
Dayan, Moshe, 231
Death Valley of the Soul, 65, 66, 68, 70, 73, 78, 81, 101

Deissmann, Adolf, 42
Demons, evil powers, 60, 214, 215, 235
Demosthenes, 190
Depravity, 67, 68, 216, 273
Desiring God (John Piper), 257
Devil, the, 66, 67, 150, 213, 214, 215, 216,
    217, 218, 219, 226, 232, 235, 239, 242,
    243
Dillard, Annie, 82

Edwards, Jonathan, 41, 83
Election, 23, 24, 25, 26, 31, 37, 41, 46, 53
Eli, 201
Eliphaz, 153
Elisha's servant, 54
Employers/employees, 206, 207, 208, 209,
    210, 211
Epistle of Aristias, the, 183
Epistle of Diogenes, 93
Eve, 51, 190, 217
Ezekiel, 68, 126, 148

Faith, 19, 49, 50, 52, 76, 77, 78, 79, 85, 125,
    219, 227, 228, 234, 235, 236, 240, 246,
    250, 255, 257, 264, 265, 266, 267, 273,
    285
    saving, 49, 51, 266, 267
Fallen angels see *Demons, evil powers*
Felix, 255
The flesh, 66, 67, 273
Ford, Gerald, 227
Forgiveness, 19, 31, 33, 34, 35, 36, 37, 42,
    75, 94, 151, 233, 235, 270
Fuller, Charles, 69

Gaius, 205
Gerstner, John, 67
Gideon, 219
God, the Creator, 82, 83, 84
    Fatherhood of, 26, 27, 28, 37, 60, 94, 99,
    102, 109, 114, 124, 125, 164, 176, 186
    love of, 23, 24, 75, 117
    sovereignty of, 24, 41, 253
    wrath of, 67, 159, 160, 273
God's Order (John A. Mackay), 15
Goliath, 231, 236
Gospel, xii, 58, 73, 78, 92, 109, 110, 133, 235
    of peace, 219, 232, 255, 283
Grace, 18, 27, 28, 31, 35, 36, 37, 53, 58, 69,
    70, 75, 76, 77, 78, 81, 92, 107, 131, 132,
    144, 153, 185, 215, 219, 235, 241, 264,
    266, 267, 270, 272, 273
Graham, Billy, 126, 133, 227, 228
Grudem, Wayne, 183

Haustafel, the, 181, 182, 183, 184, 190, 194,
    198, 201, 205, 206, 210, 211
Headship, 183, 184, 185, 186, 192, 280
Heavenly realms, the, the heavenlies, 19, 20,

23, 27, 37, 43, 47, 65, 68, 69, 73, 81,
    215, 218, 226
Hemingway, Ernest, 122
Hill, Rowland, 151
Hodge, Charles, 35
Holiness, 19, 20, 25, 26, 28, 143, 147, 192,
    194, 227, 235, 240, 255
Holy Spirit, xi, xii, 18, 19, 20, 21, 26, 34, 45,
    46, 50, 52, 54, 60, 68, 73, 84, 86, 101,
    105, 115, 124, 136, 143, 144, 147, 148,
    150, 152, 153, 160, 173, 175, 176, 177,
    185, 235, 242, 249, 250, 251, 255, 256,
    257, 265, 266, 275
    baptism of, 148, 173, 277
    down payment (deposit), 41, 45, 46, 47,
    53, 174
    filled with (fullness of), 124, 172, 173,
    174, 176, 177, 178, 182, 186, 192, 211,
    219
    fruit of, 46, 116, 173
    seal, 45, 46, 47, 148, 173
    unity of the, 124, 125
The Holy War (John Bunyan), 239
Hope, 19, 53, 90, 125, 235, 241, 276
Hopkins, Hugh Evan, 123
Hume, David, xii
Humility, 122, 123, 124, 127, 128, 184, 185,
    235, 252, 276
Husbands, 182, 183, 184, 185, 186, 189,
    190, 191, 192, 193, 194, 210, 280

"In Christ," 42, 43, 44, 47, 51, 60, 73, 83, 101
Ironside, Harry, 244
Israel, 18, 46, 90, 174, 201, 225

James, P. D., 105
Jeremiah, 126
Jesus Christ, and the Church, 15, 32, 185,
    190, 191
    ascension of, 59, 60, 132, 272
    Bridegroom, 190, 191, 192
    Creator, 24, 37, 60, 61, 62, 83, 218, 271
    Headship of, 20, 37, 38, 61, 62, 110, 136,
    182, 183, 184, 185, 271, 273
    High Priestly prayer of, 44, 51, 60
    Incarnation of, 24, 109, 132, 176
    "light of the world," 163, 164, 165, 166,
    167, 168
    Lordship of, 16, 60, 61, 62, 63, 124, 125
    love of, 113, 117, 118, 186, 190, 191, 194
    resurrection of, 54, 58, 59, 62, 70, 93,
    109, 110
    return of, 125, 192, 264
    sacrificial death of, 32, 33, 58, 68, 91
    second (last) Adam, 61, 190
Jews and Gentiles, 37, 41, 46, 67, 75, 89, 90,
    91, 92, 93, 98, 101, 106, 108, 265
Job, 153, 184
John, the Apostle, 25
John the Baptist, 67

Johnson, Ben, 156
Johnson, Samuel, 226
Joseph, 109
Josephus, 91, 183, 232

Kelley, Thomas, 251
Kingdom of God (Christ), 59, 61, 75, 160,
    192, 235, 271
Knox, John, 85
Krauthammer, Charles, 225

Lewis, C. S., 164, 216, 235
Light, 143, 144, 164, 165, 166, 167, 168,
    216, 226
Lightfoot, Bishop, 46
Livy, 89
Lloyd-Jones, Martyn, 62, 173
Love, 20, 27, 49, 50, 51, 52, 63, 116, 119,
    123, 124, 127, 128, 136, 144, 147, 182,
    183, 185, 186, 190, 191, 192, 194, 229,
    264, 265, 266, 267, 276, 284, 285
Lukasse, Johanne, 108
Luke, Dr., 262, 263
Luther, Martin, 24, 85, 150, 164, 175, 217,
    219, 224

Mackay, John A., 15, 16, 21, 150
MacLaine, Shirley, 141
Maclaren, Alexander, 43, 114
Manton, Thomas, 158
Marriage, 155, 181, 182, 183, 184, 185, 186,
    189, 190, 191, 193, 194, 211, 280
Marriage Ring or the Mysteriousness and
    Duties of Marriage, The (Jeremy Taylor),
    191
Martyr, Justin, 211
Mary, the mother of Jesus, 251
Masters, 182, 183, 205, 206, 207, 210, 211,
    280
Michael, 215
Michelangelo, 84
Montaigne, 207
Moody, D. L., 126, 151, 175
Moses, 101, 109, 166, 218, 242
Moule, Bishop, 141
Muggeridge, Malcolm, 44
Müller, George, 251
Mystery, 15, 36, 100, 105, 106, 108, 109,
    110, 111, 113, 189, 190, 262, 275, 276

Napravnik, Joseph, 122
Narcissus, 193
Nee, Watchman, 213
Newton, Isaac, 61
Newton, John, 35
Nichomachian Ethics (Aristotle), 205
Nicklaus, Jack, 227
Northern Ireland, 44

Ockenga, Harold John, 25, 209

Owen, John, 61
Oxenham, John, 93

Packer, J. I., 26
Palau, Luis, 133
Parable of the Talents, 209
Parents, 182, 183, 186, 198, 199, 200, 201,
    202, 210, 280, 284
Pascal, 77
Paul, the Apostle, 17, 24, 33, 42, 51, 107,
    164, 254, 255, 262, 263, 264
Paxson, Ruth, 15, 213
Payson, Edward, 250
Peace, 18, 20, 77, 91, 93, 94, 116, 127,
    128,201, 232, 233, 234, 236, 240, 246,
    257, 264, 265, 267, 285
    of God, 233, 236, 240, 250, 255, 264
    with God, 232, 233, 236, 240, 255, 264
Pentecost, J. Dwight, 123
Perelandra (C. S. Lewis), 216
Pharaoh, 218
Philemon, 263
Philo, 183
Picturesque Notes of Edinburgh (Robert
    Louis Stevenson), 94
Pierson, Floyd, 252
Pilate, 201, 233
Pilgrim's Progress (John Bunyan), 239
Pink, Arthur W., 24
Piper, John, 257
Plato, 89
Pliny, 175
Politics (Aristotle), 205
Polybius, 283
Power, 20, 44, 53, 54, 57, 58, 59, 60, 86,
    115, 123, 132, 173, 211, 215, 216, 218,
    219, 220, 235
    resurrection, 54, 57, 58, 63, 69, 70, 83
Practice of the Presence of God, The
    (Brother Lawrence), 252
Prayer, 20, 51, 52, 54, 58, 60, 85, 94, 113,
    114, 119, 128, 144, 148, 166, 168, 184,
    191, 192, 211, 220, 223, 226, 234, 235,
    240, 249, 250, 251, 252, 253, 254, 255,
    256, 257, 258, 265, 266, 272, 276
    All-Prayer, 250, 251, 252, 253, 254, 284
Predestination see Election

Rader, Paul, 69
Radzevil, Prince Carol, 209
Ransom, Professor, 216
Reconciliation, 18, 89, 93, 94, 98, 99, 100,
    102, 105, 109, 110, 173, 233, 264, 265,
    267
Redemption, 18, 19, 25, 31, 32, 33, 35, 36,
    37, 45, 60, 100, 270
Reed, Bishop John, 92
Righteousness, 77, 165, 166, 168, 201, 219,
    226, 227, 228, 229, 232, 240, 241, 246,
    250, 255, 257

Robinson, Armitage, 54, 60
Rockefeller, John D., 35, 115
Roman Empire, the, 98, 205, 206, 255
Rutherford, Samuel, 118

St. Francis of Assisi, 127, 175
St. John of the Cross, 17, 50
St. Patrick, 143
Salvation, 17, 27, 41, 46, 68, 73, 74, 75, 76,
    77, 78, 79, 83, 84, 144, 192, 219, 227,
    240, 241, 242, 246, 250, 255, 273
Samuel, 201
Sanctification, 25, 28, 37, 58, 165, 190, 192,
    194, 224, 228
Sanders, Oswald, 250
Sangster, W. E., 107
Sankey, 151, 175
Satan see *Devil, the*
Saul, King, 17, 231
Sayers, Dorothy, 105
Scheffler, Johannes, 101
Schleicher, Renate, 183
School of Hillel, 190
Schweitzer, Albert, 42
Scott, Sir Walter, 81
Self-love, 190, 193, 194, 235
Seneca, 33, 34
Shalom, 18, 94, 127, 201, 233, 240, 255,
    264, 265
Shimei, 84
Simeon, Charles, 113, 123, 175
Slaves/slavery, 182, 183, 205, 206, 207, 208,
    209, 210, 211
Snows of Kilimanjaro, The (Ernest
    Hemingway), 122
Socrates, 190
Solomon, King, 114
South Africa, 44
Sovereignty of God, The (Arthur W. Pink), 24
Sowell, Thomas, 225
Spafford, H. P., 18
Spartacus, 205
Speer, Albert, 33, 34
Spencer. Herbert, 90
Spinks, Michael, 241
Spiritual riches, 35, 53, 69, 75, 107, 108, 115
Spiritual warfare, 213, 214, 223, 224, 239,
    242, 246, 249, 254, 257
Sproul, R. C., 227
Spurgeon, Charles, 19, 117, 126, 147
Stevenson, Robert Louis, 94
Stott, John, 24, 44, 66, 93, 109, 110, 133,
    140, 176, 219
Submission, 176, 177, 181, 182, 184, 185,
    186, 194, 210, 211, 251, 280, 281
Swift, Jonathan, 50
Symmachus, 183

Tacitus, 90
Tauler, 176

Taylor, Dr. and Mrs.Howard, 244
Taylor, Hudson, 244, 254
Taylor, Jeremy, 191
Ten Boom, Corrie, 165
Terkel, Studs, 210
Tertullian, 175
Testament of Devotion (Thomas Kelley), 251
Theodocian, 183
Theognes, 90
Third race, the, 93, 97, 99, 101, 105, 108, 109,
    110, 113, 114, 116, 119, 122, 139, 262
Timothy, 207, 245
Tolkien, J. R. R., 223
Toscanini, 107
Tozer, A. W., 117
Trajan, 175
Trust, 77, 78, 234, 236, 266, 267
Truth, xii, 53, 136, 141, 149, 165, 166, 168,
    193, 194, 219, 224, 225, 226, 229, 232,
    240, 246, 249, 255, 257, 266
Tychicus, 262, 263
Tyson, Mike, 241

Unity, 43, 44, 92, 121 (Chapter 14 *passim*),
    131, 135,270

Van Dyke, Dick, 51
Vision, 53, 54
Von Rad, Gerhard, 233

Wedding Sermon from a Prison Cell
    (Dietrich Bonhoeffer), 183
Wesley, Charles, 175
Wesley, John, 126, 150, 164, 224, 252
Weston, Dr., 216
Whitefield, George, xii, 126
Whyte, Alexander, 153
Wilberforce, 150
Wives, 182, 183, 184, 185, 186, 190, 191,
    192, 193, 194, 210, 280, 281
Word of God, 100, 136, 144, 167, 177, 192,
    211, 220, 226, 229, 234, 235, 236, 240,
    242, 243, 244, 245, 246, 250, 251, 255,
    257
*Working: People Talk About What They Do
    All Day and How They Feel About What
    They Do* (Studs Terkel), 210
Workmanship, God's (Christians), 81
    (Chapter 9 *passim*), 93, 105
Works, 25, 74, 75, 76, 77, 78, 81, 84, 85,
    134, 144, 266, 273
World, the, world-system, 42, 66, 67, 141,
    215, 236, 240
Wycliffe, John, 123

Xenophon, 190

Yoder, John Howard, 184

Zedekiah, King, 52

Index of Sermon Illustrations

Adoption
J. I. Packer on the truth of adoption being
essential to healthy Christianity, 26-27
The woman who always forgot her daughter
was adopted, 27

Alienation
Theognes' despair (c. 500 B.C.), 90
The Roman poet Catullus' despair (c. 50
B.C.), 90
The "peace march" that ended because the
marchers could not get along, 91
The two aged sisters who drew a line across
their shared room and never spoke again, 94

Anger
F. Buechner on how when you are angry "the
feast is you," 151

Attitude
The happy beggar who never had a bad day,
for he was always giving thanks, 176
The "poor" pastor who thanked God for the
sunshine, 176
"Mommy, why do all the idiots come out
when Daddy drives?", 209

The Bible
Allan Bloom on how his uneducated grand-
parents lived a noble life, surpassing the
wisdom of their educated progeny, 35-36
John Bunyan on the power of the sword
(God's Word) in Christian's hand, 243
D. G. Barnhouse's memorization of
Philippians, 245
Hudson Taylor's reading the Bible from 2 to 4
A.M., 245
Thomas Cranmer's collect on how we must
study God's Word, 246

Bitterness
The two aged sisters who drew a line across
their shared room and never spoke again, 94
The slave whose very breath became poison,
153

Blasphemy
Playboy's *parody of the Virgin Birth, 141*

Busyness
Time *magazine, "How America Has Run out
of Time," 171*
The Queen to Alice regarding running to keep
in the same place, 171

Chastity
Jeremy Taylor on how chastity is the wedding
ring which protects marriage, 191

Children
The author's realization of how little time we
have to raise our children, dramatized in the
birth of his children and then grandchildren,
197, 198

Christ
Quotation regarding Christ being the center of
cosmic unity, 16
J. Owen on eleven glories of Christ, 61-62
Toscanini saying Beethoven is "every-
thing"—an example of how Christians
ought to see Christ, 107
How Christ adds to life, 108
St. Patrick's poem on the centrality of Christ
in a believer's life, 143

Christ's love
S. Rutherford on Christ's unquenchable love,
118

Citizenship
Memorial Day 1987 at the American
Cemetery in Cambridge, England, 97, 98

Conversion
The conversion of Princeton's John Mackay,
16
The conversion of Charles Fuller, 69

The Creator
Isaac Newton's rejoinder "Nobody!" to an
acquaintance who asked him who made the
mechanical solar system upon which
Newton was tinkering, 61
The author's experience of seeing the beauty
of the Creator at Cabo San Lucas, 82
Annie Dillard "knocked breathless" by seeing
the Creator's work in a tree, 82

The Creator's glory in the complexity of a newborn child, 82, 83

Deadness
Jeremy Bentham's corpse, though annually seated at the board meeting of University College Hospital, will never answer roll call, 66

Demons
Unhealthy preoccupation with demons, 214

Depravity
The little girl who knew the evil wasn't the Devil's fault, but her own, 67
John Gerstner regarding room for "deprovement," 67
Suppressing the truth regarding sin, 141
Shirley MacLaine proclaiming "I am God!," 141

Depression
M. Luther's *Anfectung*, 217

Despair
G. N. Clark's pessimistic inaugural lecture at Cambridge about the future of history, 37
Theognes' despair (c. 500 B.C.), 90
The Roman poet Catullus' despair (c. 50 B.C.), 90
The man who set fire to his wheelchair, 122

Dishonesty
Mortimer Adler on how contemporary writing flaunts truth, 149
The farmer who used a "pound" loaf of bread from the baker to weigh the "pound" of butter he sold to the baker, 149
An outrageously hypocritical rejection notice from a Chinese publisher, 225

Disobedience
"I'm sitting down on the outside, but . . .," 199

Disunity
List of the exotic denominational choices which exist in America, 43
The "peace march" that ended because the marchers could not get along, 91
The two aged sisters who drew a line across their shared room and never spoke again, 94
The church that split over a small serving of ham, 123

Education
Allan Bloom on how his uneducated grandparents lived a noble life, surpassing the wisdom of their educated progeny, 35-36

Election
H. J. Ockenga regarding how we are elected to holiness, 25
Jonathan Edwards on the sweetness of the doctrine of election, 41

Envy
St. John of the Cross on how we envy others' accomplishments, 50

Evangelism
How when a heterogeneous group of missionaries began to love each other, evangelism took place, 108

Faith
The man who was crawling on all fours across the solidly frozen St. Lawrence, 49
The school which installed a fire safety sprinkler system but failed to hook it up, 57
When converted, Thomas Chalmers left his "good work" to become a working dynamo—faith works!, 85

Family
The author being himself when he is with "family," 99-100

The Fatherhood of God
J. I. Packer on the truth of adoption being essential to healthy Christianity, 26-27
Our love for our children is a window to God's love for us, 114

Forgiveness
Albert Speer's sense of never having attained forgiveness, 33-34
D. L. Moody regarding how a leader's making things "right" made way for revival, 151

Fulfillment
Chinese proverb which humorously lists vacuous ways to "satisfaction," 44
M. Muggeridge on how none of his considerable attainments satisfied, except drinking from Christ, 44-45

Giving
How J. D. Rockefeller gave *from* his riches, not *according* to his riches, 35

Glory
J. Owen on eleven glories of Christ, 61-62
C. Lewis on how believers will somehow pass into the splendor, 164

God's Care
C. H. Spurgeon describes how God cares for his own, 19

God's Love
J. Swift on having enough religion to hate, but not enough to love, 50
Our love for our children is a window to God's love for us, 114
D. G. Barnhouse on how love is a key to each of the nine fruits of the Spirit, 116
The author's finite, but unmeasurable, love for his wife as a window to God's infinite love, 116-117

C. H. Spurgeon on the *length* of God's love, 117

A. W. Tozer on the infinitude of God's love, 117

Grace

How J. D. Rockefeller gave *from* his riches, not *according* to his riches, 35

The judge who considered that it took greater grace to save him than a criminal, because it was harder for the judge to see his need, 76

Pascal on the necessity of grace, 77

The man whose life totalled ten points on Heaven's 1,000-point scale and exclaimed, "At this rate I'll never get in except by the grace of God!," 266

Guilt

Albert Speer's sense of never having attained forgiveness, 33-34

Hatred

The two aged sisters who drew a line across their shared room and never spoke again, 94

Hell

A place where people can only eat by feeding one another with long-handled spoons, 50

Holiness

H. J. Ockenga regarding how we are elected to holiness, 25

Michelangelo: "I'm liberating an angel from the stone," 84

The Holy Spirit

The author's experience of the power of the Holy Spirit in preaching, 85, 86

How we develop an increased capacity for the fullness of the Holy Spirit, 118

The unity we experience with other believers because of the indwelling Spirit, 124

The average Christian has a theological "black hole" when it comes to knowledge of the Holy Spirit, 147

C. H. Spurgeon on the passibility of the Holy Spirit, 147

How music has historically reflected the fullness of the Spirit, 175

How the Holy Spirit leads us to pray prayers which he is pleased to answer, 250-251

Honesty

Samuel Johnson on why we must always make our children tell the truth, 226

Humility

The judge who considered that it took greater grace to save him than a criminal, because it was harder for the judge to see his need, 76

Paul saying he was the "leaster" of God's people, 107

Charles Simeon declaring that his curate "must increase," 123

Humor

The danger of *morologia*, moronic talk, 157

Hypocrisy

An outrageously hypocritical rejection notice from a Chinese publisher, 225

Integrity

Corrie ten Boom's father's integrity with his customers, 165

How Billy Graham's silent presence made a pro golfer feel he was having "religion stuffed down his throat," 227-228

Intolerance

"The one thing I will not tolerate is intolerance," 167

Jealousy

St. John of the Cross on how we envy others' accomplishments, 50

Knowing Christ

How knowing *about* someone is not knowing that person, 51

Loneliness

The man who set fire to his wheelchair, 122

The man who got his hair cut once a week, just to be touched, 122

Lordship

John Owen on eleven glories of Christ, 61-62

Love

J. Swift on having enough religion to hate, but not enough to love, 50

How when a heterogeneous group of missionaries began to love each other, evangelism took place, 108

D. G. Barnhouse on how love is a key to each of the nine fruits of the Spirit, 116

The author's finite, but unmeasurable, love for his wife as a window to God's infinite love, 116-117

Dietrich Bonhoeffer on the husband's great responsibility as head of the home, 184

Winston Churchill's remark that he would like to Lady Churchill's second husband, 189

The little boy who brought "something green that he loved" to school: his little sister in a green dress!, 265

Lying

John Mackay regarding lying being a sin against the Body of Christ, 150

Marriage

Dietrich Bonhoeffer on the husband's great responsibility as head of the home, 184

Winston Churchill's remark that he would like to Lady Churchill's second husband, 189

Jeremy Taylor on how chastity is the wedding ring which protects marriage, 191

Music
How music has historically reflected the fullness of the Spirit, 175

Narcissism
E. W. Bullinger on how so many people are asphyxiated with the exhalation of self, 52
The legend of Narcissus, 193

Negativism
G. N. Clark's pessimistic inaugural lecture at Cambridge about the future of history, 37

Peace
H. P. Spafford's hymn of peace over his family's watery grave, 18
The couple which moved to the Falkland Islands to find peace, 264

Pessimism
G. N. Clark's pessimistic inaugural lecture at Cambridge about the future of history, 37
Theognes' despair (c. 500 B.C.), 90
The Roman poet Catullus' despair (c. 50 B.C.), 90

Power
The school which installed a fire safety sprinkler system but failed to hook it up, 57
The Pauline bouquet for power, 57-58
The author's experience of the power of the Holy Spirit in preaching, 85-86

Prayer
E. Payson: "Prayer is the first thing, the second thing, the third . . .," 250
How the Holy Spirit leads us to pray prayers which he is pleased to answer, 250-251
John Bunyan's definition of prayer, 251
Thomas Kelley on how one can continually pray, 251
Brother Lawrence on his life of continual prayer, 252
John Wesley on his life of continual prayer, 252
Hudson Taylor's discovery of why a certain mission station was uniquely blessed: a single faithful intercessor in faraway England, 254
Former IVCF president John Alexander's Saturday night intercession for pastors, 256-257
John Piper on how we will only succeed in prayer if we plan to succeed, 257-258

Preaching
W. E. Sangster's sense of privilege at being called to preach, 107

Prejudice/Racism
Jewish/Gentile hatreds, 89
Bishop J. Reed making both his bickering white and black students say they were green, 92

"Christians" who doubt that primitive Indians have souls, 106

Pride
Memorial Day 1987 at the American Cemetery in Cambridge, England, 97-98
E. Hemingway's white hunter, 122

Redemption
The little boy's "twice bought" boat, 32

Relativism
Today's desolate moral relativism, 216
Charles Colson on moral AIDS, 225

Respect
Montaigne on how geographical distance enhances one's respect, 207

Salvation
The little boy's "twice bought" boat, 32
The judge who considered that it took greater grace to save him than a criminal, because it was harder for the judge to see his need, 76

Sanctification
H. J. Ockenga regarding how we are elected to holiness, 25
Michelangelo: "I'm liberating an angel from the stone," 84

Satan
C. S. Lewis on the utter evil of Satan, 216-217
Satan's intelligence, 217
God's power over Satan, illustrated by Aaron's rod, 218

Satisfaction
Chinese proverb which humorously lists vacuous ways to "satisfaction," 44
M. Muggeridge on how none of his considerable attainments satisfied, except drinking from Christ, 44-45

Selfishness
Hell, a place where people can only eat by feeding one another with long-handled spoons, 50
E. W. Bullinger on how so many people are asphyxiated with the exhalation of self, 52

Sensuality
Ben Johnson's poem describing the danger of dwelling on sensual topics, 157

Serving
God is not so much interested in our being the star of the show, but that we do the best with the part he has given us, 134-135

Temptation
The "cookie jar syndrome," 155

Testimony
D. G. Barnhouse on how the Church, like the moon, reflects Christ, 164

To "shine in the night, keep me in the light," 166

The happy beggar who never had a bad day, for he was always giving thanks, 176

The "poor" pastor who thanked God for the sunshine, 176

How Billy Graham's silent presence made a pro golfer feel he was having "religion stuffed down his throat," 227-228

Thanksgiving

The happy beggar who never had a bad day, for he was always giving thanks, 176

The "poor" pastor who thanked God for the sunshine, 176

Truth

Mortimer Adler on how contemporary writing flaunts truth, 149

Samuel Johnson on why we must always make our children tell the truth, 226

Unity

List of the exotic denominational choices which exist in America, 43

D. M. Lloyd-Jones on the organic unity of Christ's body, 62-63

The author being himself when he is with "family," 99-100

How when a heterogeneous group of missionaries began to love each other, evangelism took place, 108

The supernatural unity we experience with other believers because of the indwelling Spirit, 124

The unity of the Church is as indestructible as the unity of the Godhead, 125

Gather the great saints of the centuries and there will be amazing *diversity*, but also amazing *unity*, 126

Wisdom

Allan Bloom on how his uneducated grandparents lived a noble life, surpassing the wisdom of their educated progeny, 35-36

Works

The pelagian frog whose works were his "salvation," 74

The non-swimmer, the average swimmer, and the Olympic swimmer—none of these could save himself in the mid-Atlantic, 75

The sparrow on its back, legs up, doing its best to keep the sky from falling, 84

How when converted, Thomas Chalmers left his "good works" to become a working dynamo; faith works!, 85

H. J. Ockenga's account of a Polish worker whose hard work was a witness to his master, 209

Studs Terkel describing how work can demean, 210

About the Book Jacket

The design of the book jacket brings together the talents of several Christian artists. The design centers around the beautiful banner created by artist Marge Gieser. The banner is more than eight feet tall and was displayed in College Church throughout Pastor Hughes' series of sermons on Ephesians. It is photographed here on the jacket at about one-twentieth of its original size.

Concerning the symbolism used in the banner for *Ephesians* Marge Gieser writes:

> The Book of Ephesians speaks to us about the mysterious union of Christ and the Church. Through the work of the Holy Spirit the body of believers joined together rejoices in the promise that there is something beyond this earthly sphere. Christ is the Head over the Church (the *chai rho* symbol), relating this body of believers to the "heavenly places," with the promise that someday they will rule and reign with Him forever.

Other artists contributing their talents to the creation of the jacket include: Bill Koechling, photography, and Mark Schramm, overall design and art direction.